LEARNING BEHAVIORAL ECONOMY EDITION 3

AF514918

JOHN LOK

Contents

Preface

Preface

This book is concerned how to apply behavioral economy method to predict consumer behavior. This book divides two parts, first part introduce what is behavioral economy and second part explains how environment influences consumer behavior.

In Behavioral economics part , it can provide more realistic psychological foundations. This book is intended to explain why consumer behaviors and economy has close relationship and apply economic concept to explain how the consumer chooses to do whose consumption of decision.In part one, it shall indicate how the process of behaviour economic field develops, then I shall show what methods are used to measure behavioural economy. Next, I shall indicate what the main two categories of behavioural economy are as well as I shall explain what risky and uncertain outcomes of individual behavior economic theories are as well as what behavioral game theory is. Finally, I shall explain how policy makers or decision makers can apply behavioral economy concept to do whose policy decision as well as I shall also indicate why behavioral economy and psychology which has close relationship to influence consumption of decision.

In part two, environment and consumer behavior relationship, I shall explain what psychological method means and how to apply psychological method to predict consumer behavior. Consumer behavior is comparatively a new field of study. It led every manufacturer's attention from product to consumer and specially focused on consumer behavior. The evaluation of marketing concept from selling concept to consumer oriented marketing has resulted in buyer behavior becoming an independent discipline. The growth of consumerism and consumer legislation emphasizes the importance that is given to the consumer. Thus, consumer behavior is a study of how individuals make decision to spend their available resources (time, money and efforts) or consumption related aspects (what who buy? when why buy? how who buy? etc.) Hence, marketers need to obtain an depth knowledge to know to use what psychological method(s) is(are) the suitable to predict consumers buying behavior to raise customer numbers easily . Finally, this knowledge acted as a tool to the marketers to forecast the future buying behavior of customers to reduce any new products of investment risk before who decide to manufacture to sell to the market.

I write this book aims to give my opinions to indicate whether what factors can influence householder resource , such as, gas, electricity energy behavior at home as well as what factors influence householder rent or house purchase choice at housing market in any countries as well as to explain why and how what factors can cause householder food and energy waste behaviors and how to influence their food and energy waste behaviors to be changed to reduce or avoid at home.

I write this book second part gives opinions to explain whether the country's government rent subsidies support to its householders to pay lesser rent amount assistance. It will bring what influences to impact its householders rent spending behavioral choices or decisions. The questions include such as , whether rent subsidies assistance can encourage the country's householders choose to spend more rent expenditure to rent higher quality of private properties to live, due to their government can support some sent subsidies to assist them to pay higher rents in order to reduce their rent burdens, or whether rent subsidies assistance can encourage the country's low income working age group householders choose to rent cheap rent expenditure of public houses to live, or whether it will bring the raising of shortage of public house number supplies, due to it encourages many low income working age group householders choose to rent public houses to live , or whether it encourages many high income working age group householders to choose to rent private properties to live in the country's housing market, due to they can pay lower rent amount to rent high quality of private houses to live , or whether rent subsidies assistance can bring private properties number growth or expansion, due to it is sudden that the country has many high working age group householders choose to rent private properties to live, due to rent subsidies assists them to pay less rent , or it will bring negative private properties rent raising effect, due to the country has many householder choose to rent any kinds of private properties to live to cause the challenge of the demand to private properties is sudden increased, but the supply of private properties is limited. So, it encounters the shortage of private properties shortage supply challenge, or whether the government's rent subsidies strategy can bring good or bad influences to the country's householders' living changing needs in society etc. different rent subsidies assistance questions.

I write third part aims to let readers to analyse whether future (AI) artificial intelligent machine can assist humans to learn how to reduce food waste or food loss to consumers' food habits or manufacturers' manufacturing processed in order to avoid the actual food or energy shortage challenges are caused from human's food or energy consumption negligent behaviours. Consequently, I hope my readers can make judgement whether future (AI) artificial intelligence can help human to reduce or avoid environmental pollution or food/ energy waste challenges to cause social cost to be raised to influence human future living quality to be poor.

In third part, I shall indiate how and why what factors can impact or influence householders or any energy users to waste to consume energy to use at homes or offices or any places or any private using, e.g. driving cars. etc. energy waste using behaviours , then I shall explain why (AI) technology can impact energy users to reduce to use excessive energy behaviours more easier than education method.

In my this book, the main important aim, I give examples to explain how to apply psychological and behavioral economic both view point related methods to predict consumer individual behavior to let businessmen learn how to choose the reasonable or right methods to attract consumers to choose to buy whose products or consume whose services to win competitors more easily. In this book final part, I shall indicate clear reasons to explain why I agree behavioral economy method and psychological method can be used to predict consumer behavior in nowadays society.

Prologue

Table Of Contents

How can constructive consumer choice processes influence consumption behavior?

How can economical environment factor predict consumers consumption?

How can auctions or online experimentation respond to predict consumer behavior and sale forecast accuracy?

Chapter 5
Environment influences consumer behavior
How to apply online psychological
advertising method to predict behavioral
consumption p.91-128

How can store atmosphere environment influence
consumer individual shopping behavior

How can constructive consumer choice processes influence consumption behavior?

What is consumer neuroscientific research method to predict consumer behavior

Can food consumption for trust cooperation influence food consumption choice

Does habit strength moderate the intention behavior to consumption?

How can economical environment factor predict consumers consumption

Can firm's conduct and behavior factor influence consumer consumption

spending at homes

Factors influence householder energy
efficient consumption behaviors
at homes

How artificial intelligence impacts energy
consumers using behaviours
How to apply (AI) technology to improve
energy efficiency and better climate change
and the security of energy supply as well
a resource efficiency?

CHAPTER I

The historical development of behavioral economics and function

Behavioral economy is consisted from psychology and standard economic model. Standard economic model is the way most economists think about consumer welfare and consumer choice in microeconomic environment. I shall apply behavioral economic model to explain underground train and Disney entertainment theme park and University and unground train transportation and environmental protection businessmen etc. enterprises which rationality in the standard economic model relies heavily on the assumption that consumers are rational. In this case of consumer individual behavior consumption process, I assume that consumers are fully aware of all the options who have, who can always and consistently to rank their options in accordance will whose preferences and always choose the option who like best.

Thus, these assumptions of the standard economy model of consumer include such as: consumers have known preferences and consumers choose the best option available. The advantages of the standard model, from there three assumptions, such as a logically consistent theory of consumer behavior can be biult, that theory can be used to make predictions about consumer behavior and those predictions can be compared with reality. These models often correspond to actual consumer behavior. But behavioral economy model can give evidence from psychology to show that consumer often are irrational and also who are predictably irrational. Clearly, psychology has shown that the rationality assumptions of standard economics are wrong. For example, if irrational consumers were irrational in randomways, who would cancel each other out, leaving the overall outcome determined by the behavior of rational consumers. In that case, economic theories that ignored irrational between would work just fine. But psychology has shown that consumers are irratonal in similar and predictable ways, therefore, irratonality doesn't cancel out and can't be ignored. Moreover, the fact that consumers are predictably irrational means that whose predictably irrational behavior can be relatively easily inserted into economic theories to make economic predictions more accurate. In fact, consumers often are unable to make use of what who know about their available options and their preferences to figure out the best available option, and even when who know what is best for them, evidence shows tht who often make bad choices anyway. Unfortunately for economic view point, there's plenty of reliable evidence of predictably unselfish behavior to consumers. It is true, that the free market competitiion will encourage consumers to make the best option.

In summary, standard economic theories assume that consumers are rational and self interested. However, behavioral economic theories assumes that psychology shows who are not rational usually. I shall indicate how consumer's psychological decision to choose their behavioral consumption in actual life environment for
underground train and Disney entertainment theme park and University and unground train transportation and environmental protection businessmen etc. enterprises. Some consumption of these enterprises evidences also show that consumer individual irrationality , these enterprises have predictable features in these enterprises consumption suitation. I shall use these enterprises to explain why behavioral economy can make economic predictions more accurate by using these enterprises' consumption evidences on their predictabl irrational behavior to these enterprises. Although, these global enterprises' market competition is serious, consumers may be expected to learn to reduce irrational behavior over time, these processes may not work well and may take. You can read these underground train and Disney entertainment theme park and University and unground train transportation and environmental protection businessmen etc. enterprises to make judgement why behavioral economic model is more accurate to

predict consumer behavior to compare standard economic model.

In behavioral economy view point, if the manufacturer expect to advertise whose products to achieve the maximum sale numbers. So, the manufacturer must expect to pay the most reasonable advertisement cost to achieve the maximum sale numbers. How can marketing of advertisement information influence consumer has positive attitude to influence many consumers choose to buy the manufactuer's consumption behavior? Consumer attention to advertisement or any marketing communication depends on four levels of consumer involvement: pre-attention, focal attention, comprehension and elaboration. Each calls for different level of message processing. Pre-attention demands only limited message processing, the consumer only identifies the product. Focal attention involves basic information as product name on use. In comprehension level, the message is analyzed, through elaboration, the content of the message is integrated with other information that helps to build attitude towards the product. It is suggested that marketers make advertisement with can induce elaboration. In general, steps in consumption decision making process include: first step, consumer feels need recognition. Second step, who will search any information concerns to the product. Third step, who will evaluate of alternatives. Fourth step, who will make purchase decision. Finally, who will do post purchase behavior to judge whether the product's price is reasonable or unreasonable to decide whether to consume the product again in the future. Thus, advertisement can be one factor to influence consumer choice in behavioral economy view point.

Behavioral economics studies all human environment behavior: all types of consumer spending and saving behaviors, entreprepreneurship and all work related behavior including job choice and investments in human capital, all types of business behavior ranging from decisions on prices, output, investment, finance and preferences and reactions to economic policies and programs by consumers as well as businessmen. In addition, the analysis could be focused on the micro or the macro level. So, insights from behavioral economics would naturally be incorporated into the discriplines of economics as well as psychology. Thus, behavioral economy focuses on the rationality of the process of decision making when economics was mainly focused with the rationality of the outcomes.

Economics is used equailibrium conditions to define the apprpriate outcomes, but psychology's main focus is on how consumers learn and adapt to a constantly changing environment. Economic theory indicates cnsumers learn from whose mistakes, so that their behavior will change to the rational and optimum outcomes in equibilrium . However, consumption was not a passive, variable completely is determined by the rational calculation of economic factors. So, it explains that how behavioral economy theory can be applied to predict consumer behavior.

In general, human economic activities include production, distribution, consumption and resource maintenance. Economic actors can be individuals, small groups (such as a family, or a group of roommales) or large organizations, such as a government or a multi-national corporation. Economics is about how these actors behave and interact as who engage in economic activities. In conclusion, I agree that every consumer's realistic behavior is in economic theories that deal with judgemetn under uncertainty.

Psychological method predicts consumer behavior characteristics

Consumer behavior is comparatively a new field of study. It led every manufacturer's attention from product to consumer and specially focused on consumer behavior. The evaluation of marketing concept from selling concept to consumer oriented marketing has resulted in buyer behavior becoming an independent discipline. The growth of consumerism and consumer legislation emphasizes the importance that is given to the consumer. Thus, consumer behavior is a study of how individuals make decision to spend their available resources (time, money and efforts) or consumption related aspects (what who buy? when why buy? how who buy? etc.) Hence, marketers need to obtain an depth knowledge to know to use what psychological method(s) is(are) the suitable to predict consumers buying behavior to raise customer numbers easily . Finally, this knowledge acted as a tool to the marketers to forecast the future buying behavior of customers to reduce any new products of investment risk before who decide to manufacture to sell to the market.

Consumer behavior is the study of individuals or organizations and the processes consumers use to research, select , use and dispose of products or services, experience or ideas to satisfy needs and its impact on the consumers and society. The term " customer" is specific in terms of brand , company or shop. It refers to person who customarily or regularly purchases particular brands or purchases from particular company's products or purchases from particular shops. Whereas, the " consumer" is a person who generally engages in the activities, search, select, use and dispose of products, services , experiences or ideas. Thus, consumption behavior concerns to predict how the consumer activities to be done to influence who chooses to buy the product or consume service among of all competitive and similar products or services provision to the market. However, consumer purchase decision and nature of motive which have close relationship. For example, in the psychological view point, when the consumer desires for saving money, who will decide to purchase when the price falls down; when the consumer feels fear, who will feel purchasing insurance policy need; when the consumer feels health need, who will choose to buy health foods to eat or/and to join to be membership in health clubs; when the consumer has possession need, who will decide to buy antiques for appreciating whose future values for saving. Thus, businessmen ought need to predict what the nature of motive will be whose target customer group, then who can persuade whose target customer group to choose to buy whose products or consume whose service more easily.

How to explain consumer behavior? Consumer behavior is said to be an applied discipline as some decisions are significantly affected by their behavior or expected action. The two significantly perspective that are micro and societal perspectives. The micro perspectives involve understanding consumer for the purpose of helping a firm or organization to achieve its objectives. Whereas, the societal or macro perspective applies knowledge of consumers to aggregate-level faced by mass or society as a whole. The behavior of consumer has significant influence on the quality of the standard of living.

Consumers can divide either organization buyer or individual buyer. First, organizational buyers are more geographically concentrated than consumer markets, who are fewer in number , but who are bulk buyers compared to individual buyers, whose markets are either vertical or horizontal. (vertical structures who cater only one or two industries, whereas, in horizontal structure , the buyer base is too broad. Organizational demand is derived from consumer demand. The nature of demand is influential and inelastic. Organizational buying lot of formalities have proposals , quotations, procedures are to be followed unlike consumer buying, e.g. decision process is much complex with high financial risk, technical aspects, multiple influencing factors etc. Also, it requires more extensive negotiation over larger time period than consumer buyer. Second, in psychological view point, individual consumer whose personal and/or product and/or situational factors can influence consumer decision making? self-concept, needs, and values are the three psychological factors that influence individual consumer how who chooses to buy one product or consume one service. For example, the more number of consumers share a certain self image, certain value and needs. They tend to use products and services the reflect whose life style. They get highly involved in purchasing products like designer wear, imported cars, health care products etc. On the product factor aspect, e.g. the consumer involvement grows as the level of perceived risk in the purchase of a product on or service increase. It is likely that consumers will feel more involved in the purchase of their house than in the purchase of tooth paste. It is a much riskier purchase. Beside, product differentiation can also affect consumer have to choose from increases. This may be due to the fact that consumers feel variety which means greater risk. On the situational factor aspect, the product is brought or used can generate emotional involvement. For example, buying a pair of socks for yourself is far less involved than buying a gift for a close friend. Social pressure can significantly increase involvement. One is likely to be more self conscious about the products and brand one looks at when shopping with friends than when shopping alone. So, individual consumer shopping decision will be influenced by whos friends, when whose friends give ideas to influence whose buying choice decision easily.

Models of consumer involvement have two level: First, low involvement products are those, which are at low risk, perhaps by important of being inexpensive and repeatedly used by consumers. Marketers may try to sell the product without changing the attitudes of consumers. For example, writing pen with the " uninterrupted flow" and tooth paste with " mouth wash" positioning attracts new consumers. Some buying decisions are taken will let of thinking or great feelings. Some are made through force of habit and others are made consciously, that attributes consumer choice to information (learn) , attitude (feel) and behavior (do) issues. Second, high involvement products are purchases in first requires more information, both because of the importance of the product to the consumer and thinking issues related to the purchases. Major purchases , such as cars, houses and other expensive and infrequently buying items. The purchases decisions in high involvement product involve less of information than feeling. Typical purchases tied to self-esteem, jewelry, apparel, cosmetics and accessories. The strategy model is feel-learn-do. To encourage purchases much approach customers with emotion and appeal. Otherwise, the purchase in low involvement product is primarily by the need to satisfy personal tastes, many of which are influenced by self-image products like newspaper, soft drinks, liquor etc. Marketers can promote these low involvement products through reference groups and other social factors . Because low involvement product involves less in thinking and more of habitual buying. Products like stationery, groceries , food etc. The role of information is to differentiate any point of difference from competitors. Brand loyalty may result simply from the habit. It suggests marketers induce trial through various sales promotion techniques.

What is the relationship between behavioral economics and psychology

At the core of behavioral economics is used psychology of economics analysis to improve economics on its own terms generating theoretical insights, making better prediction of field consumption of behavioral phenomena, and suggesting better policy to any company or government decision makers. It rejects economic theories based on utility maximization, equilibrium and efficiency. It is useful because it provides economists with a theoretical framework that can be applied to almost any form of economic (and even non-economic) behavior to predict behavioral consumption more easily to businessmen. So, behavioral economy is different to general economy concept, it applies psychological methods to attempt to predict consumption behavior.

Simpifying much assumption that are not central to the economic theory to apply to psychological behavior. Other assumption simply acknowledge human limits on computational power and self-interest. These assumptions can be considered procedurally rational because human needs to solve problems that are often so complex that who can't be solved exactly by even modern computer technology. So, if businessmen apply psychological method to predict behavioral consumption to earn the more benefits or profit, it is more reasonable to compare to apply computer methods to predict consumption behavior.

Theories in behavioral economics should be judged by reality, generality and tractability concepts to apply why we (consumers) do our behavior (consumption of choices) from psychological analysis. We share the positivist view that the ultimate test of a theory is the accuracy of its predictions. But we also believe that better predictions are likely to result from theories with more realistic assumptions. In psychology, such as connectionist models that capture some of the essential features of neural functioning, which are based on utility maximization, yet are reaching the point where they are able to predict many judgemental and behavioral phenomena. Contrary to the positivistic view, however, businessmen ought believe that predictions of consumers‘ feelings (e.g., of subjective well-being) should be an important goal to earn more profit more easily.

Most of the ideas in behavioral economics are not new. When economics first became identified as a distinct field of study, psychology didn't exist as a discipline to apply to economy subject. For example, "invisible hand" and "the wealth of Nations" which belong to theory to moral sentiments, which laid out psychological principles of individual behavior that are arguably as profound as whose economic observations. Another example, such as a simple model of social utility means that one (consumer) or person's utility was affected by another person's , such as whose family or friends' influence why to choose to buy this product or use this service in consumption market.

Nowadays, economists hoped their discipline could be like a natural science to apply psychological methods to predict behavioral consumption to assist businessmen to earn more economic benefit or to reduce cost or profit to win whose competitors. But psychology was not very scientific. However, later economists are very much appealed to psychological insights to attempt to assist businessmen how to predict consumers how who will prefer to choose to consume to buy this product or use this service.

Throughout the second half of the century, many criticisms of the positivistic perspective took place in both economics and psychology. The economists of the time had less disagreement with psychology than they realized. They assume without foundation that behavior always aims at the goal of maximum pleasure and minimum pain; but behavior is not goal-oriented. Also the economists of the time believed false conclusions are drawn from false psychological assumptions to predict consumer individual behavioral consumption wrongly.

The importance of psychological measures and bounds on rationality. These commentators attracted attention, but did not alter the fundamental direction of economics. One development was the rapid acceptance by economists of the expected utility and discounted utility models which are making decision under uncertainty and choice, respectively. Whereas the assumptions and implications of utility analysis are rather flexible, and the expected utility and discounted utility models have numerous precise and testable implications. So, it seems economy and psychology can have close relationship to be connect to be applied to predict consumer individual consumption of behavior to assist any enterprises can earn more profit or more economic benefit more easily in global competitive consumption market nowadays.

In behavioral economy view, economists began to accept counter examples that could be not be permanently ignored, developments in psychology identified promising directions for new theory to be applied how to assist businessmen to predict behavioral consumption to earn economic benefits or profits. Beginning around 1960 year, psychology became to be dominated by the brain as an information-processing device replacing the behaviorist conception of the brain as a stimulus-response machine. The information-processing permitted a fresh study of neglected topics like memory, problem solving and decision making. These new topics were more obviously relevant to the conception of utility maximization than behaviorism had appeared to be to apply how to predict behavioral consumption in traditional psychological method.

However, behavioral economy and psychological consumption prediction method, psychologists began to use economic models as a benchmark against which to constrast their psychological models. Early research in behavioral consumption methds have followed these steps. First, identify assumption or models that are used by economists, who expected utility and discounted utility. Second, the assumption or model is a rule out alternative explanations (such as subjects' confusion or transactions costs). And third, the assumption or model creates alternative theories that generalize existing models. The final is to construct economic models of behavior using the behavioral assumptions to test them from the third step. This final step of economic models of behavior has only been taken more recently to be applied to predict why the consumer prefers to choose to do this behavioral consumption of decision finally.

In behavioral economy method, what is the standard economic model? It is the standard economic model, the way most economists think about consumer welfare and consumer choice. What is the rationality in the standard economic model? The standard economic model relies heavily on the assumption that consumers are rational. Standard economic model assumes that consumers are fully aware of all the options who have, who can always and consistently , rank whose options in accordance with their preferences, and always choose the option, who like the best option. Thus, what the assumptions of the standard economic model of consumer are? The assumptions include consumers act with full information, consumers have known preferences, consumers choose the best option available. In behavioral economic view point, It concerns consumers will compare cost to make decision to choose to buy which kind of product which can satisfy whose needs among of similar products of comparision.

The standard economic model of consumer behavioral prediction method advantages includes: A logically consistent theory of consumer behavior can be built, that theory can be used to make predictions about consumer behavior and those predictions can be compared with reality and those models often correspond to actual behavior of consumption reasons. What is the inconvenient truth? It includes clear evidence from psychology has shown that the rationality assumptions of standard economic model are wrong. Evidence from psychology has shown that consumers often are irrational and also who are predictably irrational. So these are wrong view point to influence how economists judge what cause consumption of behavior. Thus, it beings this question? What is mean of predictably irrational? It means that of irrational consumers were irrational in random ways, who would cancel each other out, leaving the overall outcomes determined by the behavioral consumption of rational consumers. As that case, behavioral economic theories that ignored irrational behavioral consumption would work just fine. But, psychology has shown that consumers are irrational in similar and predictable ways. Therefore, irrationality doesn't cancel out and can't be ignored to judge why the behavioral consumption has been caused.

How can behavioral economists judge each behavioral consumption cause? Economists will see evidence that consumers often are unable to make use of what consumers know about whose available options and whose preferences to figure out the best available option. However, although economic theory doesn't always assume self- interested behavior to any consumers, as a practical matter, most applications of economic theory assume that consumers act according to self- interest to decide every behavioral consumption of choice. For insurance industry is one good behavioral economy market example, insurance market competition can make rational consumption. Such as competitive market in auto vehicle accident insurance will charge very high rates to some insurance buyers who might to drive a fast speed, but unsafe motorbike, this one might argue will protect the driving insurance buyers from taking stupid risk. So learning can make rational consumers. Even if consumers are predictably irrational, who can learn from their families and other consumer' or friends behavioral mistakes, therefore, over time irrational consumers will learn to be rational to make the most irrational consumption. As a result, there are few opportunities to learn from consumer individual mistakes of any consumption of decision. Finally, if there are many potential; bad choices and one good consumption of choice, it might take a lot of costly experimentation to figure out the right consumption of choice. Thus, the standard economic model of behavioral consumption of prediction method, which is standard economic theories assume that consumers are rational, strong-willed , and self-interested, but evidence from psychology shows that who are not and that evidence also shows that consumer individual irrationality has predictable features. So, it seems behavioral economic model can make economic predictions more accurate by using the evidence on consumer individual predictable irrational behavioral prediction in any kind of the similar products in competitive market nowadays.

CHAPTER II

How to apply psychological method to predict consumption of behaviors

The methods how to predict to cause the (consumer's) person's consumption of behavior are the same as those in other areas of behavioral economic and psychological methods. In fact, behavioral economics relied heavily on evidence generated to predict behavioral consumption by experiments. More recently, however, behavioral economists have moved beyond experimentation and the full range of methods are employed by economists. The experiements played a large role in the initial phase of behavioral economics because experimental control is exceptionally helpful for distinguishing behavioral explanations from standard ones.

Suppose we observed this phenomenon in these any one of cares, in the form of failures of legal cases to settle before trial, costly divorce proceedings, and labor strikes. They are phenomenons of human‘ behaviours are caused by costs and benefits measurement of result. It implies the married people or the legal compensatory amount or labor strikes compensatory benefits will evaluate whether thier economic benefit is more or loss is more to decide divorce behavior or legal trial behavior or labour strikes compensatory behavior . So, consumer individual psychological behavior and economic benefits has close relationship to cause how consumer who prefers to make any consumption of choice every day. As the failures of legal cases to settle before trial , the behavioural economy concept would be difficult to tell whether rejection of offers was the result of reputation-building in repeated games, agency problems (between clients and lawyers) confusion why the lawyer' client (appellant) who choose to continue to attempt to pay legal fee to find the lawyer to appellate the case if the case is fail at the first time . However, in these game experiments of failures of legal cases to settle before trial, costly divorce proceedings, and labor strikes. These explanations are ruled out because the experiments are played once, have no agents, and are simple enough to rule out confusion. Thus, the experimental data clearly establish that subjects are expressing concern for fairness.

Other experiments have been useful for testing whether judgment errors which individuals commonly make in psychology experiments also affect prices and quantities in markets, such as shareholder's individual investment behavior. The lab is especially useful for these studies because individual and market-level data can be observed. Although behavioral economists relied on experimental datato predict shareholder's individual investment behavior, however, behavioral economics subject is seen as a very different method from experimental economics. As noted, behavioral economists are methodological profession. They define themselves, not on the basis of the research methods that who employ, but rather their application of psychological insights to economics.

Experimental economists, on the other hand, define themselves on the basis of use of experimentation which is as a research tool. Also, economists have made a major investment in developing experimental methods that are suitable for addressing economic issues, and have achieving among themselves on a number of important issues. For example, experimental economists often make instructions and software available for precise replication, and raw data are typically shared for reanalysis. Experimental economists also insist on paying performance-based. However, experimental economists have also developed rules that many behavioral economists are likely to find excessively . For example, experimental economists rarely collect data like demographics, self-reports, reponse times and other cognitive measure which behavioral economists have found useful. Descriptions of the experimental environment are usually abstract rather than which are carried on experiment in the outside world because economic theory rarely makes a prediction about how a happen would matter, and experimenters are concerned about losing control over incentives if choosing strategies with certain labels is appealing because of the labels themselves. Finally, economic experiments also typically use "stationary replication", in which the same task is repeated over and over in each period. Data from the last few periods of the experiment are typically used to draw conclusions about equilibrium behavior outside the lab. When economists believe that examining behavior after it is of great interest, it is also obvious that many important aspects of economic consumption of individual behavior to every individual consumer. The consumer's individual consumption of behavioral choose is like the first few periods of an experiment rather than the psychological methods to predict behavioral consumption.

Supposing if we need to make decision of marriage, educational decisions, and saving for retirement, or the purchase of large durables like houses, sailboats, can cars, which happen just a few times in a person's life, a focus on behavior is clearly not warranted. All said, the focus on psychological realism and economic applicability of research promoted by the behavioral-economics perspective suggests the usefullness research outside the lab and of a broader range of approaches to laboratory research. So, economists realize that who have ideal opportunity to learn by trial-and-error, in a stationary environment, and uses the opportunity to learn how to carry on experimenting any psychology and behavioral researches in lab experiment environment.

What is psychology of consumption behavior?

Psychology is the science of human behavior and mental consumption processes. In consumption process behavior, it is any consumption behaviors as well as consumer mental consumption process is consumer individual internal experiences, comparison with alternative products, products choice of the best, making decision to consume or not consume for the product. So, advertisers often persuade to influence consumers' behavior to attract them to choose to buy whose products.

Why businessmen need to learn consumer psychology? Because psychology can help businessmen scientifically to evaluate common consumer beliefs and misconceptions about consumption behavior and consumption decision making mental processes. Consumption scientific psychology has four basic goals: To describe , explain, predict and change consumption behavior and consumption decision making mental process. Consumption psychological information is based on evidence, this is information based on direct observation and measurements with consumption behavior with scientific method. How are typical images of psychology? Consumption psychologists need to use scientific method to help businessmen to think what predicts who own, make a list of words would who use to describe a psychological scientist and what use to describe a psychological scientist and what images the businessmen have. However, consumption psychologists have difference ways of looking at the same problem for the businessmen, which is why there are so many sub-fields of consumption psychology. Consumption psychology's roots began in philosophy, but the focus changes to a scientific focus consumer.

Behaviorism is focused on consumer buying behavior that can be measured and observable. This returned the scientific approach to consumption psychology. Consumption behaviorist's believe consumers are controlled by their environment. Consumption behaviorism focuses on consumption observable behavior. However, consumption cognitive psychology believes that consumption behaviors are preformed because of the product ideas and thoughts. The cognitive perspective focuses on such consumer decision making and choice processes, such as perception, memory and thinking to the product.

The two categories of consumer's behavioral consumption of decision

The field of consumer's behavioral consumption of decision research, on which behavioral economics has drawn more than any other subfield of psychology, typically classifies research into two categories: judgement and choice. Judgement research deals with the processes people use to estimate probabilities. Choice deals with the processes people use to select among actions, considering of any relevant judgements who may have made. Everyday, we, such as consumers need to make probable judements. Due to judging the likelihood of events is central to economic life. For example: Will you lose your job in a poor economic environment? Will you be able to find another house you like as much as the one you must bid for right away? Will the government raise interest rates in this year or next year? Will a merger strategy increase profits? These questions are answered by some process of judging likelihood. The standard principles used in economic to model probability judgement in economic are concepts of statistical sampling, which are concerned probabilities in the face of new evidence. However, it requires a separation between previously judged probabilities and evaluations of new evidence. However, (consumers) people often overestimate the probability who previously attached to events which later happened. This leads to "secondguessing". For example, Monday morning quarterbacking and may be partly responsible for lawsuits against stockbrokers who lost money for their clients. (The clients think the brokers should have known). For example, anybody has tried to learn from a computer distance learning manual has seen the classroom learning of knowledge in action. Another example for making probability judgements is called "representativeness": People judge conditional probabilities like P(hypothesis /data) or P(example/class) by how well the data represents the hypothesis or the example represents the class. Representativeness is an economical shortcut that delivers reasonable judgements with minimal effort in many cases. For example, in judging whether a certain student (University customer) described in a profile is, say, a psychology major or computer science major, the student decides how well the profile matches the psychology or computer science career to the student generally. So, University can read the student profile to predict whether the student will choose to study psychology subject more prefer or computer subject more prefer to predict whose computer or psychology student numbers more accurate in the year.

Many studies show how this sort of feature-matching can lead people to underweigh the "base rate", in this example, the overall frequency of the two majors. Another byproduct of representativeness is the "law of small numbers": Small samples are though to represent the properties of the statistical process that generated them (as if the law of large numbers, which guarantees that a large sample of independent draws does represent the process, is in a hurry to work). Field and experimental studies with basketball shooting and betting on games that people believe that there is positive attitude that players experience the "hot hand", when there is no evidence that such an effect exists.

For example, how the government tax department can judge whether the company's financial report has not been misled from accounting auditor's moral behavior, how to predict consumer's brand choice behavior and how to control students' learning behavior in classroom . It is important to judge whether it is either a good attitude or bad attitude from the consumer's personal behavior in the past. A consumer's good attitude to the product or the service consumption provides good consumption experience, close to optimal, answers when time or capabilities are limited, but it also needs logical principles and leads to situations. So, optimal is largely a critique (a reasonable one) of the later applied research. Otherwise, a consumer's bad attidude to the product or the service consumption provide poor consumption experience to buy the product or use the service again. Thus, the consumer's good or bad past buying experience to the product or to use the service will have help to assist the businessman how to predict whose consumption behavior next time.

Assume that people misspecify a set of hypotheses, or encode new evidence incorrectly. For example, assuming that people believe hypothesis A is more likely than B will never encode pro-A evidence mistakenly, but will sometimes encode pro-B evidence as being supportive. For another example, investors will think there is wide variation in skill of, say, mutual-fund managers, even if there is no variation at all. (A manager who does well several years is a surprise if performance is mistakenly thought due to nonreplacement, so concluding that the manager must be really good.) A question concerns stock market, such as: Overreacts in the long term. In their model, earnings follow a random walk but investors believe, mistakenly, that earnings have positive attitude. After one or two periods of good earnings, the stock market can not be confident that exists and hence expects, but since earnings are really a random walk, the stock market is too pessimistic and is underreacting to good earnings news. After a good earnings, however, the stock market believes many investors are increasing. Since, it is not the stock market is too optimistic and overreact. So, investor's past experience to earn or loss from the share, which will influence whose invetment behavior to choose to buy the share next time.

For another example, valuable consumer products (A $100 wireless keyboard, a fancy computer mouse, bottles of wine, and a box of chocolate) are sold to postgraduate (MBA) business students. The students were presented with a product and asked whether who would buy it for a price equal to the last two digits of their own social security number (a roughly random identification number required to obtain work in the United States) converted into a dollar figure, e.g. , if the last digits were 99, then the postgraduate business students will accept the hypothetical price was $99 to buy any of it for a price to the last two digits of their own social security number . After giving a yes/no response to the question. Would you pay $99? subjects were asked to state the most who would pay (using a procedure that gives people an incentive to say what who really would pay). Although subjects were reminded that the social security number is essentially random, those with high numbers were willing to pay more for the products. However, many studies have also shown that the method used to elicit preferences can have dramatic consequences.

Nevertheless, when required to make an economic decisions-to-choose a brand of toothpaste, a car, a job, or how to invest, people do make some kind of decision. Behavioral economists refer to the process by which people make choices with ill defined preferences as "constructing preferences". So, psychologic methods can be used to predict why the consumer choose to buy the product as well as any consumer seems who needs to evaluate whether who will earn more benefit or low to choose to buy the brand of product or use the service to achieve the best benefits. However, in classical consumer theory, preferences among different commodities are assumed to be invariant with respect to an individual's current consumption. Specifically, people seem to dislike losing commodities from their consumption much more than they like gaining other commodities. For example, the research of "contingent valuation" studies that attempt to establish the dollar value of products which are not routinely trades. Contingent valuation is often used to do government cost-benefit analysis or establish legal penalties from environment damage. These surveys typically show very large differences between buying prices (e.g. paying to clean up oil of beaches) and selling prices (e.g. having to be paid to allow beaches to be ruined) to reduce environmental pollution from the low cost method for government spending.

Nowadays, there are many USA manufacturers use behavioral economy methods to predict consumer individual behavior, a quarter of the wealth in the USA has more interesting opportunities to do behavioral economies. They find that motivated sellers should regard the price who paid as a sunk cost and choose at a nominal loss from the purchase price. Sellers‘ listing prices and subsequent selling behavior reflects to nominal losses. There are some cases in which no effect would be expected, such as when products , such as house or antique dealers' products are purchased for resale rather than for utilization. For example, Do art or antique dealers like with pieces who buy to resell? What about surrogate mothers who agree to bear a child for a price paid in advance? Reference points can also serve as social focal points for house or antique products or surrogate mothers whose behavioral judging performance.

For an interesting example from corporate finance. In general, when managers whose firms face possible losses (or declines from a previous year's earnings) are very reluctant to report small losses. As a result, the distribution of actual losses and gains show a very large at zero, and hardly any small reported losses (compared to the number of small gains). A manager who does not have the skill to shift accounting profits to erase a potential loss (i.e. has some earnings in his pocket.) is considered a poor manager. It seems that the bad performance manager whose behavior is bad to mislead public to believe his firm have better performance in this year. Hence, in the mental accounting view, people(accountants) set up mental accounts for outcomes which are psychologically separate, much as financial accountants lump expenses and revenues into separated accounts to guide managerial attention. Otherwise, mental accounting stands in opposition to the standard view in economics that it predicts, accurately , that people will spend money coming from different sources in different ways. So, a generalization of the notion of mental accounting (the accountant's mislead financial report performance) , which aims to let investors and consumers have more confidence to choose to invest or to choose to buy it's products or consume its service more easily. So, it explains why the accountant needs to mislead to report it's earns are more than loss in every year.

CHAPTER III

Explanation behavioral consumption

What is preferences over risky to behavioral consumption. Such as prospect theory is experimental choices more accurately than (EU) because it gets the psychological of judgement and choice right. It consists of two main components, a probability weighting function, and a "value function" which replaces the utility function of (EU) to any consumer when who needs to choose to buy any product or consume any service by more than one choice. The weighting function P(P) combines two elements: (1) The level of probability weight is a way of expressing risk and (2) Captures how sensitive people are to differences in probabilities. New information of any products can help any decision maker to feel better to make better final purchase decisions. These theories effect may explain demand for information in settings like medicine or personal finance, where new information usually does not change choice, but relieves anxiety people have from knowing there is something who could know to choose to buy the medicine or borrowing loan of low interest payment. So, new information of any products can reduce consumer individual risk to choose to buy.

However, the planning problem for economic agents who would like to behave in fashion and discussed the important time discounting for choice. Most big decisions, e.g. savings, educational investments, labor supply, health and diet, crime and drug etc. decisions use have costs and benefits which occur at different point in time. Thus, time discounting is basically standard time discounting plus an immediacy effect, a decision discounts delays in equally at all moments except the current one, caring differently about well being. This functional form provides one sample and powerful model of the taste to individual to make right or reasonable behavior economic decision. However, most analyses of choice assume that people integrate new consumption with planned consumption. It is infeasible and perhaps for this reason, descriptively inaccurate. When people make decisions about new sequences of payments or consumption, they tend to evaluate them in isolation, e.g. treating negative outcomes as losses, rather than as reductions to their existing money flows or consumption plans.

How to decide fairness and social preferences. The assumption that people maximize their own wealth and other personal material goals just self-interest is a correct simplification that is often useful in economics. However, people may sometimes choose to spend their wealth to punish others who have harmed them, reward whose, so who have helped, or to make outcomes more fair. Just as understanding demand for products requires specific utility function. So. on economic view point, utility function concept can influence consumer choice. if the consumer feels the product has more utility, then who will prerfer to choose to buy the product. Otherwise, if who feels the product has less utility, then who will not perfer to choose to buy the product.

Behavioral economy can also use to assist firms to choose right behavior to decide to do any matters. I show hypothesis to establish any reference level of consumer surplus and product profit. Both sides are entitled to any firm's levels of profit, so price changes which threaten any matter are considered unfair. So raising any product price, it will reduce consumer surplus and is considered unfair. But the cost of a firm's inputs rises, subjects said it was fair to raise prices. Because not raising prices would reduce the firm's profit (compared to the reference profit). Everyday observation that firms don't change prices and wages as frequently commonly.

For example, when the fourth hary potter story book was released in summer 2000 year, most stores were allocated a small number of books that were pre-sold in advance. Why not raise prices or auction the books off? It is possible that it concerned about customer goodwill and excess demand to cause book stores limit such book price increases. Offended consumers are often able to affect firm behavior by media attention or provoking legislation. For example, scalping tickets for popular sports and entertainment events (resulting them at a large premium over the printed ticket price) is constrained by law in most countries. For example, some countries have "anti-laws" penalizing sellers who take advantage of shortages of water, fuel and other necessities by raising prices after natural disasters. So, the countries' governments can protect which citizen benefits to balance the natural resource supply and demand to sell in the reasonable price fairly after the natural disaster occurrence. This is utility function concept. Because the book store believes the fourth hary potter story book will be excess demand and reader goodwill is good. So the books' utility function is enough to prepare to sell to readers, which do not need to raise price to attract readers to read. Also, scalping tickets for popular sports and entertainment events will rise ticket price to be limited level because the popular sports and entertainment players believe who have attrative ability to attract full ticket buyers and whose numbers will exceed seats demand. So, the ticket numbers utility are enough and which are not need to raise ticket price too much. Also, shortages of water, fuel and other necessities by raising prices after natural disasters, because government make whose citizen has limit number of water, fuel and other necessities supply to keep enough utility function to satisfy whose needs. So, the nature resources do not need to raise price when natural disaster occurs.

A few years ago, responding to public anger at rising CEO salaries when the economy was being restructured through downsizing and many workers lost their jobs. Otherwise, some countries passed a law prohibiting firms from deducting CEO salaries for tax purposes beyonded $1 million a year. However, because some countries need to earn much tax income from these high salary CEO income every year. So, these countries do not suggest to pass a law to probibit firm from deducting CEO salaries for tax purpose. So, utility function can be applied to company benefit. If the company hopes to limit the CEO salary, then it will limit whose CEO 's duty (reducing utility funtion to whose duty). Aim to avoid to pay more salary expenditure to the CEO , when the country's economy is poor and it believes there are less consumers prefer to consume more. Otherwise, if the company does not hope to limit the CEO salary, then it will not limit whose CEO'duty (increasing utility function to whose duty). Aim to hope who can help whose company to earn more profit, when the country's economy is good and it believe there are many consumers prefer to consume. On the other side, if the country tax department hopes to earn more salary tax income, it will choose not to pass a law prohibiting firms from deducting CEO salaries for tax purposes beyonded $1 million a year. In the behavioral economy concept, the government tax department hopes to earn more salary tax when the economy environment is not good or it is worse to compare last year's economy environment. Thus, behavioral economy concept will be applied to company profit intention or country income intention or individual consumption intention.

How can behavioral game theory apply to company income intention?

How can behavioral game theory apply to company income intention ? Behavioral game theory has rapidly become an important foundation for many areas of micro economic theory to any organizations, such as bargaining in decentralized markets, outsource contracting and organizational structure. The descriptive accuracy of game theory in these application can be questioned because equilibrium predictions often assume strategic reasoning and direct field tests are difficult to any organizations. In fact, behavioral game theory uses any experimental evidence and psychological research to generalize the standard assumptions of game theory to any organizations how which choose to make profit intention.

One component of behavioral game theory is a theory of social preferences for allocations of money to oneself and others. Another component is a theory of how people choose in one shot games or in the first period of a repeated game. For example, in share buying and selling market, shareholders shall buy or sell shares from their judgement in the economic cycle market everyday. So share investment is seemed as allocation of game to these shareholders. Also, shareholders whose mind can influence whose psychological behavior to decide how to invest whose shares in their share investment economic activities. The component of behavioral game theory can include a model of learning to either individual or a population. Also, game theory is one area of economy in which serious attention has been paid to the process by which can equilibrium comes about. Many learning theories have been proposed and carefully tested with experimental data. Theories about population never predict as well as theories of individual learning through who are useful for other purposes. So, behavioral game theory can be applied to these complex environments. e.g. consumer supermarket purchase, share market etc. for these business organizations research.

How to apply behavioral game theory to macroeconomics and saving aspect? Many concepts in macroeconomic probably have a behavioral style that could be influenced by research in psychology. For example, it is common to assume that prices and wages are in nominal terms, which has important implications for macroeconomic behavoir. Behavioral economics suggests some ideas for among consumers and workers, perhaps it is influenced by workers' concern for fairness.

An important model in macroeconomics is the life cycle model of savings or permanent income hypothesis. This theory assumes that people make a guess about their lifetime earnings profile, and plan their lifetime earnings profile, and plan their savings and consumption in each period has diminishing marginal utility; and preferences for consumptions streams are time-separable (i.e. overall utility is the sum of the discounted utility of consumption in each separate period). The theory also assumes people lump together different types income when they guess how much money who will have (i.e. different sources of wealth are different). So, why many young people won't spend too much money for unnecessary expenditure, e.g. entertainment easily. Because who plan to save for their old age to use in their long time life time.

A behavioral life cycle theory of savings in which different sources of income are kept track of in different mental accounts. Mental accounts can reflect natural perceptual or cogitive divisions. For example, it is possible to add up the travellers' paycheck and dollar value of whose frequent flyer miles, but it is simply unnatural to do so. It is important to note that many key implications of the life-cycle hypothesis have never been well supported ,e.g. consumption is far more closely related to current income than it should be according to theory. However, predictions can be improved by introducing utility functions with habit formation in which utility in a current depends on the reference point of previous consumption, and by more carefully accounting for uncertaining about future income.

For example, in the accountancy (economic) professional view point mental accounting is only one of several behavioral approaches that may prove useful. Economics is money illusion, it is the tendency to make decisions based on nominal quantities rather than converting those figures into real terms by adjusting for inflation. Money illusion seems to be pervasive in some domains. So, it appears that employees don't seem to mind if their real wage falls as long as their nominal wages doesn't fall.

How can behavioral game theory apply to company income intention? Labor macroeconomics is involuntary unemployment. Why can some people not find work beyond of switching jobs, or a natural rate of unemployment? A popular account of unemployment pushs that wages are deliberately paid above the market clearly level, which creates an excess supply of workers and hence unemployment. But why are wages too high ?
As efficiency wage theory shows that paying workers more than who deserve is necessary to ensure that who have something to lose if they are unemployed, which motivates them to work hand and economizes on monitoring.

How Another viewpoint indicates that employer and worker is such as into a gift exchange relationship. Employers pay more than who have to as a gift and workers repay the gift by working harder than necessary. They show how gift exchange can be an equilibrium and show some of its macroeconomic implications. In labor economics, gift exchange is clearly evident of experimental labor markets. In practical working environment, firms offer wages; workers who take the jobs than choose a level of effort, which is costly to the workers and valuable to the firms.

For example, firms and workers can enforce wages, but not effort levels. Since workers and firms are matched for just one period, and do not learn each other's identities, there is no way for either side to build reputations or for firms to punish workers who chose low effort. However, self interested workers should shirk, and firms should anticipate that and pay a low wage. In fact, firms deliberately pay high wages as gifts and workers choose higher effort levels when they take higher wage jobs. It seems that it has strong relationship between wages and effort is stable over time.

For another example, standard life-cycle theory assumes that if people can borrow, they should prefer wage profiles which maximize the present value of lifetime wages. Holding total wage payments constant, and assuming a positive real rate of interest, present value maximization implies that workers should prefer declining wage profiles over increasing ones. However, in fact, most wages profiles are clearly rising over time which is such as a phenomenon. Rather, workers derive utility from positive changes in consumption, but have self-control problems.

If any company has any good wages profiles would prevent them from positive changes in consumption, but have self-control problems that would prevent them from saving for later consumption of wages were more front-loaded in the life cycle. In addition, workers seem to derive positive utility from increasing wage profiles, it is perhaps because rising wages are a source of self-esteem and the desire for increasing payments is much weaker for non wage income. The standard life-cycle of labor supply also implies that workers should substitute labor and leisure based on the wage rate who face and the value who place on leisure at different points in time. If wage fluctuations are temporary workers should work long hours when wages are high and short hours when wages are low. However, because changes in wages are often persisting and because work hours are generally fixed in the short-run. So, it is difficult to tell whether workers are substituting. So, if the company can have good method to decide when to rise salary or wage level , even reduce salary or wage level, as well as how much rising or reducing salary or wage level is the suitable in different time. If the wage fluctations are reasonable in the most suitable time, the labor turnover numbers will not be reduced easily.

How can behavioral game theory apply to individual business income intention? For example, taxi drivers who target daily will drive longer hours on low income days and will drive less hours early on high income days. This behavior is exactly the opposite of substitution. Also inexperienced taxi drivers support the daily targeting prediction. But experienced taxi drivers don't have negative elasiticies, either because target minded drivers earn less and self select or taxi drivers learn over time to substitute rather than target. Perhaps the simplest prediction of labor economics is that the supply of labor should be upward sloping in response to a increase in wage. Suppose to the inexperienced taxi drivers will attempt to drive long hours if who can feel or predict the taxi passengers number will reduce on the low income day. Otherwise, the experienced taxi drivers will attempt to drive less hours if who can feel or predict when the taxi passengers number will increase on the high income day. So, these experienced or inexperienced taxi drivers whose decison of driving long hours or less hours is depended on whose feeling of taxi passengers number who is high or low.

How, behavioral game theory applys to investor behavior. In finance, standard equilibrium models of asset pricing assume that investors only care about asset risks if who affect marginal publicly available information to forecast stock returns as accurately as possible the efficient markets hypothesis. When those hypotheses do make some accurate predictions and some investors in assets have limited rationality of behavioral finance. Also, in share stock market, it is common, shareholders should not want to trade with them, but the volume of stock market transaction is large. So, it presents data on individual trading behavior which suggests that the extremely high volume may be driven, in part, by overconfidence on the part of investors. Thus, if the company's share numbers buying and selling transactions are very large in the year. Then, it will influence many investors have more confidence to be encouraged to choose to buy the firm's shares in the year. Otherwise, if the company's share numbers buying and selling transactions are less in the year. Then, it will also influence many investors have less confidence to be encouragd to choose to buy its' shares in the year.

For another example, behavioral game theory applys to property agent's behavior. Property agent's individual behavior is similar to share agent's individual behavior. In the economy view point , property agent bases a list price for a house on the selling prices of nearly houses that is similar ("comparables"). Every nearest neighbour techniques bases on similarity is also used in credit scoring and other kinds of evaluations. Also, one firm whose every share sale on the selling price is comparable to its similar firms whose every share price in its same business industry. The shareholder will evaluate whose every share issued sale price in the stock (share) market. Otherwise, in behavioral economy view, for example, property or share buyer who has risky choice to decide to buy in the property or share market. It is a process of comparing the similarity of the probabilities and outcomes in two gambles and choosing on dimensions which are dissimilar.

As we mentioned above, behavioral economics simply includes an interest in psychology. In fact, we believe that many familiar economic distinctions do have a lot of behavioral content, they are implicitly behavioral, and could surely benefit from more explicit ties to psychological ideas and data. However, some people do not feel psychology and economy which have close relationship. Such as, substantial debate is ongoing in psychology about whether knowing the precise details of how the brain carries out computations is necessary to understand functions and mechanisms of driving car skill at higher levels, (knowing the mechanical details of how a car works may not be necessary to turn the key and drive it). So, the drivers who concerns more safe to their families and themselves, who will prefer to pay more money to buy the more safe vehicle to driver. Otherwise, the drivers who disconcern safe and concern money save, who will choose to pay less money to buy the less safe vehicle to drive.

Behavioral game theory can apply to price behavioral elasticity for how firm's price decision. For example , it is the distinction between short run and long run price elasticity which concerns behavioral economy. In fact, economy needs have theories concepts to support any evidence to prove any matter has happened. Concerning short run and long run price elasticity cause and effort issue, with a casual suggestion that the run is the time it takes for markets to adjust, or for consumers to learn new prices, after a demand or supply stock. Adjustment costs undoubtedly have technical and social component, but probably also have some behavioral factors influence in the form of gradual adaption to loss and learning. So, if there are many consumers who believe the product is reliable to use and the brand is famous, the product's price won't be push down often and it has less price elastic. Otherwise, if there are many consumers who do not believe the product is reliable to use and the brand is not famous, the product's price will be push doen often and it has more price elactic tendency.

Another macroeconomic model which can be interpreted as implicitly behavior is that business cycles can emerge if it is not general price inflation, so why the consumers shall not decide to buy this kind of product in the competitive market. So price when the market price inflation, consumers will not choose to prefer to spend to buy more food to eat or products to use. Otherwise, when the market price is stable, consumers will choose to prerfer to spend to buy more food to eat products to use. So, inflation will influence consumption of behavior.

Behavioral economic simply includes an interest in psychology. In fact, we believe that many familiar economic distinctions do have a lot of behavioral content, they are implicitly behavioral and could surely benefit from more explicit ties to psychological ideas and data. However, some people do not feel psychology and economy which have close relationship. Such as psychology is about whether knowing the precise details of how the brain carries out computations is necessary to understand functions and mechanisms at higher levels. (knowing the mechanical details of how a car works may not necessary to turn the key and drive it.)

Most psychology experiments use indirect measures like response times, error rates, self reports and natural experiments due to brain has been fairly successful in codifying what we know about thinking. However, pessimists think brain scan studies won't add much. The optimists think the new tools will lead to some discoveries and the potential is great that they cannot be ignored. However, economy needs have theories or concepts to support evidence to prove why any matters had happened. An example, is the distinction between short term and long term price elasticity. This distinction, mentions between of them, with a casual suggestion that long run is the time it takes for markets to adjust, or for consumers to learn new prices, after a demand or supply shock. Adjustment costs undoubtedly have technical and social components, but probably also have some behavioral factors influence in the form of gradual adaption to loss and learning.

However behavioral economy theory can be applied to organizational behavior, organizational behavioral theory concerns that organizatonal contracting are shot through with implicitly behavioral economics. Some economists motivate the incompleteness of contracts as a consequence of rationality in foreseeing the future, but do not tie the research directly to work on memory and imagination. For example, agency theory begins with the presumption that there is some activity the agent doesn't like to do. Why markets are better at making dramatic changes than managers influence cost. So, influence costs are the costs managers preform for projects who like or personally benefit from like promotion or raises. A lot of influence costs are undoubtedly inflated by optimistic, each division manager really does think their division desperately needs funds and social comparison of pay and benefits. Otherwise, why are salaries kept so secret? In all these cases, conventional economic behavior has deeper psychological questions of where adjustment costs, effort and influence costs come from. So, it beings these questions: Could these phenomena surely produce surprising testable prediction? Is psychology regularity an assumption or a conclusion?

Behavioral economics generally begins with assumption rooted in psychological regularity and asks what follows from those assumptions. An alternative approach is to work backward, regarding a psychological regularity as a conclusion that must be proved an explanation that must be derived from deeper assumption before we fully understand and accept it. The alternative approach is caused by a fashionable new direction in economic theory and psychology too, which is to explain human behavior as the product of evolution. However, we may not believe that behavior of intelligent, modern people lived in socialization and cultural influence can only be understood by guessing what their lives were like and how their brains might have adapted generally. There are other models that treat psychological regularity as a conclusion to be proved rather than an assumption to be used. Such models usually begin with an observed regularity. However, I think economic factor can influence consumers to make who feel the more reasonable psychological decision to make the more right behavior. Thus, economy and psychology has close relationship to influence consumer individual decision.

Economists have for deriving behavior from first principles and rationalizing apparent irrationality. Theories of this sort are useful behavioral economics and what fresh predictions do they make. However, critics have pointed out that behavioral economics is not a unified theory, but is instead a collection of tools and ideas. This is true. However, some economists believe that economic models do not derive much predictive power from the single tool of utility maximization. The goal of behavioral economic is to develop better tools that, in some cases, can do both jobs at once.

Economists like to point out the natural division of labor between scientific disciplines: Psychologists should concern to individual minds, and economists to behavior in games, markets, and economies. But the division of labor is only efficient if there is effective coordinaton, and all too often economists fail to conduct intellectual trade with those who have a comparative advantage in understanding individual human behavior. The only question is whether the implicit psychology in economics is good psychology or bad psychology. We think it is simply unwise, and inefficient to do economics without paying some attention to good psychology.

Can predict consumer behavior with web search?

In behavioral economy view point, it can be applied to predict why consumers buy products from internet. Recent work has demonstrated that web search volume can "predict the present", meaning that can be used to accurately track outcomes, such as unemployment levels, auto and home sales and disease prevalence in near real time. Consumers are searching what for online can also predict their collective future behavior days or even weeks in advance. For example, specifically businessmen can use search query volume to forecast the opening weekend box-office revenue for feature films, first month sales of video games and the rank of songs, finding in all case that search counts are highly predictive of future outcomes from online google research. Finally, businessmen can reexamine previous work on tracking trends and show that, perhaps surprisingly, the utility of search data relative to a simple auto regressive model is modest.

Nowadays, people increasingly use the internet for news, information and research purposes. From this perspective, it is a short step to conclude that what people are researching for today is predictive of what who will do in the near future. For example, consumers may search to prepare to buy a new camera, moviegoers may search to determine the opening date of a new film, or to locate cinemas showing it and individuals planning a vacation may search from a places of interest, to find airline tickets, or to price hotel rooms. So online can aggregately count of search queries related to retail activity. Movie going or travel might be able to predict collective behavior of economic, cultural, or political interest. Determining the nature of behavior that can be predicted using search, the accuracy of such predictions and the time scale over which predictions can be usefully made are therefore all questions of interest.

Researchers have focused on the observation that search " predicts the present". For example, Ettredge et al (2005) found that counts of the top 300 search terms during 2001 to 2003 year were correlated with US Bureau Of Labor statistics Unemployment Figures; Cooper (2005) et al found that search activity for specific cameras during 2001 to 2003 year correlated with their estimated incidence and Eysenbach (2006) found a high correlation between clicks on sponsored search results of flu-related keywords and epidemiolopical data from the 2004 to 2005 year Canadian flu season.

Thus, motivated , I indicate one example how investigates whether search activity is a systematic leading indicator of consumer activity by forecasting. For first example, supposing to opening weekend Box-office revenue for 119 feature films released in the united States between Oct. 2008 year and Sept. 2009. For second example, supposing to first month sales of video games across all gaming platforms, e.g. Xbox, Play station etc.) for 106 games released between Sept. 2008 and Sept. 2009 year. These search data can be collected from yahoo using research rank from the current and previous weeks.

Can online search also predict the near future? A finding that may apply usually to a wide range of consumer behaviors , e.g. airline travel, hotel vacancy rates and auto sales and economic indicators , e.g. real-estate prices, credit card and confidence indicators. It seems all research based predictions simply models to build on publicly available information. For movies, baseline predictions can be used a linear model that includes production budgets, the number of screens on which each movie opened and box office projections from the Hollywood Stock Exchange (HSX) (hsx.com) on online, play money prediction market that is known to generate information prediction. For video games, many of the key indicators of revenue, including production budgets and initial available. Thus, it seems that businessmen can attempt to use internet (online) search technological method to search past information to concern whether what number of customers will be estimated.

Can firm's conduct and behavior factor influence consumption of behavior ?

In behavioral economy view point, it can explain how firm conduct and behavior factor can infuence consumption of behavior. The usual assumption about the objectives of firms made by economists is that firms seek to maximize profit. The means that firms feel that who are protected against the possibility of new entrants, and proceed to maximize short-run profits. Firms feel that the barriers against new entrants ensure that their profits won't induce new firms to enter the industry and to reduce competitors enter to industry to raise consumers' choices to buy any similar products.

A major challenges to the profit maximization objective has come from proponents of the view that modern larger corporation are under a managerial control, which it is argued leads to the pursuit of other objectives, such as growth. The pursuit of non-profit objective is not unique to managerial-controlled firms, although the growth of such firms and of theories about than have emphasized these types of objectives.

Another view has focused on the controllers of the firm, whether owners or managers, having a wider range of objectives and that the achievement of profit maximization and the cost minimization requires considerable time and effort by the controllers. Thus, the controllers have incentives to forge profit maximization, unless who are forced to do so. Under oligopoly, firms can earn profits above the normal level, e.g. one country has only two electricity power companies are existing in the country's energy supply market. They may change a profit maximizing price, but actual reported profits may be less than potential profit.

This could raise from technical inefficiency or from higher than necessary payments to the factors of production. The technical inefficiency can arise since it takes effort by the controllers to reach full efficiency and which may be willing to make necessary effort. The higher payments can involve higher salaries to the controllers of the firm. For either reasons, company needs to concern how to report profit fall below true profit of the firm, with the difference used to finance inefficiency and higher factor payments in fair business conduct behavior. Particularly, company also need to concern how to carrying on fair business conduct behavior, e.g. none mislead advertising information, correct profit differentiation financial information, product reputations of the existing products presentation, none mislead consumption motives performance (which favor the established over the unestablished) and lower trade-in values of second –hand products of entrants (particularly in the car market). So, it seems that any one firm none mislead conduct behavior factor can influence consumer choices to increase or decrease to buy the firm's products in fair buying and selling transaction.

Another view point, for same products differentiation none mislead conduct factor is also important to influence each consumer behavior. For example, cars don't have a common prototype and each manufacturer must design its particular model. In constant , for a product like sugar , there is a common prototype, and differentiation through branding is within the discretion of the firm involved. This for some good product differentiation may be benefit whereas, for other products differentiation depends upon the activities of the firms involved, although the costs and benefits to the existing firms varies between profits. However, the height of the barrier to entry by product differentiation is likely to be influenced by the conduct and behavior of the firms involved, and thus in the case , there is an element of firm's behavior and conduct can influence any consumer buying behavior of choice to its products.

CHAPTER IV

Apply behavioral economic principles to assist policy makers

Behavioral economics theories can also apply to assist any policy makers to make right and reasonable decision in right time. I shall indicate new principles to recommend and I also shall give any psychological cases to explain how policy makers can apply behavioral economic theories to judge how to make their any decision is the most right and the most reasonable.

Behavioral economy is an independent and demonstrates real economic well-being. It aims to improve quality of life by promoting innovative solutions that challenge mainstream thinking on economic, environment and social issues. Also, behavioral economy is different branches of more alternative economies into a form that is useful primarily for policy-makers. I think behavioral economy can be given an aid to policy makers how who use economic tools to the broader policy making community by providing a theoretical behaviour for many policy approaches to be used. The standard economic analysis assumes that humans are rational and behave in a way to maximize their individual self-interest. This rational man assumption indicates a powerful tool for analysis. However, it has many shortfalls that can lead to unrealistic economic analysis and policy-making. Also, I think behavioral economics and psychology has these principles to influence human behaviour. These principles include, such as below:

In common, people do many things by observing others and copying; people are encouraged to continue to do things when they feel other people approve of their behaviour. People do many things without consciously thinking about time. These habits are hard to change. There are cases where money is de-motivating as it undermines people's intrinsic motivation. People want their actions and commitments to be values usually. People put undue weight on recent events and who can't calculate probabilities well and worry too much about unlikely events and who are strongly influences by how the problem/information is presented to them. People need to feel effective to make a change, even just giving who the incentives and information is not necessarily enough in any environment usually. So any policy maker ought concern about what the acceptable degree is when who choose to decide to make any new policy in whose country. If who can predict whether whether whose country's citizen will or won't accept whose new policy implement and know why some won't accept whose new policy implement and why some accept whose new policy implement, then who can decide to do any economic activities more reasonable, e.g. investment to build public hospital or public school in the location; spending this expenditure to education or medical more.

In fact, much of our behaviour is strongly influenced by other people's behaviour. Social learning is a process by which we take in the behavior of others to learn how to behave. In more complex situations with which we are unfamiliar, we consciously watch and learn from the behavior of others. For example, when use a new library for the first time. When we make a conscious decision on how to behave, our sense of social identity is important, we think: how would other from my group behave in this situation? So, the policy marker will need to make to compare the economic benefits to choose to build either library or public school between of them to satisfy readers need or students need more in the location.

In situations where there is high social capital. i.e. where there are strong networks between people and a high level of mutual trust, so its seems other people's behaviour and our sense of social identity may be extremely important in influencing our own behavior and policy makers ought need to know how to judge their behaviour whether their behavior is either right and reasonable or wrong and unreasonable in any learning process of environment. The standard economic theory is tried to explain where people's preferences come from, so it does not take account of the direct influence of the people's behaviour and social norms on our behaviour. The theory assumes we independently know what we want and that our preferences are fixed. This standard theory is very good at explaining short-term decision making for policy makers only. In decision marker view point, for example, I want green vegetables and choose fruits as they are on special offer in short term, but it cannot explain longer term changes in preferences. Now, I only choose organic food for long term because orgnic food can have more clean and no pollution to compare general green vegetables and fruit. Thus, the learning process environment will influence the food consumers who prefer to choose to buy organic food more than general green food in supermarket.

For driving example, it would require too much effort to look up all the rules when driving in a new country, to find out all the fines/punishments for failing to meet the rules, to work out the probability of being caught and the possible costs, before deciding how to drive there. Instead we just copy other people, and perhaps adjust our behaviour according to the feedback we receive. However, some psychologists indicate to see people how to behave, especically in crises situations and when others are experts. These psychologists have identified that we are open to influence from people in authority or people we like. When we are influenced by authority, an expert, someone with legitimate power to direct our actions, someone who can either reward or punish us. The effects are less likely to be lasting than we are influenced by someone we like. Thus, learning process of environment can influence any person's psychological behavior change easily. However, some people's psychological behaviour is similar to economic behaviour to judge to make any decision. For example, why do you wear a seatbelt in your car? Most of us wear seatbelts as it has became normal behaviour, everyone does it. We neither evaluate the likelihood of having an accident, nor the chance of getting caught without our seatbelt on and incurring a fine. The enforcement of seatbelt wearing is now hardly necessary, as it has become a social norm.

What does this mean for policy makers? Policy makers focusing only on economic analysis may often devise a system that has an immediate effect. In psychologists view this issue point, knowing that there is a fine for speeding and a high likelihood of getting caught, the driver will probably drive more slowly, but who will drive just as fast one who realise the chance of being caught is low. However, of policy makers can change the social norm, perhaps in this case by encouraging us to frown on others who drive dangerously fast with campaigns against dangerous driving, then less enforcement will be needed after the change. In other words policy makers might want to take preferences as fixed in the short term, but they should consider shifting preferences in the medium term.

An example where policy appears to have successfully changes people's preferences in the US and Singapre and Hong Kong is banning smoking in public places. This change appears to reduce the social proof of the amount people smoke in private places and public places both also. It seems that government policies can influence the decreasing numbers of consumers require to buy cigeratte to smoke habitually, due to fine and punishment is regulated to be ban effectively. Such daily routines quickly became habits. Even when we consciously think about what we do, it can be difficult to change our behaviour. Perhaps I think it is a good idea for people to use public transport, but I do not know where the bus stop is or when the bus runs. I think to use private car to drive to work place is more preference choice. The reward feeling , my journey by car was easy and free to reinforce my old bad habit. Psychologists theories on changing habits generally involve raising it to a conscious level where we can consider the merits of alternative behaviour.

In our learning process in environment, this is followed by adopting the new behaviour, which, with time, becomes frozen as a new habit. Thus, I think that we need have regulation to control my behaviour, then we can change my behaviour to be new habit from old habit of behaviour easily, such as consumption behavior.

For example, human blood sale is an economic product, due to paying donors for blood would increase supply. Supplies would be provided at a cost advantage in the future, if demand continued to rise. Such as supplies to hospitals for blood will has cost from donors when there are many patients need much blood to use to treat any diseases in any hospitals. Otherwise, if there are not many patients need much blood to use, but there are many donors have effort to provide blood to any hospitals, then it will be economic inefficiency and it is highly wasteful of blood. Thus, the hospitals need to predict when there are many patients need much blood or there are less patients need less much. Then, hospitals can pay cheap cost to donors for blood supply. Thus, the learning processing for donors for blood supply is needed for hospitals.

For shareholder behavioual learing process in share investment environment example, if you hold some shares in a firm that has gone down in value. What do you do? Many people hold on to their shares in this situation, in the hope that they will recoup their losses. Conversely, when shares have gone up in share, people are happy to sell them to realise their gain, A similar behaviour is also observed for professional traders who tend to hold on to shares with a loss for longer than those with a gain. The traders who exhibit this type of loss to a lesser degree tend to be the more successful ones.

For another learning process environement example, this is a case where the theory is directly applicable within economic cost-benefit-type analyses that include valuations of no-market products, such as valuations of pollution damage. Policy makers have a choice as to whether-to-accept, and as these may vary by up to a factor, the outcome of such an analysis many well depend on which value is chosen. When a policy maker reasonably has a right to something that might be taken away from them, the willing-to-accept value would be used. On the other hand, when the policy maker only reasonable has a right to the status quo and an improvement is proposed, then the willingness-to-pay is the correct value to use. Thus, for valuations of pollution damage, policy makers need to learn whether pollution damage cost is higher or pollution bringing benefit is higher to make reducing pollution decision for long term. In generaly, people are expected to rationally make the best choices given their preferences, independent of how these choices are presented. Therefore more information and choice is always considered good. Using this theory, policy makers should ensure that people always have as much information and as many things to choose between as possible, the process of introducing policy is irrelevant. Thus, gathering information can assist policy makers to choose right decision for pollution damage benefit or cost behvioral choice to their society for economic benefit.

So, a participatory approach not only improves policy, it also makes to any policy makers more happier. In most cases these principles cannot be used directly as part of any mathematical economics analysis, but highlight situations where this standard analysis will not accurately describe human behaviour and therefore might have unintended consequences when implemented in policy. However, that the policy implications could be quite powerful as the behavioural approach provides quite different lines of analysis to the standard economic model. It is heartening to see policy makers focusing more on the psychology of behaviour when devising policy. So behavioral economics is a relatively new field of economics that attempts to incorporate insights from psychology into economic models and analyses. As above cases seem any policy maker's economic activities which are relative to whose psychology's decision.

However, psychologists are often interest in understanding at the level of individual or social group of behaviour, the primary interest in economic is usually in understanding how behaviour and interactions play out in a system to shape economic outcomes. Economists are interested in system-level outcomes, such as the level and path of wages, the effect of taxes on economic output, how rates of savings respond to interest rates etc. However, those economic outcomes depend on complex interactions of individuals.

So, behavioural economy concerns to how to judge individual to do the reasonable or right behaviour to hope to get the reasonable economic result as well as it's goal rather to help improve any policy makers to understand their behaviour in ways that allow economists to make better predictions and suggest better economic policies. However, new elements about information processing or individual preferences might impact economic models and analyses in any learning process environment.

Is psychology influencing all field of economics? It is possible that behavioral economy needs theoretical contributions and laboratory evidence to support to make any reasonable or right decision to any policy makers. This type of work generally uses existing observational data and estimates relationships between variables of interest by either using naturally occurring variation in the data i.e. natural experiment.

Perhaps more than any other field, behavioral economics has had a large impact on finance to the point that behavior finance is often considered a separate field as opposed to being of behavioral economics. Also, public economic is the study of how government policies in fluence economic markets. A primary emphasis of public economic involves the topic of taxation. Otherwise, the biggest impact that the behavioral approach has had in economic is the analysis of retirement saving to influence any employees' decisions about their retirement savings. However, when employees can do make any active savings choices to prepare their retirement. If employers can assist whose employees to design any methods to allocate fund, then accumuates interest and is tax free until the retirement funds are withdrawn to every retirement employee. The tax advantage make effort to save for retirement.

Behavioral economic is in understanding how individuals do or do not smooth consumption over time. Smoothing consumption is a standard economic models. It suggests that individuals should borrow or save in order to consume a similar amount throughout one's lifetime. For example, a teacher who is paid a salary 12 months a year, who should not spend all whose salary within one year. Rather, the teacher should smooth whose consumption over the 12 month period. How to allocate to spend paychecks, food and social security payments which concerns the teacher decide to spend whose salary efficiently. Hence, who needs to plan how he shall spend whose one year salary to be reasonable use in the future.

Public economic is to understand how people respond to taxation and social benefit programs. This has been an area that has seen an explosion of behavioral work in recent year. i.e. how taxpayers can experience over-withholding and receive tax refunds from tax department. Policymakers and insurers are also increasingly turning to psychology for approaches to improve health behavior. Traditionally health-policy focused largely on information provision, assuming that as long as individuals were well informed, their decisions would maximize their health choices. For example, influential work on the effects of smoking taxes, however, well being of smokers appears to increase with higher taxes to influence health behaviours are not completely rational.

Behavioral economic has also had a small impact on the study of criminal behaviour. For example, individuals are not less likely to commit a crime when who are 18 age and the pubishment of doing so increases dramatically. However, some economists explain the motivations people have for giving to charity and who understand the psychological motivations for charitable giving. So, it seems that charity award giving has probable to reduce 18 age people who choose to do crime behaviour easily because who feel who have effort to assist charity in their life time.

Industrial organization economists study why firms exist and how which function and compete with each other. Insights and psychology and behavioral economics have made a significant contribution to develop that model the interactions of profit maximizing firms with their customers. In fact, firms often need to evaluate whether their products if prices are needed to set what of price of level is the most reasonable and attractive to customers to choose to buy their products.

For cell phone plan sale example, individuals choose cell phone plans with fixed minute allotments and steep charges for going over the minute limits, but frequently exceed their plan limits. This behavior is the best explained by a model in which people overestimate the precision of their demand forecasts. So, cell phone firms need to research how cell phone plans with fixed minute allotments and steep charges of cell phone call fee charge plan is the most acceptance method to cell phone clients generally. However, cell phone call charge plan and various cell phone product features and the way cell phone clients allocate their limited attention affects cell phone products markets which are external important factors can influence any cell phone clients why who will choose to use the cell phone call plan because any cell phone will be very large durable product to any cell phone consumer after who choose to buy the cell phone product. Hence, who will not often choose to use the old cell phone firm call charge plan if who feel it provides the excellent cell phone call service and reasonable phone call plan to use to compare other cell phone call plans in the cell phone call market.

Hence, the cell phone call firm needs to make marketing research why consumers need to choose to use which cell phone call plan among of other cell phone call plans in the cell phone call market. Also, researching the cell phone buyers' choice behaviour why who choose to buy the cell phone to use issue, which will have influence to the cell phone buyer why who choose to use the cell phone call charge plan because expensive cell phone is needed to use excellent quality of cell phone call service usually. Otherwise, cheap cell phone is needed to use poor quality of cell phone call service usually. So, cell phone call plan is needed to follow the cell phone quality and price to be used and they ought have direct relationship to influence why the cell phone buyer who chooses to use the cell phone call plan.

Finally, behavioral economy can also apply to be used to labor supply as a motivating in negative or positive labor supply elasticities in taxi driving example. For example, it is possible that taxi drivers work fewer hours when wages are high-consistent with a model of daily income targeting. This finding is that when wages are high (perhaps it is raining and thus it is easy to find people who want a taxi ride), taxi drivers are able to hit their daily target quickly and then go home. However, when wages are low, taxi drivers are not able to hit their target quickly and thus work additional hours in order to hit their target. It means taxi driver's behaviour produce the effect that taxi driver works more when wages are low than when wagers are high. This work has resulted to analyze taxi driver of labor supply decisions with daily reference points in non taxi domains. So, instead of the weather and client numbers and taxi charge factors, the factors of taxi drivers‘ hours worked and the quality of service is produced is another important factor to influence any taxi drivers' numbers to supply to the taxi market.

Behavioral economic has also influenced the understanding of how staffs can impact worker productivity and job satisfaction. For example, it is possible that poor cooperation can cause worker productivity decreases and it can also cause poor job satisfaction to the worker. So, when working environment can impact productivity, social comparisons can have an impact on job satisfaction as well as the worker's job satisfaction and search intentions are affected by knowing about the salaries of their peers in whose firm. Hence, the worker's positive or negative psychological feeling to whose employers which will have effort to influence whose working performance and productivity to whose firm in possible.

Behavioral economic is increasingly being used in the field of development economics or low income countries. Such as, how Philippines can offer commitment to individuals who wanted to save money in whose country or how Philippines can change to smoking behaviour when commitment devices were offered to Philippine smokers. So, Philippines policy makers need to concern resource scarcity and resource allocation issue to solve how to let its low income level householders can raise to the middle income level to achieve the high income level householders and the low income level householders whose income level is not distant very much.

Have behavioral economy and psychology methods close relationship.

Finally, I shall analyze whether it has close relationship between the discipline of behavioral economy and psychology which two branches are totally opposite or if the behavioral theories is only complement that mainstream economics. I think study of economy is the behavior of the complex human beings; this science examines how people choose to act and allocate resources in different market situations. So the economic analysis, is based on the implications that arise from a series of simple assumptions (which are sometimes cited as unrealistic) regarding the human nature. However, in psychological view, the individual is characterized by unlimited rationality and by the ability to follow time consistent, in every situation, his self-interest. In these conditions, behavioral economic attempts to consider a field of analysis in the study of economic phenomena.

Because economics deals with the study of human behaviour on the market, it highlights the human character of the science and the fact that, besides of all the patterns and models, the analysis refers to the real individual. It is also behavioural because it attempts to combine approaches from several sciences mainly from economics and psychology, and also from sociology, philosophy, anthropology or biology. This is not an easy mission, in the conditions in which these various disciplines have adopted in time different approaches that became, in many ways, contradictory. So, behavioural economics is that a multidisciplinary approach will increase the explanatory power of economics.

On one hand, there are specialists two argue that behavioural economic is a field of economics that continues the hand, there are others who see it as a distinctive school of thought, which proposes a new paradigm. However, behavioural economists propose a multidisciplinary study, criticize certain assumptions on which the traditional model is built (such as rationality and self-interest, in their unlimited form), resource to experiments (the classical method of psychology) to validate some assumptions, propose new theories (such as the prospect theory) and advance different interpretations of the economic behaviour, e.g. how to maximize consumers satisfy their needs. This issue is concerned to concern consumption of psychology and social economic situation research aspect.

Also, I think that behavioural economics can help the economic science by describing more realistically the utility functions of the individuals. This field of study is based rather it is a natural extension of the basic approach. However, it is can be claimed that behavioural economics is also built on the premise that psychology methods and assumptions are equally important. Also, models of behavioural economics, allow the utility to depend on the differences between one's own level and a reference level. People are sensitive to changes and preferences are not stable in time. The vision of behavioural economics concerning the inter-temporal choice (which assumes that individuals prefer immediate gains and delay unpleasant activities) seems to be more appropriate to the human behaviour that the one of the traditional model (which assumes that utility is updated over time). I shall give below suitations to explain how to apply behvioral economy method to predict consumption behavior.

How can consumer debt management psychological factors influence consumption behavior?

In behavioral economy view point, it can be applied to explain why consumer debt management psychological factors can influence consumption behavior. Some consumption psychologists had investigated several psychological variables which have been suggested as causes or effects of debts. Economic and demographic factors can predict debt category well to support this influence of factor. How can consumer manage money skills to pay debt which can influence when who plan to consume? Debtors were more likely to buy cigarettes and Christmas presents for children than non-debtors. Conclusions must be qualified because of low return rates, but the results suggest that a complex of psychological and behavioral variables affect debt and are affected by it. It is argued that these variables are linked to the psychology.

In general, economical environment is poor, it will cause many unemployed people, even some people will loan debt to pay daily essential expenditure from banks. If those debtors can't manage whose debt to be better to spend. Whose behavior will cause who do not have more spending desires often. Because these debtors will feel themselves as being in a community where debt was more common and more tolerated than non-debtors. The whole question of the classification of products a necessities or luxuries and its consequences for purchasing behavior is of current interest in economic psychology. Since debt is associated with poverty and poor people tend to give external reasons for economic phenomena, such as poverty and unemployment, causality may run the other way. In either case, however, there should be a positive correlation between external control and debt. There have different variables offer explanations of debts at different levels. One factor may be a consequence of another, or the mechanism by which it takes effect (for example, different patterns of economic socialization might generate different attitudes towards debt).

Some debtors need to borrow debt (loan) for house purchasing need. So, if the house loan debtors who need to pay back whose house loan to bank for long time. It is possible that their house loan will influence to reduce to spend much of daily consumption behavior to buy non luxury and daily essential products for long time. Thus, the result is these house loan debtors will reduce every day essential expenditure, such as food and soft drink, entertainment etc. to consume too much to compare to non house loan debtors for long time. It seems that retailers can attempt to apply debt management behavior to predict consumer shopping of desires.

In conclusion, I shall indicate two theories to explain why economy and psychology has close relationship to influence human do any behavioural economic activities daily. For example, through the prospect theory, behavioural economics adds new parameters to improve the mathematical modelling method, which was advanced by economists for decisions taken under uncertainty. However, the theory also proposes a slightly different interpretation. The results are interpreted by the individual as positive or negative deviations from a reference point, which has a neutral psychological value. Last but not least, in addressing social preferences, behavioural economics adds parameters that increase the concern of decision-makers to also assess their utility function in relation to others. For another example, the choice theory; secondly there is not a common consensus between the specialists of behavioural economics regarding the variables that should be included; and finally, many variables that affect the behaviour are not quantitative, but qualitative, and cannot be precisely measured. The findings of behavioural economic are relevant and can help the mainstream theory by providing a more realistically base of study. However, this argument has contributed to the development of behavioural economics, because there are a large number of phenomena that cannot be entirely explained by the mainstream economics.

So, why in the beginning, I indicated why behavioural economics does not imply the totally exclusion of the neoclassical approach and the most studies in this area try to provide a more realistic base of the standard theory. In the concluding, I believe that in time, behavioural economic models will replace the simplified ones, based on unlimited rationality. Also, economists have provided a great importance to the quantitative structures, departing from the human nature. However, behavioural economics can become truly revolutionary only it will always be receptive and will provide a critical insight to their own theories and perspectives, and especially the ones regarding the aspects that they reproach to the traditional economic theory. However, I also feel that the individual's behaviour on the market is determined only be economic factors. In brief, individual choices and, by this, the demand variation are explained only and the variations in the prices of products/services and the available personal income. Am important discussion in the field of determine directly the economic behaviour of an individual (like the sociological and psychological of factors) are actually active elements in the process the reshaping of the utility functions. Finally, in my view, I believe that the conduct of the market phenomena, as it occurs in reality. In this sense, the research of behavioural economics aims to see how the neoclassical model could be improved, using mainly psychology concepts. Although, there are some specialists who argue that behavioural economics can be an alternative to the neoclassical theory.

Finally, most findings, of my study conducted in this book, modify some of standard economical assumptions, in order to provide a greater psychological realism. However, the additions proposed by behavioural economists simply recognize the human limitations on (mentally) calculations, will and self-interest. So, I think psychology and economy has close relationship to assist any policy makers or decision makers to do any economic psychology daily. Because the purpose of economics is to better understand and explain the conduct of the economic activities as which occur in reality. Otherwise, human being is complex and its behaviour and constitution is studied by all the social sciences. Consequently, multi and interdisciplinary approaches can bring real benefits to the economic science, by providing a more realist foundation to cause any policy makers or decision makers how to decide to make any behaviours or economic activities by behavioural economic activities support daily.

Can price change influence consumer behavior?

In behavioral economy view point, it can explaine why price change can influence consumer behavior. In general, under short –run profit maximization, the price was seen as a mark –up marginal cost with the marketing determined by the elasticity of demand. However, economists have used these methods to determination of how prices change behavior. The first is the indicated prices are determined relative to costs by firms in the pursuit of objectives. In the view point, the first is firms are price-makers and let prices in a way which think will achieve these objectives. Subject to constraints arising from demand and cost conditions. The second is theory of perfect competition, firms are effectively price-takers and the interaction between demand and supply in the market set price. So, firms are regarded as price-takers, and hence not in position to set prices, such as price-adjuster . The third is the idea of observing the process of price decision-making and seeking observation is on the prices of price determination. Their view is expressed as price is based on full average cost , including a conventional allowance for profits and full average cost . Is determined as follows? price or direct cost per unit is taken as the base, a percentage addition is made to cover overhead or on cost or indirect cost, and a further conventional addition of percentage is made for profit. This, it seems price change behavior can influence consumer individual consumption behavior to any products.

Can constructive consumer choice processes influence consumption behavior?

Consumer decision making has been an interest in consumption behavior research, e.g. how technological changes, an information explosion factor can influence consumer individual choice decision to buy any products. Due to limited processing capacity, consumers often don't have well-defined existing preferences, but construct them using a variety of strategies contingent on task demands. Rapid technological changes for instance, has led to multitudes of new products and decreased product lifetimes. In addition, new communications media, such as the world wide web have made amounts of information on options potentially available (Alba et al. 1987). It seems time pressure, such as fast product lifetimes and new communications, media, internet advertisement can influence consumers how to make decision to buy any thing which is the best to them, e.g. choice of gathering products of advertisement information to buy products from internet (electronic shopping) instead of traditional visiting shops consumption behavior. So, new information advertisement media, e.g. internet advertisement consumer information media will influence consumer individual decision tasks. For example, a consumer may be fairly certain about the values of some of the attributes to choose to buy which kind of mobile phone from electronic shopping easily at home. However, the consumer may not have information for all of the mobile phone options on some attributes (e.g. reliability information would not be available for a new mobile model) from internet advertisement. In addition, some attributes, such as safety may be difficult for consumer to trade off; making trade off requires possibly accepting a loss on such an attribute with potentially threatening consequences.

What is characteristics of consumer decision strategy in product choice process? It includes the total amount of information processed, the selectivity in information processing, the pattern of process, (whether by alternative brand or by attribute). First, the amount of information processed is very a great deal. For example, a mobile phone choice may involve detailed consideration of much of the information available about each of the available mobile phone, as implied by more rational choice models, or it may have a consideration of a limited set of information (e.g. repeating what are choices last time). Second, different amounts of information can be processed for each attribute or alternative (selective processing), or the same amount of information can be processed for each attribute or alternative (consistent processing). For example, suppose a consumer considers the mobile phones to decide that life time is the most important attribute, processed only that attribute and chooses which mobile brand, with the famous brand value on that mobile phone attribute. Third, choice process would involves on that attribute. This choice process would involve highly selective processing of attribute information (since the amount of information examined differs across attributes), but consistent processing of alternative mobile phone brand information, since one piece of information is considered for each mobile phone. The fact that working memory capacity is limited effectively requires selective attention to information, e.g. internet advertisement media.

In general, the more selective consumers are in processing information, the more susceptible their decisions may be to factors that influence the salience of information, some of which may be irrelevant, such as different mobile phone brands of product life time comparing information. Information may be processed primarily by alternative, in which multiple attributes of a single option are processed before another option is considered, or by attribute, in which the values of several alternatives on a single attribute are examined before information on another attribute is considered. For example, a consumer might engage in attribute processing by examining the price of each of the mobiles, concluding that mobile brand (A) was the most expensive, another mobile brand (B) was the least expensive, and the another mobile brand (C) had a very good price . However, the consumer could process in an alternative-based fashion or is design by examining the reliability, price, safety of mobile phone brand (A) in order to form an overall valuation of that mobile phone brand (A).

Finally, an important distinction among strategies in the degree to which are compensatory. A compensatory strategy is one in which a good value on one attribute can compensate for a poor value on another. A compensatory strategy thus requires explicit trade off among attributes. Deciding how much more one is willing to pay for very good rather than average reliability or long useful life time in a mobile phone involves making an explicit trade -off between reliability long useful life time and price for examples. Thus, in general, constructive consumer choice processes attribute , such as the product's price, quality, life of time , reliability, design , brand information of media sources as well as electronic internet shopping or visiting shopping buying channels of these factors will influence the consumer to do the final decision to choose to buy which kind of product in the consumption market. Also, any retailers need to concern whether which is the major influence of attribute to the product. Because wrong evaluation of the major attribute of the product will influence the consumer to make final buying decision when who compares the retailer's product to other retailers whose similar products in the consumer's choice process.

How can economical environment factor predict consumers consumption?

The dominant approach to industrial economics is
the one which is usually described as the structure-conduct-performance approach. So, predicting the performance of an industry in terms of profitability and advertising growth can predict consumer consumption in possible. The structure of an industry covers factors like the relative and size of firms, involved the ease of entry into the industry and the elasticity of demand for the output of that industry. The conduct of firms covers the objectives of the firms, price setting behavior, and attitudes to competitors (actual and potential), and from that the performance of that industry predicted, particularly in respect of profitability.

What are the main features of the structure of an industry? Many consumption psychologists discuss on the structure-conduct-performance topic, the number and relative size of the firms and the extent of barriers to entry into the industry to influence the product suppliers to consumption choices in the market. The number and relative size of firms is usually placed under either the size distribution of firms or individual concentration. Most industries don't fit into the category of a large number of small firms or of one firm.

Barriers to entry into an industry comprise all the factors which lead to new entrants into the industry being at a disadvantage to the existing firms because consumers have more choices to buy the similar products from the competitors . The first factor is the existence of economies of scale which means that a new entrant would have to produce on a relatively large scale increasingly. The second factor, the brand of products are supplied by a significant amount and thereby depressing price a significant amount , differentiation and advertising, so that a new entrant has to incur costs to overcome the loyalty of consumers to existing products. A third factor is the ability of existing firms to produce and distribute at lower costs than new entrants. Although, for example, access to cheaper new materials, accumulated knowledge of the industry etc. So, these external marketing environment factor will influence consumption behavior choices. For example, if the industrial structure determines or influences performance, the governments concerned with aspect of industrial performance (particularly aspects like price changes, technological progress and employment levels).

Consumption psychologists have often been assigned that the level of concentration in an industry is largely technological determined and that increases in concentration reflect impact of technological advance with increase the desired size of factory or firm. For example, mobile phone manufacturing industry, if the brand of mobile phone manufacturer had technological advance to manufacture any new model to attract consumers have more buying choices from their mobile products. Then, technological factor will influence consumers have more choices to buy the brand of mobile phone products. Other some psychologists believe the way in which unit costs change with the scale of production (cost conditions and economies of scale) factor which can influence consumers choice behaviors. When public policy favor active industrial intervention to change industrial structures, some indication is required as to whether the minimum efficient scale is small or large relative to the total market to supply their product numbers to influence consumers' behaviors. In the former case a policy favoring small units would be indicated, whereas, in the latter case large units may be favored.

Increasing returns to scale and economies of scales are usually defined as a situation when all inputs into the productive process are increased in the same proportion the volume of output increases in a greater proportion . How can economies of scale influence products supplying numbers? For example, that is the scale of output increases the degree of capital intensity rises. But within that change the type of the capital equipment is likely to be varied. Further, the balance between skilled and unskilled or between manual and non-manual labor may change. Thus , it is necessary to adopt a view of both increasing and decreasing returns.

The definition of unit costs of output declining with increased output. This must refer to all costs(including capital costs, and can only relate to a particular set of relative prices for inputs from which the unit costs are calculated. It would include any change in the price of input usage, such as mobile phone products which need to use different materials to manufacture any mobile phone products Thus, if a mobile phone firm had to pay more wages as its use of labor increased, that would have to be included. It is generally assumed that, for any scale of output, the firm is combining the impacts in an efficient manner. This efficiency includes economies efficiency (choosing the least cost combinations of inputs) and technical efficiency (producing the maximum feasible output from given inputs). The measurement of returns to scale under this definition may be only relevant to a particular economy, as it depends upon the particular relevance prices used.

Such as, each mobile phone product price will influence consumer individual behavior of choice to buy only one among the different brands of model mobile phones. So, mobile phone manufacturers need to concern how to reduce cost to gain economies of scale input to raise mobile phone output. For example, from a reduction in the effective price of an input to the model of mobile phone, as the volume of the styles of mobile phones purchases increased arising from an increase in monopsony power. For example, three mobile phone plants, A, B, C are assumes to have a fixed mobile phones output, and initially produce with unit costs A1, B1, and C1. Respectively. Supposing plants A and C would make subnormal profits and plant B super-normal profits, when capital costs are based on the historical cost of the mobile phone plant. Now the capital values of plants A and C are, it is argued, unlikely to fall and that of plant B to rise , for the amount which another mobile phone firm could be prepared to pay for a plant will reflect its profit prospects. If the decline in capital value fully reflects the initial deviations for normal profits, unit costs shift to A2, B2 and C2 respectively. Thus, there is a tendency at work towards mobile phone constant unit costs being observed. How far this tendency operates depends upon the based on which mobile phone firms value their assets. When the value is based on historic cost, the tendency does not operate. But the tendency does operate when the value is based in some way on the assets' profit prospects. Thus product manufacturers need to concern how to earn economic of scale to cost to avoid each product price will be changed often to influence consumer choices to other competitors more easily.

How can auctions or online experimentation respond to predict consumer behavior and sale forecast accuracy?

Nowadays, in UK suggests that consumer buying behavior has changed significantly. Consumers caan buying different things, at different times and through different channels. As a result, forecast accuracy is very poor and many companies feel automated forecasting systems can not predict buying behavior more accuracy and relying on analysts to predict buying behavior by psychological methods. Automated forecasting systems weaknesses are such as: Historical data alone can't be used to predict feature sales in times and drawing together a wider range of internal and external data would help improve forecast accuracy. The impact on revenue manager varies widely. When sales forecasts are important, adjustments to revenue management system outputs are needed to retain credibility. When customers' behavior are poor to understand, there may be a need to sell from auctions or online experimentation to predict the market response. So, these automated forecasting system have these weaknesses to cause companies feel technological method can not be better than psychological method to predict further consumption behavior for whose products.

In psychological consumption of prediction view point, learning how to predict changes in consumers' attitudes and behaviors which is important to any companies. For example, in part behavior has changes as a result a recent major disruptive events, such as recession and exchange rate changes etc. economic factor, but there are other non economic factors to change consumers' attitudes and behaviors. For example, consumers are becoming smarter in their use of the internet to research products based on previous customers' view, seek out the best, deals and offers and then buy online, with a corresponding increase in the number of price comparison sites. So , companies are percentage seeing the rise of the strategic consumer who observes the dynamic of supplier pricing and adapts their buying strategy in response. However, some observers suggest that these changes to consumers' attitudes and behaviors are fundamental long, lasting and likely to continue to be disruptive.

Some consumption psychologists feel sales have become less predictable. In general, sales forecasts based on historical patterns in time series have become less accurate and hence less useful in the past year in many industries, not just these traditionally served by revenue management. Does forecast accuracy easily? For some revenue managers may be not too much, in some businesses prices are set by reference to the main competitors and forecasts have limited impact on operating and decisions about capacity. Marketing forecasting is aim to setting prices, maximizing revenue and managing operations.

However, forecast accuracy is very important to find why changing consumer attitudes and the implications for customer segmentation and forecasting of buying behaviors are not just relevant to revenue management. They are also fundamental to sales, marketing , brand management, customer loyalty, product design and beyond. Perhaps it has an opportunity for revenue managers to take a lead in influencing thinking of their colleagues in these areas. Some consumption psychologists forecast the future, who concern the historical data of companies collection before the recession, it can no longer be applied to forecast consumer behavior during the recession or after. At the opposite extreme, companies can simply continue to between auto prediction system to predict when the market stability will return soon and how to influence consumer behavior.

Sales are likely to depend on the economic situation, the competition and consumer behavior. However, these are external environmental factor to influence consumption of behavior. If it is possible to separate out these effects, then the forecasting model can take account of them by either building the economy/market into the model or segmenting consumers in an economy/market invariant way. External data, for example on the economic situation can also provide a good indicator of future sales. For example, internet (online) web site research technology is one possibility for combining and processing data from different sources on the web using automated tools. If buying behavior is changing and every consumer demand is becoming elastic, not only to increase revenue, but also to improve knowledge of the customers. For example, online auctions are mainly used in the travel and hospitality industries for offloading surplus capacity have been shown when facing only uncertain consumer demand. However, analyzing external economy environment factor is not effective to minimize risk to the sellers. Because sale forecasts are never going to be completely accurate and there is an argument for moving the focus away from being smarter with existing data towards making the business less dependent on sale forecasts. For example, taking close look at increasing flexibility in the supply chain or operations or re-examine the strategy for setting price.

What the current situation really emphasizes however is that there is certainly a need for forecast accuracy to be taken seriously by revenue managers and reported on by revenue management system. Thus, revenue managers need to concern how to predict whose consumers' psychological emotions to find why the reasons can influence whose consumption attitudes and behaviors changing to cause their product sale numbers had been falling. So, it seems that consumers' emotions can be influenced whose buying behavior by online auctions factor.

CHAPTER V

Environment influences consumer behavior

How to apply online psychological advertising method to predict behavioral consumption?

Online advertising can give relevance information to represent the similarity between advertisement and queries. These existing online advertisement works mainly focused on interpreting advertisements clicks in term of what consumers seek. (i.e. relevance information) and how consumers choose to watch TV or magazine or online advertisement etc. from different promotion media. (historically to know the product is selling on the market through advertising information). However, few of manufacturers or sellers attempted to understand why consumers chose to watch the advertising from TV or magazine or internet etc. different media.

Online Advertisement can be as a commercial search engine for manufacturers or sellers to gather data to concern how behavioral consumption is. The online advertisement's each observations motivate who to systemically model to test what each consumer individual psychological desire in order for a precise prediction on behavioral consumption after online advertisement promotion from internet media.

Today, internet is one kind of effective psychological advertising promotion method. For example, an online advertisement system, sponsored search has been one of the most important business models for commercial web search engines. It generates most of the revenue of search engines by presenting to users sponsored search results, i.e. advertisements (ads), along with organic search results. To deliver the most interesting ads to the users, a sponsored search system consists of technical components, including query-to-ads matching, online click prediction for matched ads, online click probability and auction to determine the ranking, placement, and pricing of the remaining ads. To aim to attempt to predict behavioral consumption for any kinds of product sale from online advertisement media.

In today's industry, generalized second price auction (GSP) is the most widely-used auction mechanism , in which the price that an advertiser has to pay depends on the predicted online click probability of the online buyers, whose own ads as well as the bid price and predicted online click probability of the ads ranked in the next position. The online sponsored search systems typically employ a machine learning model top predict the probability that an online user clicks an advertising from internet.

However, in practical sponsored search system. There are many ads without adequate historical click through data, even after query levels. Then online ads can been click improved prediction accuracy to consumer individual behavioral consumption when each click is occurred to the seller individual website. For example, online ads, such as : free Nike coupons ad. It shows " Go-Get_couptons.com/Nike, Download and print Nike coupons (100% Free)" ; another Nike-sales prices ad. It shows www.calibex.com, clothing, latest fashions and styles on sale. Buy Nike Fast!" ; another Perfume.com official site ad. It shows "www.perfume.com, 10,000 + brand name perfumes and colognes-up to 80% off retail!" ; another Luxury English Perfume Ad. It shows " www.florislondon.com, shop online for luxury perfumes for men, women and the home". Above of these are example online ads. For two queries, "Nike" and "Perfume" , and two ads under the same query field similar relevance to the query.

Despite the usefulness of the relevance and historical of what users click and how users click. Specially, relevance information can indicate what relevant content users seek to click from online (internet) media. However, as it is well-known that users are not active to search for ads., the search engine, instead has to recommend ads. To users during their generic web search. Therefore, the relevance between query and ad can't perform as the key driver for click. In my opinion, in order for more click prediction, businessmen need to examine why users click.

How to apply psychological research to analyze of online user desire in sponsored search for behavioral consumption of reasons? First, according to literatures on consumer behavioral analyses, many factors will influence the decision making for consumption, including thought based effects and feeling-based effects. Though-based effects are basically win or loss analysis (e.g. trade-off between price and quantity), when feeling-based effects are more subjective (e.g. brand loyalty and luxury seeking). Note users online clicking the ad. Usually are with the intention to purchase something. In this situation, it is natural that the factors mentioned in consumer behavior analyses will influence their online click behaviors. So, advertisers can gather online advertisement data to choose how to design whose online advertisement to follow either is based on win or loss analysis, either focusing on product price and quality features or is based on more subjective analysis , focusing on brand loyalty and luxury seeking features to attract any consumer individual attention to choose to watch whose online advertisements from online advertisement media more easily. So, it seems that online advertisement is a promotional and gathering data channel to persuade consumer individual attention to predict whose behavioral consumption for any manufacturer or seller how to design whose online advertisement to sell whose products more accurate.

The application of consumer psychology, and in particular to branding, has gained popularity over the past decade in academic research and business practice. What neuroscience can bring to advance manufacturers' understanding of the consumer psychology of brands choice of behavioral consumption. The brand preference formation over time has four basic components: (1) representation and attention, (2) predicted value , (3) experienced value and (4) remembers value and learning.

First, on representation and attention component, it means that the amount of information consumers are exposed to is enormous, yet consumer's processing capacity is limited. How consumers represent, attend to, and perceive incoming information may have a profound influence on their behavioral consumption , i.e. brand identification. Representation is the first process in brand decisions , which involves forming the representation of the choice alternatives, that is brand identification. For example, different beer brands provide different options for choice are identified to consumers. At the same time, the consumer needs to integrate information on internal state , (e.g. thirst level) and external states , e.g. (location , social context) that drive attention. For example, when faced with a choice between a consumer's choice is likely to depend on whose own level of thirst (an internal state) and level of thirst chooses to drink (an external state). However, the brand image is a visual system allows for rapid brand and product identification. One of the key questions at this stage is what consumers pay attention to (i.e. focus on) once who are exposed to a number of rapidly identified choice alternatives (i.e. brands).

Attention is the mechanism responsible for selecting the information that gains preferential status above other available information for researching on branding. Thus, if the product brand image is attractive, then it will be probable attract the initial eye movement of consumers and thus may have a profound effect on related consumer behavior. For example, Pieters and Wedel (2007) showed that ensuring that consumers pay attention to the brand displayed in a print ad. It is the most effective way to ensure that who will transfer their attention to other elements of the print ad. So, brand image of attractive visual selection and eye movement can enhance the quality of incoming information to consumer individual behavioral consumption for the product of choice. The suggestion of eye-tracking is as a useful tool for determining the extent to which consumers find different brand extensions plausible. In sum, representation and attention are complex processes that influence all subsequent steps in our brand decisions framework.

Next, the step is predicted value, it is of each brand that is available for choice to represent the consumer's belief about the experienced value of that brand at same time in the future. In other words, the predicted values involves the consumer's evaluation of how much enjoyment who will desire form consuming among of different brands of product choice. For example, clothes are at different retail stores (e.g. H&M vs. Zara), consumer who are loyal to a store as measured by real purchasing behavior. (i.e. amount spent, frequency and recent of purchases based on loyalty card data) show more activation in the compared to consumers who are less loyal. The cloth brand inviting loyalty card holders who will be persuaded by the brand . So, the loyalty card of the brand of cloth seller can be the predicted value to the brand of the cloth to persuade the loyalty card holders to choose to buy.

Next, the step is experienced value , it is based on the pleasure derived from consuming a brand. It is a concept of motivational value to the consumer. Motivational value is a concept that is related to how predicted and experienced values interact is the motivational value or incentive of an option to the consumer. So building good brand image memory us important to influence consumer psychology. For example, the information of channel ,.e.g. ad. can build brand image memory to consumer more easily. Thus, good brand image can build good memory to consumers to prefer to choose to buy the brand of product easily. Otherwise, bad brand image can build bad memory to consumers to not prefer to choose to buy the brand of product easily. Thus, manufacturers or sellers can not neglect how to build good brand image to attract any consumer individual attention by attrative advertising because good brand image has close relationship with psychological consumption for shopping. It seems brand loyalty of famous degree can help businessmen to predict whether consumers are accepting or are not accepting to choose to buy their products or consume their service provision more accurate. For example, if the product brand is very famous long term, it seems consumers are accepting to choose to buy the product. Otherwise, if the product brand is not famous long term, it seems consumers are not ccepting to choose to buy the product.

How can store atmosphere environment influence consumer individual shopping behavior?

On the one hand, some consumption psychologists suggest in-store variable factor can influence consumer emotion to feel either pleasure or displeasure of intended shopping behaviors within the store, thus these consumption psychologists who believe retail store environment can influence consumption behavior. On the other hand, some employment psychologists also suggest work environment can influence employee individual emotion to work, work environment include hospitals, schools and prisons etc. public work environment. It seems consumers and employees whose emotion will be influenced by environment factor. It brings this question. Can store atmosphere environment predict consumers buying decision?

These consumption psychologists feel the component of store image, physical in-store variable , such as aisle width, brightness and crowding, when clearly these physical variables are store environment's major factor which can influence consumption behavior will be changed. Some retailers have claimed large effects from manipulating store atmosphere via layout, lighting, color and music (Wysocki 1979; Stevens 1980).

Some consumption psychologists also show these avoidance behaviors can cause consumer individual shopping emotion. First, physical approach and avoidance, which can be related to store patronage intentions at a basic level. Exploratory approach and avoidance can be related to in-store search and exposure to a broad or narrow range of retail offerings. Second, Communication approach and avoidance can be related to interaction with sales personnel and floor staff. Third, performance and satisfaction approach and avoidance can be related to repeat shopping frequency as well as reinforcement of time and money expenditures in the store.

In consumer psychological view point, pleasure or displeasure refers to the degree to which the consumer feels good, joyful, happy or satisfied in the situation. Then, another degree to which a consumer feels excited, stimulated, alert or active in the situation. Thus, if the consumer feels the shopping environment is comfortable, joyful, happy or satisfied. The shopping environment, it will have more chance to influence the consumer chooses shopping. Otherwise if, the consumer feels the shopping environment is excited, alert, stimulated or active. The shopping environment will have less chance to influence the consumer chooses shopping. It seems each consumer individual emotion will influence whose consumption behavior as well as store atmosphere environment has close relationship to influence each consumer individual emotion also.

Thus, retailers need to concern how to design whose store environment, e.g. what kind of furniture color, style and size; how much area of the store. For example, the store area is either large or middle or small area to let many or small number of consumers to stay in the store at the same time. How to let consumers to enter or leave the store? For example, how to let consumers to feel to leave the store easily when the fire is happening in store, it can make the consumers feel more safe, so who will have more probable to stay in the store to consume. How to display whose products to let consumers feel to touch or see to find any products on the shelves more easily. Choosing what kind of music to let consumers to listen during who are staying to shopping in store, e.g. soft music or none any music (quiet environment). These different store external feeling factors will influence each consumer individual emotion to feel more comfortable or uncomfortable feeling to decide to spend more long time or short time to stay in the store. Thus, it seems store atmosphere environment can influence consumer individual shopping behavior, so retailers can not neglect how to design store atmosphere environment to let whose customers feel more comfortable and safe to stay in stores.

Can model for understanding service encounter evaluation that can synthesize consumer satisfaction, services marketing, and attribution to influence consumption behavior to the retailer?

These factors concern on the service industries how to influence consumption behavior, which focus on service encounter satisfaction and service quality to both the importance and the complexity of the issues. First and foremost, customer satisfaction depends directly and most immediately on the management and monitoring of individual service encounters (Parasuraman, Zeithaml, and Berry 1985; Shostack 1984, 1987; Sollmon et al. 1985).

What is the conceptual definition of service encounter? The model of service encounter evaluation relies on Shostack's (1985, p.243) definition of the term" service encounter" as " a period of time during which a consumer directly interacts with a service." The author identified all aspects of the service firm with which the consumer may interact, including its personnel, its physical facilities and other tangible elements, during a given period of time. I give this hypothesis, such as when an employee offers to compensate the customer for service failure, the offer may influence attributions. The employee performance will lead the customer to have negative beliefs about the firm, when the bad employee offer leads the customer to think bad image to the firm. So, the employee's bad service attitude can influence the offer is made to compensate for service failure to build bad service image to the company. Moreover, physical surroundings also are hypothesized to influence customer emotion in service failure situations. For example, if a customer experiences service failure in an organized , professional environment, e.g. lawyer, doctor, accountant professional services. The customer may not have more confidence to find the firm to serve to him again. In contrast, in a disorganized environment, the physical cues may suggest incompetence, inefficiency and poor service. In such an environment, the customer may attribute greater responsibility to the firm and be more likely to expect the same type of problem to occur in the future. Thus, any professional service firms, whose employees' service performance can influence customers' confidence to decide to find whose professionals to give any professional service opinions again. Thus, any professional service firm, whose employees' service performance can influence customers' confidence to the service firm likely.

How can the impact of personality and emotion on post-purchase service processes influence consumption behavior? Will consumption behavior be influenced to the retailer by consumer satisfaction or dissatisfaction and post-purchase service behaviors? Such as complaints, recommendations, and repeat purchase intentions, toward loyalty and word of mouth. Developing a new customer is expensive. Particularly in mature markets, competition is strong, product differentiation is low, and promotional costs have skyrocketed. So, understanding who these customers are, why who are dissatisfied, and how or even whether to market to them is an increasingly important issue.

That a customer's level of satisfaction affects much post-purchase behaviors, such as complaining and negative word of mouth is well documented. Satisfaction itself is influenced by comparing actual product performance to expectation. So, some consumption actual product performance will be needed to expectations by the product manufacuter or seller. So, some consumption psychologists began to research that the role of consumption based emotion in consumer satisfaction formation how to make recent personality research particularly concerning. It seems post-purchase processed can be a response to influence consumption- based emotions and consumption behavior to any retailers. The degree of satisfaction is a specific consumption experience, it has a direct impact on such post-purchase processes as repeat purchase intentions and complaining. So, any retailers need to concern on how predicting post-purchase consumer behavior will be.

Because personality should be an important predictor of consumption experiences, and thereby of post-purchase processes. Post-purchase processes can include either on positive consumption-based emotions or on negative consumption-based emotions. When the consumer satisfies to use the product, the useful of product expectation will be increased. Otherwise, when the consumer dissatisfies to use the product, the useful of product expectation will be decreased and the consumer complaint behavior will be increased. So, it seems post-purchase processes can influence consumers to decide to continue to choose to buy the products from the retailer again as well as how to reduce consumers have negative emotions to the products which is an important factor to influence any consumption behavior changing to the retailer.

How can constructive consumer choice processes influence consumption behavior?

Consumer decision making has been an interest in consumption behavior research, e.g. how technological changes, an information explosion factor can influence consumer individual choice decision to buy any products. Due to limited processing capacity, consumers often don't have well-defined existing preferences, but construct them using a variety of strategies contingent on task demands. Rapid technological changes for instance, has led to multitudes of new products and decreased product lifetimes. In addition, new communications media, such as the world wide web have made amounts of information on options potentially available (Alba et al. 1987). It seems time pressure, such as fast product lifetimes and new communications, media, internet advertisement can influence consumers how to make decision to buy any thing which is the best to them, e.g. choice of gathering products of advertisement information to buy products from internet (electronic shopping) instead of traditional visiting shops consumption behavior. So, new information advertisement media, e.g. internet advertisement consumer information media will influence consumer individual decision tasks. For example, a consumer may be fairly certain about the values of some of the attributes to choose to buy which kind of mobile phone from electronic shopping easily at home. However, the consumer may not have information for all of the mobile phone options on some attributes (e.g. reliability information would not be available for a new mobile model) from internet advertisement.

In addition, some attributes, such as safety may be difficult for consumer to trade off; making trade off requires possibly accepting a loss on such an attribute with potentially threatening consequences.

What is characteristics of consumer decision strategy in product choice process? It includes the total amount of information processed, the selectivity in information processing, the pattern of process, (whether by alternative brand or by attribute). First, the amount of information processed is very a great deal. For example, a mobile phone choice may involve detailed consideration of much of the information available about each of the available mobile phone, as implied by more rational choice models, or it may have a consideration of a limited set of information (e.g. repeating what are choices last time). Second, different amounts of information can be processed for each attribute or alternative (selective processing), or the same amount of information can be processed for each attribute or alternative (consistent processing). For example, suppose a consumer considers the mobile phones to decide that life time is the most important attribute, processed only that attribute and chooses which mobile brand, with the famous brand value on that mobile phone attribute. Third, choice process would involves on that attribute. This choice process would involve highly selective processing of attribute information (since the amount of information examined differs across attributes), but consistent processing of alternative mobile phone brand information, since one piece of information is considered for each mobile phone. The fact that working memory capacity is limited effectively requires selective attention to information, e.g. internet advertisement media.

In general, the more selective consumers are in processing information, the more susceptible their decisions may be to factors that influence the salience of information, some of which may be irrelevant, such as different mobile phone brands of product life time comparing information. Information may be processed primarily by alternative, in which multiple attributes of a single option are processed before another option is considered, or by attribute, in which the values of several alternatives on a single attribute are examined before information on another attribute is considered. For example, a consumer might engage in attribute processing by examining the price of each of the mobiles, concluding that mobile brand (A) was the most expensive, another mobile brand (B) was the least expensive, and the another mobile brand (C) had a very good price . However, the consumer could process in an alternative-based fashion or is design by examining the reliability, price, safety of mobile phone brand (A) in order to form an overall valuation of that mobile phone brand (A).

Finally, an important distinction among strategies in the degree to which are compensatory. A compensatory strategy is one in which a good value on one attribute can compensate for a poor value on another. A compensatory strategy thus requires explicit trade off among attributes. Deciding how much more one is willing to pay for very good rather than average reliability or long useful life time in a mobile phone involves making an explicit trade -off between reliability long useful life time and price for examples. Thus, in general, constructive consumer choice processes attribute , such as the product's price, quality, life of time , reliability, design , brand information of media sources as well as electronic internet shopping or visiting shopping buying channels of these factors will influence the consumer to do the final decision to choose to buy which kind of product in the consumption market. Also, any retailers need to concern whether which is the major influence of attribute to the product. Because wrong evaluation of the major attribute of the product will influence the consumer to make final buying decision when who compares the retailer's product to other retailers whose similar products in the consumer's choice process.

How can be survey research measured that is applicable to intentions, attitude or satisfaction data to predict consumer behavior? Whether surveyed consumers will be predicted how consumers behavior are more easier than non surveyed consumers. Most academic studies of satisfaction use consumers' intention to repurchase as the criterion variable (for an exception, see Bolton 1998), and most companies rely on consumers' purchase intentions to forecast their adoption of new products or the repeat purchase of existing ones (Jamieson and Bass 1989).

In practice, some consumer psychologists' studies adjust the intention scores by analyzing that actual purchase behavior of consumers whose purchase intentions have been measured previously. For example, the popular ACNIELSEN BASES model forecasts aggregate purchase rates by applying conversion rates to measured purchase intentions (e.g. it seems that 75% of consumers who checked the top purchase-intentions box will actually purchase the product). To obtain these conversion rates, BASES uses previous studies that measured the purchase intentions of consumers and then tracked their actual purchases. However, investigating whether survey research is useful to measure consumer behavior. It has a weak point, a limitation of these studies is that companies (businessmen) focus on the internal rather than the external accuracy of purchase-intention measures. That is, the company studies measure the improvement in the ability to forecast the behavior of consumers whose intentions who previously measured for survey research experiments, not the behavior of consumers whose intentions who did not measure. Therefore, the studies assume that the companies can predict the intention-behavior relationship of non-surveyed consumers on the basis of the relationship that surveyed consumer exhibit.

It would suggest that studies measure the strength of the association between intentions and behavior on the same sample of consumers overstate that external predictive accuracy of purchase intentions by survey method. This would explain why so many new products fail even after which are performed well in purchase-intention tests by survey method. I shall suggest survey framework distinguished between two sources of measurement reactivity. The first is self-generated validity effects, it is as a strengthened relationship between latent intentions and behavior, due to the measurement of intentions from post-survey research. The second source includes all measurement effects that are independent of latent intentions, such as those that social norms or post-survey intention modifications create.

I also suggest a two stage procedure to detect whether the act of measurement alters the strength of the relationship between a latent construct that is measured through surveys, experiments or observations and its consequence (e.g. intentions-behavior, attitudes-intentions, attitudes-behavior, satisfaction behavior) and to determine the time relationship in the absence of the difference between non-survey and survey consumers behavior measurement. For example, prediction of consumer behavior purchase intention to achieve more profitability. Survey method can measure to these products , such as groceries, mobiles and personal computers etc. Companies can show the strength of the relationship between latent intentions and behavior is stronger for surveyed consumers than for similar non surveyed consumers.

I also suggest the survey questions can concern to compare with other inputs for purchase decisions. e.g. tastes, mood, competitive environment may make subsequent purchase behavior more consistent with prior intentions. For example, Feldman and Lynch's (1988) survey method predictions, Fitzsimons and Morwitz (1996) found that measurement of general intentions to purchase automobiles increase the likelihood that buyers will repurchase the automobile brand that they also previously consume and that first time buyers will purchase brands will large market shares. Under the assumption, if the survey's result showed the automobiles brand-specific purchase intentions. Thus, Fitzsimons and Morwitz's results suggest that the measurement of general intentions increases the association between latent, brand-specific intent and brand choice. So, brand is a factor which can influence consumers to choose to buy which automobiles. In conclusion, it seems companies can attempt to use survey method to investigate consumer behavior to predict what kind of factor is the most influential to attract consumers to choose buy whose product or consume whose service.

What is consumer neuroscientific research method to predict consumer behavior?

The key motivation has not been possible to directly observe the mental processes when subjects perceive marketing stimuli, such as advertisement or when who make purchasing decisions. Despite the long history of consumer research, little is known about the neural representation of how marketing stimuli affects consumers' perceptions, their decision-making processes and their consumption experience.

In the past, consumer researchers had to rely on varying the stimuli , e.g. prices or packaging and context factors, e.g. putting subjects in a good or bad mood in order to measure participants' reactions , e.g. choice behavior or brand preference. However, same researchers suggest scientific tools can observe brain activity to predict consumers behavior (Ambler et al., 2000 and Shiv and Fedorikhin, 1999 et al).

However, some consumer psychologists showed advertising research studies have often pointed out the important role of emotions for advertisement memorization (Ambler, 2000). In advertising research, who suggest that emotion and ratio are represented in different hemispheres of the brain. Research on the neural representation of stimuli-induced emotions, however, could show that emotions are not only processed in the left brain hemisphere, but are also processed bilaterally (e.g. in the left and right hemispheres of such cortical structure.

Customer loyalty is as an example, which can be defined as " a deeply held commitment to rebuy or a preferred product/service consistently in the future (Oliver, 1999). Consumer loyalty is a popular predictable consumer behavior topic for marketing researches, early research tried to establish whether customer loyalty has impact on aspects of business performance (such as profit margin and sales).

Loyalty is a psychological construct that develops over-time during a learning process of the consumer. Thus, loyalty research can benefit from insights in neuroscience and neuro-economics about how learning processes are represented in the brain. Some brain psychologists also explained how people learn to be loyal. They showed the following three processes in order to learn to be loyal.

(1) The brain should be able to memorize and retrieve positive and negative outcomes of former decisions, such as positive experiences after choosing brand A over brand B.

(2) The brain should be able to predict several outcomes of choosing between alternatives (buying A or B).

(3) The brain needs to integrate the information from processes 1 and 2 into the decision process.

Thus, it seems retailers need to concern how to develop loyalty and advertment promotion method and commitment to let consumers to have more confidence to choose to buy whose products or consume whose services more easily.

I shall indicate brain image and psychological feeling can influence consumer behavior. Such as digital signage is a new technology, where people broadcasting displays adapt their content to the audience demographic and features. In some shopping centers, retailers like to use machine learning methods on real-world digital signage viewer data to predict consumer behavior in a retail environment. Digital signage systems are nowadays primarily used as public information interfaces. They display general information, advertise content or serve as media for enhanced customer experience.

Interaction design studies show that the interaction level of users with digital signage systems will increase, including also the mobility of users around the display. Since digital signage systems can have a significant effect on commerce, which are also rapidly shopping centers ad retail stores. Retail generalization studies reveal that in-store digital signage increases customer traffic and sales (Burke, 2009).

Some consumer psychologists believe purchase decision processes can be described with five stages. The first stage is problem recognition, where consumer recognizes a problem is a need. The second stage is search for information via heightened attention of consumer towards information about a certain product, which can even resolve in actual proactive search for information. The third stage represents the evaluation of alternatives , which usually involves a comparison between various options and features based in the models of the expected value and beliefs. In the fourth stage of the purchase decision process, a provider, place, time, value , type and quality of the selected product or service and determined. The fifth stage are the final stage describes the post purchase use, behavior and actions.

Why will digital signage influence consumers choose to buy the product? It is possible that some consumers who like to use visa card to go to shopping as well as who like to use digital signage to confirm who are the visa card holders to let the businessmen to feel who are rich to let bank give trust to issue visa card to them to use. So, who do not need to bring much money to leave home to prepare to buy anything and who only bring one visa card to leave home safely. Thus, the digital signage systems are a new approach to automatic modelling of in-store consumer behavior based on audience measurement data. It is a unique machine payment method, which can also be used to predict more distinctive characteristics, such as an consumer individual's role in the purchase decision process. So, I believe digital signage audience measurement data can be used to model various user behavior for one kind of in-store consumer behavior prediction of method.

Can food consumption for trust cooperation influence food consumption choice?

Whether has it relationship between food consumption for trust and cooperation to influence eating similar vs dissimilar food consumption? Some consumption psychologists have attempted to do research to prove that food consumption with strangers who are assigned to eat similar food cooperating more in a labor negotiation and therefore earning more money. I image meeting for coffee with a colleges that just met. Is it possible that eating the same snack could increase your trust in that person? Similarly, could eating the same snack as a salesperson increasing your trust information about the similar food.

In general, people prefer to gather to share in a meal with others rather than eat alone, cultures define themselves partially through shared tastes and cooking traditions, and religious improve food regulations and restrictions meant to increase bonding among in-group members. Some psychologists had examined the relationship between food consumption and social connection. Development research finds that attraction increases similarly in food preference and also that similarity, in food preference increase attraction. Whereas, past research focused on the outcome of goods for food choice and consumption behavior is possible that group's food consumption results in social connection as increases liking and smoother interactions, presumably leading to interpersonal closeness. If the psychologists' research of social group similar food consumption is proved which can influence the people like to consume more than one person alone eats dissimilar food consumption, then restaurant businessmen only need to arrange what kind of similar food can attract group customers to eat as well as what kind of dissimilar food can attract one person customer to eat alone by their design food product advertising information.

We define incidental similar food consumption as group people choose to consume similar good more than dissimilar food with one restaurant table that is assigned and unrevealing of either preferences or prosocial intentions. Such that people eating together could become closer and more similar, with benefits for work performance. Eating may thus serve as a strong cue for signaling liking and closeness and more importantly trust and cooperation.

Our main focus is on understanding how food can be used as a connecting device that increases consumers' cooperation and trust.

To the extent that similar food consumption promotes closeness and liking, it follows that it would increase trust and cooperation, and this would be particularly true for strangers who can't rely on past behavior to establish trust. Unlike preference , such as taste in music or political beliefs, some food consumption psychologists feel that the role of food consumption on trust and cooperation is influenced by food product information. Thus, consumers can be strategic in food who consume, utilizing food when eating dinner on adapt or when out for lunch with a colleague . Similarly, marketers can use incidental similar food consumption to increase trust in product information when advertising a non-food product. Some food psychologists believe that similar food consumption lead to increase in cooperative behavior, such that those who consume similarly will be better at resolving a negotiation conflict than those consuming dissimilarly. Additionally, who also believe consequences of similar consumption for trust in product information. So, some food psychologists predict group close friend or family relationship consumers assigned to eat similar food as a product advertiser will like the advertiser more, which will translate into increased trust in the information presented about the similar food product.

Summarize incidental similar food consumption should increase closeness and liking, when group people are absence of dissimilar food choice, when people are influenced to consume similar food by food product information. Thus, the increase in closeness and liking should subsequently lead to an increase in trust and cooperation for the group of consumers who consume similarly. So, some food psychologists predict similarity in food consumption serves as a storage cue of trust compared with other incidental similarity and is therefore an important domain for examining implications of similar food consumption. These food psychologists suppose to consumers who eat the same food as product advertiser will trust information about the similar food product is more consumption as well as consuming similar food can increase cooperation resulting in a faster resolution of a labor conflict and more beneficial outcomes to both parties. Finally, who indicate similar food taste includes, sweet food ,e.g. sweet bread or ice cream or cookie as well as salty food , e.g. potato or chip etc. So, restaurant food shall divide sweet or salty taste similar food. If one person chooses to eat the restaurant food, the restaurant can advertise dissimilar sweet and salty taste food both product information to let the person to choose. Otherwise if one group people chooses to eat the restaurant food, the restaurant can advertise either all sweet taste food or all salty taste food product information to let the person to choose.

Does habit strength moderate the intention behavior to consumption?

Scientific evidence provides a sufficiently strong basis to justify the systematic development of intervention programs to increase healthy nutrition behaviors (World Health Organization, 2003). Such as an adequate consumption of fruit, a high consumption of fruit is associated with lower risk of cancer (Kremers et al., 2005, World Health Organization, 2003).

Will the concept of habit influence consumption behavior? Such as, fruit is a kind of health food. If the consumer has habit to choose to buy different kinds of fruit to eat everyday. Is habit as a factor to influence the consumer to choose to buy fruit to eat? Otherwise, if the consumer has no habit to choose to buy different kinds of fruit to eat everyday. Is non-habit as a factor to influence the consumer individual consumption behavior to choose any kinds of fruit to eat everyday.

Traditionally, habit has been measured by the number of times that behavior has already been performed in the past by an individual. Evidence to date indicates direct effects of past behavior on current behavior (Conner & Abraham, 2001). Some consumption psychologists had done experiment to research whether habit factor can influence fruit consumption. Their showed fruit consumption was assessed with a five item questionnaire, which was validated against seven day dietary records and biomarker for fruit intake (Bogers et. al 2004).

According to this consumption questionnaire result, it showed that intention is hypothesized to be the most immediate determinant of consumption behavior, yet several recent lines of research suggest that intentional control of behavior may be difficult to change, due to habit behavior consumption is caused to the individual consumer. Thus, it is difficult to change the consumer's behavior, when who have habit to choose to consume different kinds of fruit every week. However, results showed that the influence of intention on fruit consumption was weak and non-significant for those who had a strong habit toward fruit consumption. In constant, for those with a low or medium habit strength towards fruit. For those with low/medium habit strength, path analyses confirmed the reasoned, intentional process is for fruit consumption. In contrast, for those with high habit strength, it had the strongest influence on behavior. Thus, perceived control ability of fruit consumption seems to overrule the planned and intentional processes of fruit consumption for those with a strong habit. The environment behavior link also relates to the origins of habit, which are thought to originate from repeated performance of a given behavior in a stable situation. Thus, it seems environment can be one factor to influence strong habit consumers to buy fruit to eat every week as well as strong habit fruit consumer will buy much fruit to eat more than weak habit fruit consumer per week.

Nowadays, in UK suggests that consumer buying behavior has changed significantly. Consumers can buying different things, at different times and through different channels. As a result, forecast accuracy is very poor and many companies feel automated forecasting systems can not predict buying behavior more accuracy and relying on analysts to predict buying behavior by psychological methods. Automated forecasting systems weaknesses are such as: Historical data alone can't be used to predict feature sales in times and drawing together a wider range of internal and external data would help improve forecast accuracy. The impact on revenue manager varies widely. When sales forecasts are important, adjustments to revenue management system outputs are needed to retain credibility. When customers' behavior are poor to understand, there may be a need to sell from auctions or online experimentation to predict the market response. So, these automated forecasting system have these weaknesses to cause companies feel technological method can not be better than psychological method to predict further consumption behavior for whose products.

In psychological consumption of prediction view point, learning how to predict changes in consumers' attitudes and behaviors which is important to any companies. For example, in part behavior has changes as a result a recent major disruptive events, such as recession and exchange rate changes etc. economic factor, but there are other non economic factors to change consumers' attitudes and behaviors. For example, consumers are becoming smarter in their use of the internet to research products based on previous customers' view, seek out the best, deals and offers and then buy online, with a corresponding increase in the number of price comparison sites. So , companies are percentage seeing the rise of the strategic consumer who observes the dynamic of supplier pricing and adapts their buying strategy in response. However, some observers suggest that these changes to consumers' attitudes and behaviors are fundamental long, lasting and likely to continue to be disruptive.

Some consumption psychologists feel sales have become less predictable. In general, sales forecasts based on historical patterns in time series have become less accurate and hence less useful in the past year in many industries, not just these traditionally served by revenue management. Does forecast accuracy easily? For some revenue managers may be not too much, in some businesses prices are set by reference to the main competitors and forecasts have limited impact on operating and decisions about capacity. Marketing forecasting is aim to setting prices, maximizing revenue and managing operations.

However, forecast accuracy is very important to find why changing consumer attitudes and the implications for customer segmentation and forecasting of buying behaviors are not just relevant to revenue management. They are also fundamental to sales, marketing , brand management, customer loyalty, product design and beyond. Perhaps it has an opportunity for revenue managers to take a lead in influencing thinking of their colleagues in these areas. Some consumption psychologists forecast the future, who concern the historical data of companies collection before the recession, it can no longer be applied to forecast consumer behavior during the recession or after. At the opposite extreme, companies can simply continue to between auto prediction system to predict when the market stability will return soon and how to influence consumer behavior.

Sales are likely to depend on the economic situation, the competition and consumer behavior. However, these are external environmental factor to influence consumption of behavior. If it is possible to separate out these effects, then the forecasting model can take account of them by either building the economy/market into the model or segmenting consumers in an economy/market invariant way. External data, for example on the economic situation can also provide a good indicator of future sales. For example, internet (online) web site research technology is one possibility for combining and processing data from different sources on the web using automated tools. If buying behavior is changing and every consumer demand is becoming elastic, not only to increase revenue, but also to improve knowledge of the customers. For example, online auctions are mainly used in the travel and hospitality industries for offloading surplus capacity have been shown when facing only uncertain consumer demand. However, analyzing external economy environment factor is not effective to minimize risk to the sellers. Because sale forecasts are never going to be completely accurate and there is an argument for moving the focus away from being smarter with existing data towards making the business less dependent on sale forecasts. For example, taking close look at increasing flexibility in the supply chain or operations or re-examine the strategy for setting price.

What the current situation really emphasizes however is that there is certainly a need for forecast accuracy to be taken seriously by revenue managers and reported on by revenue management system. Thus, revenue managers need to concern how to predict whose consumers‘ psychological emotions to find why the reasons can influence whose consumption attitudes and behaviors changing to cause their product sale numbers had been falling. So, it seems that consumers' emotions can be influenced whose buying behavior by online auctions factor.

How can economical environment factor predict consumers consumption?

The dominant approach to industrial economics is
the one which is usually described as the structure-conduct-performance approach. So, predicting the performance of an industry in terms of profitability and advertising growth can predict consumer consumption in possible. The structure of an industry covers factors like the relative and size of firms, involved the ease of entry into the industry and the elasticity of demand for the output of that industry. The conduct of firms covers the objectives of the firms, price setting behavior, and attitudes to competitors (actual and potential), and from that the performance of that industry predicted, particularly in respect of profitability.

What are the main features of the structure of an industry? Many consumption psychologists discuss on the structure-conduct-performance topic, the number and relative size of the firms and the extent of barriers to entry into the industry to influence the product suppliers to consumption choices in the market. The number and relative size of firms is usually placed under either the size distribution of firms or individual concentration. Most industries don't fit into the category of a large number of small firms or of one firm.

Barriers to entry into an industry comprise all the factors which lead to new entrants into the industry being at a disadvantage to the existing firms because consumers have more choices to buy the similar products from the competitors . The first factor is the existence of economies of scale which means that a new entrant would have to produce on a relatively large scale increasingly. The second factor, the brand of products are supplied by a significant amount and thereby depressing price a significant amount , differentiation and advertising, so that a new entrant has to incur costs to overcome the loyalty of consumers to existing products. A third factor is the ability of existing firms to produce and distribute at lower costs than new entrants. Although, for example, access to cheaper new materials, accumulated knowledge of the industry etc. So, these external marketing environment factor will influence consumption behavior choices. For example, if the industrial structure determines or influences performance, the governments concerned with aspect of industrial performance (particularly aspects like price changes, technological progress and employment levels).

Consumption psychologists have often been assigned that the level of concentration in an industry is largely technological determined and that increases in concentration reflect impact of technological advance with increase the desired size of factory or firm. For example, mobile phone manufacturing industry, if the brand of mobile phone manufacturer had technological advance to manufacture any new model to attract consumers have more buying choices from their mobile products. Then, technological factor will influence consumers have more choices to buy the brand of mobile phone products. Other some psychologists believe the way in which unit costs change with the scale of production (cost conditions and economies of scale) factor which can influence consumers choice behaviors. When public policy favor active industrial intervention to change industrial structures, some indication is required as to whether the minimum efficient scale is small or large relative to the total market to supply their product numbers to influence consumers' behaviors. In the former case a policy favoring small units would be indicated, whereas, in the latter case large units may be favored.

Increasing returns to scale and economies of scales are usually defined as a situation when all inputs into the productive process are increased in the same proportion the volume of output increases in a greater proportion . How can economies of scale influence products supplying numbers? For example, that is the scale of output increases the degree of capital intensity rises. But within that change the type of the capital equipment is likely to be varied. Further, the balance between skilled and unskilled or between manual and non-manual labor may change. Thus , it is necessary to adopt a view of both increasing and decreasing returns.

The definition of unit costs of output declining with increased output. This must refer to all costs(including capital costs, and can only relate to a particular set of relative prices for inputs from which the unit costs are calculated. It would include any change in the price of input usage, such as mobile phone products which need to use different materials to manufacture any mobile phone products Thus, if a mobile phone firm had to pay more wages as its use of labor increased, that would have to be included. It is generally assumed that, for any scale of output, the firm is combining the impacts in an efficient manner. This efficiency includes economies efficiency (choosing the least cost combinations of inputs) and technical efficiency (producing the maximum feasible output from given inputs). The measurement of returns to scale under this definition may be only relevant to a particular economy, as it depends upon the particular relevance prices used.

Such as, each mobile phone product price will influence consumer individual behavior of choice to buy only one among the different brands of model mobile phones. So, mobile phone manufacturers need to concern how to reduce cost to gain economies of scale input to raise mobile phone output. For example, from a reduction in the effective price of an input to the model of mobile phone, as the volume of the styles of mobile phones purchases increased arising from an increase in monopsony power. For example, three mobile phone plants, A, B, C are assumes to have a fixed mobile phones output, and initially produce with unit costs A1, B1, and C1. Respectively. Supposing plants A and C would make subnormal profits and plant B super-normal profits, when capital costs are based on the historical cost of the mobile phone plant. Now the capital values of plants A and C are, it is argued, unlikely to fall and that of plant B to rise , for the amount which another mobile phone firm could be prepared to pay for a plant will reflect its profit prospects. If the decline in capital value fully reflects the initial deviations for normal profits, unit costs shift to A2, B2 and C2 respectively. Thus, there is a tendency at work towards mobile phone constant unit costs being observed. How far this tendency operates depends upon the based on which mobile phone firms value their assets. When the value is based on historic cost, the tendency does not operate. But the tendency does operate when the value is based in some way on the assets' profit prospects. Thus product manufacturers need to concern how to earn economic of scale to cost to avoid each product price will be changed often to influence consumer choices to other competitors more easily.

Some consumption psychologists had investigated several psychological variables which have been suggested as causes or effects of debts. Economic and demographic factors can predict debt category well to support this influence of factor. How can consumer manage money skills to pay debt which can influence when who plan to consume? Debtors were more likely to buy cigarettes and Christmas presents for children than non-debtors. Conclusions must be qualified because of low return rates, but the results suggest that a complex of psychological and behavioral variables affect debt and are affected by it. It is argued that these variables are linked to the psychology.

In general, economical environment is poor, it will cause many unemployed people, even some people will loan debt to pay daily essential expenditure from banks. If those debtors can't manage whose debt to be better to spend. Whose behavior will cause who do not have more spending desires often. Because these debtors will feel themselves as being in a community where debt was more common and more tolerated than non-debtors. The whole question of the classification of products a necessities or luxuries and its consequences for purchasing behavior is of current interest in economic psychology. Since debt is associated with poverty and poor people tend to give external reasons for economic phenomena, such as poverty and unemployment, causality may run the other way. In either case, however, there should be a positive correlation between external control and debt. There have different variables offer explanations of debts at different levels. One factor may be a consequence of another, or the mechanism by which it takes effect (for example, different patterns of economic socialization might generate different attitudes towards debt).

Some debtors need to borrow debt (loan) for house purchasing need. So, if the house loan debtors who need to pay back whose house loan to bank for long time. It is possible that their house loan will influence to reduce to spend much of daily consumption behavior to buy non luxury and daily essential products for long time. Thus, the result is these house loan debtors will reduce every day essential expenditure, such as food and soft drink, entertainment etc. to consume too much to compare to non house loan debtors for long time. It seems that retailers can attempt to apply debt management behavior to predict consumer shopping of desires.

Can firm's conduct and behavior factor influence consumer consumption ?

The usual assumption about the objectives of firms made by economists is that firms seek to maximize profit. The means that firms feel that who are protected against the possibility of new entrants, and proceed to maximize short-run profits. Firms feel that the barriers against new entrants ensure that their profits won't induce new firms to enter the industry and to reduce competitors enter to industry to raise consumers' choices to buy any similar products.

A major challenges to the profit maximization objective has come from proponents of the view that modern larger corporation are under a managerial control, which it is argued leads to the pursuit of other objectives, such as growth. The pursuit of non-profit objective is not unique to managerial-controlled firms, although the growth of such firms and of theories about than have emphasized these types of objectives.

Another view has focused on the controllers of the firm, whether owners or managers, having a wider range of objectives and that the achievement of profit maximization and the cost minimization requires considerable time and effort by the controllers. Thus, the controllers have incentives to forge profit maximization, unless who are forced to do so. Under oligopoly, firms can earn profits above the normal level, e.g. one country has only two electricity power companies are existing in the country's energy supply market. They may change a profit maximizing price, but actual reported profits may be less than potential profit.

This could raise from technical inefficiency or from higher than necessary payments to the factors of production. The technical inefficiency can arise since it takes effort by the controllers to reach full efficiency and which may be willing to make necessary effort. The higher payments can involve higher salaries to the controllers of the firm. For either reasons, company needs to concern how to report profit fall below true profit of the firm, with the difference used to finance inefficiency and higher factor payments in fair business conduct behavior. Particularly, company also need to concern how to carrying on fair business conduct behavior, e.g. none mislead advertising information, correct profit differentiation financial information, product reputations of the existing products presentation, none mislead consumption motives performance (which favor the established over the unestablished) and lower trade-in values of second –hand products of entrants (particularly in the car market). So, it seems that any one firm none mislead conduct behavior factor can influence consumer choices to increase or decrease to buy the firm's products in fair buying and selling transaction.

Another view point, for same products differentiation none mislead conduct factor is also important to influence each consumer behavior. For example, cars don't have a common prototype and each manufacturer must design its particular model. In constant , for a product like sugar , there is a common prototype, and differentiation through branding is within the discretion of the firm involved. This for some good product differentiation may be benefit whereas, for other products differentiation depends upon the activities of the firms involved, although the costs and benefits to the existing firms varies between profits. However, the height of the barrier to entry by product differentiation is likely to be influenced by the conduct and behavior of the firms involved, and thus in the case , there is an element of firm's behavior and conduct can influence any consumer buying behavior of choice to its products.

Advertising is one kind of promotion method to any firms. Advertising is a subject on which people tend to hold strong and often opposing views, and economists are not expectations to this. Some economists regard advertising as one means by which firms concentrate on promoting whose tastes and opinions in the direction of their products and also more generally in favor of private consumption (consumer behavior). Other economists see advertising as an efficient way by which firms supply information to potential consumers. Otherwise, some economists see advertising as a barrier inhibiting new entrants into an industry thereby enabling the established firms to reap high profits, when others see advertising as evidence of competition and an aid to new entrants in establishing themselves. So, it seems advertising can influence consumer choices possibly.

Advertising relatives to sales varies considerably between industries. For example, the ratio of advertising in 1968 year varied from over 15% in the toilet preparations industry to over 10% in the soap and detergents industry to near is in a number of toilet preparation producer industries. A distinction is frequently made between information an persuasive advertising , and it is often suggested that some forms of advertising (such as classified ads.) are likely to have more informative content than other forms (such as television advertising).

What is the sale of advertising in the demand function? One response is that a firm can sell more of its products because consumers have more information on that product. The information may relate to its existence, price, quality etc. Thus advertising is seen as essentially supplying information to consumers how to choose the similar kinds of products to decide which is the suitable product to buy. The other response is that advertising seeks to persuade consumers to purchase with favored people or situations, repetition of the same message. This advertising seeks to promote tastes rather than to inform. One firms' advertising may not be successful through false judgement by that firm and its advertisers or because of the impact of the advertising of other firms. The difference between the two responses can be put in terms of the conventional; utility maximization approach top consumer demand theory. The first response regards consumers' taste (i.e. the utility function) as fixed and advertising informs the consumer about availability, price etc. So, that utility maximizing process can take place more effectively . The second response regards advertising and seeking to promote consumers' tastes and change the consumers' utility function in a manner favorable to the advertiser. So, different types of advertising have been as containing information and persuasion in varying proportions and varying in the degree of desirability. But for the firm, the intention is to sell its products, and it will present any information in a way which seeks to influence the consumer to purchase its products.

Some consumption psychologists believe utility maximization by well-informed individuals plays a central role in conventional micro-economies. However, advertising can be a part of the conduct of firms in that firms use advertising amongst many other things to seek to increase profits or whatever their objectives it. Finally, advertising can be a part of performance, influenced by industrial structure. Some consumption psychologists also believe the highly differentiated products are more suitable for advertising than undifferentiated ones. They suppose existing firms benefit from their past investment in advertising and new entrants have to overcome those advantage.

If advertising is a profitable activity for firms to undertake, then the question arises as to why other firms don't follow suit. If other firms possibly including new entrants did follow suit, then the returns to advertising are likely to be reduced. It is useful to discuss the returns to advertising in terms of the returns in increased sales per advertising message and the cost of delivering an advertising message. Increasing return would occur form a message of repeated showing of a particular advertisement led to the product demand increasing at an increasing rate. Thus, of the product demand per unit of time is same to the number of advertising message per unit of time, then increasing sale returns would be raised possibly. The implications of any increasing sale returns to advertising may depend upon whether the increasing returns operate for advertising of a single product or for advertising of a number of products. Thus, it seems advertising promotion behavior can create barriers to entry to reduce consumers have more choices from other competitors' similar products sale.

In general, under short –run profit maximization,
the price was seen as a mark –up marginal cost with the marketing determined by the elasticity of demand. However, economists have used these methods to determination of how prices change behavior. The first is the indicated prices are determined relative to costs by firms in the pursuit of objectives. In the view point, the first is firms are price-makers and let prices in a way which think will achieve these objectives. Subject to constraints arising from demand and cost conditions. The second is theory of perfect competition, firms are effectively price-takers and the interaction between demand and supply in the market set price. So, firms are

regarded as price-takers, and hence not in position to set prices, such as price-adjuster . The third is the idea of observing the process of price decision-making and seeking observation is on the prices of price determination. Their view is expressed as price is based on full average cost , including a conventional allowance for profits and full average cost . Is determined as follows? price or direct cost per unit is taken as the base, a percentage addition is made to cover overhead or on cost or indirect cost, and a further conventional addition of percentage is made for profit. This, it seems price change behavior can influence consumer individual consumption behavior to any products.

Can scientific research be predicted consumer behavior by experts?

Using scientific research methods to predict consumption behavior phenomena in this field, some experts had attempted to do research in predictive validity to evaluate whether a measure of scientific achievement to consumer behavior. There are three groups thought to have varying knowledge of and ability to predict consumer behavior are academics, marketing practitioners and consumers in general. Academic groups use their scientific knowledge of consumer behavior as a basic for such activities as teaching, consulting for corporations, and testifying in legal and regulatory proceedings. In contrast, marketing practitioners are likely to be as familiar with this scientific literature. However, practitioners gain expertise through their experience. This expertise might help them to make accurate predictions of consumer behavior. Finally, when few studies on consumer behavior reach the general public, consumer's personal experiences should help them to predict certain aspects of customer behavior. So, it seems that how to predict consumer behavior, personal experiences (psychological feeling) method is more accurate than to scientific method.

In this discussion, I shall imply two hypotheses about how experts measure consumer behavior predictions. The first hypothesis, experts can make more accurate predictions than novices as well as the second hypothesis, academics can make more accurate predictions them practitioners. Thus, these hypotheses bring the questions and asked the subjects to predict whether each hypothesis tended to be true or false. For example, whether the more frequently an adolescent interacts with peers about consumption matters is the greater the tendency to use peer preferences in evaluating products? (Moschis & Moore, 1979). Will a person be more satisfied with their recently purchased car if the car met or exceeded whose expectations? (Westbrook 1980).

Their consumer research result indicated that for the practitioner group, who worked with marketing problems, but who were unlikely to be familiar with scientific research on consumer behavior. For example, systematic sampling was used to select 100 practitioners from the 1984 year American Marketing Assocication Membership Directory (academic addresses were excluded), a self addresses envelope was enclosed in the original mailings, and two postcard reminders were sent. Replies were received from 20 academics and 13 practitioners.

Subjects were asked whether who had previously read each of the studies. Two academic had read most of the studies because few of their predictions were usable (three or fewer), all responses from these subjects were excluded. Two academic respondents said that who did not understand all of the hypotheses, so who were also excluded. This left 16 academics. Other practitioner was excluded because who said that who did not understand the instructions, which reduced the number of practitioners to 12. Six academics and one practitioner reported reading one or more studies and their responses for these studies were excluded. Finally, the predictions by expects and native subjects showed that the prediction of consumer research percentage is larger than academics experts. For example, by assuming that researchers typically found what who were looking for and as a result, predicting
" true" for all hypotheses a subject would have been correct for 74.2% of the predictions, subjects who gave a higher percentage of these answers would be expected to achieve higher level of

accuracy.

I shall indicate web site (internet) example, to judge whether which can be used to predict consumer behavior. Recent work has demonstrated that web search volume can "predict the present", meaning that can be used to accurately track outcomes, such as unemployment levels, auto and home sales and disease prevalence in near real time. Consumers are searching what for online can also predict their collective future behavior days or even weeks in advance. For example, specifically businessmen can use search query volume to forecast the opening weekend box-office revenue for feature films, first month sales of video games and the rank of songs, finding in all case that search counts are highly predictive of future outcomes from online google research. Finally, businessmen can reexamine previous work on tracking trends and show that, perhaps surprisingly, the utility of search data relative to a simple auto regressive model is modest.

Nowadays, people increasingly use the internet for news, information and research purposes. From this perspective, it is a short step to conclude that what people are researching for today is predictive of what who will do in the near future. For example, consumers may search to prepare to buy a new camera, moviegoers may search to determine the opening date of a new film, or to locate cinemas showing it and individuals planning a vacation may search from a places of interest, to find airline tickets, or to price hotel rooms. So online can aggregately count of search queries related to retail activity. Movie going or travel might be able to predict collective behavior of economic, cultural, or political interest. Determining the nature of behavior that can be predicted using search, the accuracy of such predictions and the time scale over which predictions can be usefully made are therefore all questions of interest.

Researchers have focused on the observation that search " predicts the present". For example, Ettredge et al (2005) found that counts of the top 300 search terms during 2001 to 2003 year were correlated with US Bureau Of Labor statistics Unemployment

Figures; Cooper (2005) et al found that search activity for specific cameras during 2001 to 2003 year correlated with their estimated incidence and Eysenbach (2006) found a high correlation between clicks on sponsored search results of flu-related keywords and epidemiolopical data from the 2004 to 2005 year Canadian flu season.

Thus, motivated , I indicate one example how investigates whether search activity is a systematic leading indicator of consumer activity by forecasting. For first example, supposing to opening weekend Box-office revenue for 119 feature films released in the united States between Oct. 2008 year and Sept. 2009. For second example, supposing to first month sales of video games across all gaming platforms, e.g. Xbox, Play station etc.) for 106 games released between Sept. 2008 and Sept. 2009 year. These search data can be collected from yahoo using research rank from the current and previous weeks.

Can online search also predict the near future? A finding that may apply usually to a wide range of consumer behaviors , e.g. airline travel, hotel vacancy rates and auto sales and economic indicators , e.g. real-estate prices, credit card and confidence indicators. It seems all research based predictions simply models to build on publicly available information. For movies, baseline predictions can be used a linear model that includes production budgets, the number of screens on which each movie opened and box office projections from the Hollywood Stock Exchange (HSX) (hsx.com) on online, play money prediction market that is known to generate information prediction. For video games, many of the key indicators of revenue, including production budgets and initial available. Thus, it seems that businessmen can attempt to use internet (online) search technological method to search past information to concern whether what number of customers will be estimated.

In psychology view point, implications tests have been developed in an attempt to overcome and to obtain investigates the adaptation of implicit methods to measure product preference. Two questions are for test. (I) establishing an acceptable methodology for tests using product images . (ii) determining whether response to products can produce significant effects in affective experiments.

How can design researchers predict how to design product to be more attractive? Understanding how consumers experience designed products have important implications for design research and design practice. These questions are often investigated experimentally by presenting consumers with a range of products or design variants and measuring subjective response for future design development. Measuring consumer response to design product testing, e.g. survey methods, questionnaires, interviews and focus groups. Questionnaire methods are especially popular, and often feature attitude response, such as choice questions. Although, those explicit measures can provide helpful feedback to product designers, who are also subject to a number of limitations. Consumer survey responses to a product or predict future behavior, such as purchasing decisions in the marketplace.

In some cases, participants might be motivated to answer a questionnaire dishonestly, or in a way that seems most socially acceptable. However, the survey may not be targeting the same thought processes that a consumer faces in the product use scenario or in the marketplace. There is evidence that actual product-related behavior is affected by more spontaneous or processes, as consumers are often distracted or pressed for time when consuming products or making purchasing decisions. Other methods include psychophysiological techniques, such as eye tracking, brain imaging, heart rate measurement, and voice pitch analysis for an overview of these methods applied to design product measuring to consumer responses.

Can implicit design questionnaire (survey) or /and interview methods test product preference for measuring consumer response?

Some design researchers often use interviews and/or questionnaires to measure consumer response to products. In psychology, " implicit" tests have been developed in an attempt to overcome self-report biases and to obtain a more automatic measure of attitudes. Two exploratory studies have conducted to (i) establishing an acceptable methodology for implicit tests using product images, and (ii) determining whether response to products can produce significant effects in affection.

How to contribute design-research methodological developments for measuring consumer response. For example, product design research and conventional methods need to be gathered consumer feedback. How can consumer research in product design? Understanding how consumer experience designed products has important implications for design research and design practice. Thus, product manufacturers need to attempt to develop knowledge about the relationship between product designs and the responses who elicit from consumers, e.g. borrowing which product features can contribute to consumer preference by presenting consumers with a range of products or design variants and measuring subjective responses to them. This process can offer guidance for what products or design variants might be most preferred and can give useful clues for further design development.

Consumer response can be measured by questionnaires(surveys), interviews and focus groups. Questionnaire methods are especially popular and often feature attitude response. However, consumer survey responses may not fully capture reactions to a product or predict future behavior, such as purchasing decisions in the marketplace. This is evidence that actual product-related behavior is affected any more spontaneous or impulse processes , as consumers are often distracted or processes for time when consuming products or making product decisions (Friese, Hofman & Wanke, 2009). For example, cell phone images can be replaced with cars in order to develop the experiment using a second product category. As with phones, vehicles were chose , due to their wide appeal, user involvement and variety of models for potential testing.

In these experimental studies, the consumption psychologists selected products from two categories (phone models and car models) with the intention of measuring significant differences in approach bias among product stimuli. These consumption psychologists aim to test that of the method could be defined to measure attitudes with sufficient sensitivity, variants of particular designs could also be used as stimuli, offering feedback on the viability of different design directions. The consumption psychologists feel it will be helpful to add multiple questions to the self-report stage . Instead of a single attractiveness rating, who might as about " liking" or "employing additional methods". Comparison with real would measure , such as willingness to pay, prior ownership or observed consumption behavior may also be instructive. It may also be worthwhile test a version of the task where the correct response is determined by a feature, such as class membership (product color), shape, brand etc. instead of image ,location or rotation. It seems survey method can be used to predict consumer behavior.

In economic view point, demand is a model of consumer behavior. It attempts to identify the factors that influence the choices that are made by consumers. In microeconomics, the objective of the consumer is to maximize the utility that can be derive given their preferences, income, the prices relates products and services for which the demand function in derived.

Utility is the capacity of a product or service to satisfy a want. It can explain the phenomenon of value. Since utility is subjective and can't be observed and measured directly. The objective in microeconomics is to maximize the satisfaction or utility of individuals given their preferences, incomes and the prices of products or services who buy or consume. Thus, total utility of more or less satisfaction degree be caused by consumer behavior. It is consumption psychological result (effect) and it has close relationship.

Are internet delivered electronic services being made available to consumers about how who are evaluated for potential adoption to predict consumer behavior? Some psychologists' past researches had focused primary on the positive utility gains attributable to information technology adoption. However, their results indicate that e-service is adversely affect primary be performance-based risk perceptions, when perceived ease of use of the e-service reduces risk perceptions. E-services are interactive software based information systems received via internet. E-services are important in business to consumer (B2C) e-commerce because which represent ways to provide on demand solutions and improving customer satisfaction. So, it brings this question shows that whether businessmen can predict consumer adoption of e-services.

It is important to distinguish the different between conducting basic purchase transactions and adopting e-service. The e-service adoption decision is essentially different from most typical e-commerce purchases as which create a longer-term relationship between the consumer and service provider. Hence, even, if e-services are an e-commerce application to which some adoption models exists. It requires a distinct conceptualization to businessmen and businessmen need focuses on the role of perceived risk on influencing on adopting intentions of e-services. When e-services are convenient and create efficiencies for businessmen users. Little is understand about how consumers evaluate them for adoption. So, e-service performance quality and the potential utility of the service usefulness is a difficult task for consumers, especially given the newness of the online environment. If the consumer feels e-transaction is not suitable to him/her to use for shopping, then it is possible that it will reduce the chance to the consumer to choose to use the kind of e-transaction service to buy the brand of products. So, this e-service transaction will include both risks (potential negotiations utility) and perceived usefulness (potential positive utility) to let every customer to feel either of high utility or low utility after who choose to use e-service to shopping.

How important are risk perceptions to the overall e-services adoption decision? What types of risk are influenced and therefore important to the customer of e-service? Perceived risk is commonly thought of as an uncertainty regarding possible negative consequences of using a product or service. It has formally been defined as " a combination of uncertainty plus service of outcome involved" (Bauer 1960, 1967) and " the expectation of losses associates with purchase and acts as an inhibitor to purchase behavior" (Peter & Ryam 1976). Their research's pilot test result have indicated some electronic service shoppers concern for the theft of their private information, or simply its misuse by the businessmen collecting it. Members of a focus group drawn from the population studied to concern for the loss of privacy of personal financial information as an identify-theft. So, privacy risk was gathered and modeled as a deterrent to utility evaluations and the adoption choice to influence consumers choices to buy the product from this e-service sale channel.

Overall, some consumers will feel those perceived risks to influence who decide to buy the product from e-service sale channel. Such as performance risk, it means the possibility of the product manufacturing and not performing as it was designed and advertised and failing to deliver the desired benefits, financial risk, it means the potential monetary outlet associated with the initial purchase price as well as the subsequent maintenance cost of the product (ibid). The current financial services include potential for financial loss , due to fraud, time with means consumers may lose time when making a bad purchasing decision by wasting time researching and making the purchased, learning ow to use a product or service only to have to replace if it does not perform to expectations, psychological risk means potential loss of self oneself. Consumers feel unwise if they experience a non-performing products and may experience their feelings of harm to their self-image from the frustration of not achieve their buying goals, social risk means potential loss of status in one's social group as a result of adopting a product or service, looking foolish, privacy risk means potential loss of control over personal information, such as when information about purchase used without the customer's knowledge or permission. A consumer is carrying a criminal use whose identity to perform fraudulent transactions. Overall , when any one consumer feels one of those perceived risk will occur, then any one of these risks will influence who to choose to use e-service transactions method to buy product from internet. So, internet shopping seems have bad image to influence consumer shopping choice of channel as well as consumer demand of the product will be reduced if who feel e-service transaction channel is not safe to whom.

Is online video and television service is to be affective in predicting technology adoption to influence consumption behavior choice? Nowadays, online video and television services have become one of the most promising activities in terms of advertising revenue. E-Marketer has estimated that online video or television advertising will soar at 56% to 70% in the next five years (Halleman, 2008). To predict user acceptance of online video and television services. Despite a digital growth in online video and television to service over the span of a few years.

What factors can influence consumers to choose to buy the product after who watch online video and television advertising? Some psychological experiments shows a greater influence of perceived behavioral control on intention to use this type of services. The effects of attitude toward use and subjective norm were positive, but more moderate. The lesser effect of attitude towards use may be explained by the evidence benefits of watching videos online. However, search recent consumer studies have confirmed that watching online videos and televisions has become one of the favorite online activities for internet users (Hallerman 2008. Mulligan et al. 2008).

In the past, if somebody wanted to buy a book, on little learned about from whose friends or relatives, first who had to go into more bookstores to see of that book exists and after to make some price comparisons in order to decide from where to buy it from one bookstore choice only. These activities were time and money consuming. The situation has changed how the person can learn about launching a book easily from social networks, and by simply accessing an online store, such as Amazon . com , readers who can purchase the book to save time and energy by pressing a button activity only. So, the process of buying a product simplified in terms of time and money spent, but because more difficult in terms of decision making which has become more complex. The main reason is people have too many options to choose from in terms of product or service, price, quality and time.

Can digital internet technological electronic service influence consumers to choose this shopping style when who is habit to spend time to play internet . Is lifestyle a tool for understanding buyer behavior? Consumption psychologists had examined to confirm that it has relationship between the consumers' general life styles and their consumption pattern and the brands of products are used by them. They concluded that consumers often choose products, service and others because who are associated with a certain lifestyle . The products are the building blocks of lifestyle, marketers should therefore, have a complete idea of these changing lifestyles. So, dividing to segment them and position their products successfully.

The lifestyle of individuals has always been of great interest to marketers. They deal with everyday behaviorally oriented facets of people as well as their feelings, attitudes, interests and opinions. A lifestyle marketing perspective recognize that people sort themselves into groups on the basis of the things groups on the basis of the things who like to do, how who like to spend their leisure time and how who choose to spend their disposable income. Lifestyle is an important concept used in segmenting markets and understanding target customers, which is not provided by the study of demographics alone.

Many researchers have focused on identifying the lifestyle of the consumers to have better information about them. This study used the lifestyle analysis to identify market segments. Otherwise, some consumption psychologists believe to apply life style analysis for market segmentation, the developed of product strategy and the developed of the most appropriate communication strategy. They suggested successful retailers based on general application of lifestyle analysis have begun to implement a portfolio management approach which focuses on the needs of the key target markets. So, lifestyle segmentation can provide a valuable insight into the task of creating an effective brand identity. The study of lifestyle often provides fresh insights into the market and gives a more dimensional view of the target consumers. The marketing managers may be able to develop improved multi-dimensional views of key market segments, uncover new product opportunities obtain better product position, develop improved advertising communications based on a richer more life-like portrait of the target consumer and generally improve overall marketing strategy. These consumption psychologists assume that the members of any target client groups are all similar. The first hypothesis is people differ in their lifestyle they can be grouped into segments and the second hypothesis is people belonging to lifestyle segments differ in their demographics.

Thus, in consumption environment, a consumer chooses a product or a brand , which indicates a maximum possibility of the definition of whose lifestyle identity. Alternatively, a person makes a choice in a consumption environment in order to define actualize whose lifestyle identity if through the products or brands chosen. It can be assumed that the individual's consumption behavior can be predicted from an understanding of how who represents whose would be himself/herself of the details of choosing lifestyle system are known. Thus, digital internet is one good channel to research consumer lifestyle to predict whose consumption style.

Research question: Can behavioral economy method and psychological method predict consumer behavior.

Some consumption psychologists had attempt to research whether planned behavior can predict alcohol consumption. This research aims to quantify variables between theory of planned behavior variables and (i) intentions to consume alcohol in habit and (ii) reducing alcohol consumption reasons. They showed some drunken violence alcohol consumers who will reduce to consume much alcohol if who feel driving accident or causing death or violence behavior or alcohol poison causing non-health after who have consumed too much alcohol often. Thus, it is important to understand the psychological determinants of alcohol consumption.

A model of human behavior that has been extensively utilized to predict health-related behaviors, such as alcohol consumption in the theory planned (TPB; Ajzen, 1991). This model proposes that the most important determinant of behavior is a person's intention to perform the behavior. Three variables are identified as determinants intention, attitude, subjective norm and perceived behavioral control . Attitudes are an individual's positive or negative evaluation of performing the behavior. Subjective norms reflect an individual's perceptions of social approach or disapproval for performing the behavior. It represents an individual's perceptions of control over behavioral performance in the face of internal and external barriers. These results suggest the possibility that alcohol consumer behavior that are harmful to health, such as alcohol consumption, may yield different relationships when compared with results for behaviors that are beneficial to health. Specifically, individuals may wish to emphasis a lack of control over health risk behaviors, because these behaviors are not seen as socially , desirable and may need to be explained away be reference to external causes, such as peer pressure (De Visser & Mc Donnell, 2013).

Hence, it seems fear feeling psychological factor can influence alcohol consumers to reduce alcohol consumption in these situations, such as what action is being considered (e.g. heavy episodic drinking and the action is located (e.g. driving car) and what is the time frame for the action(e.g. needs car), the staff is a company driver when needs to drive car every day. Thus, whose action will influence to reduce whose alcohol consumption. Although, who has drinking alcohol in habit, but because who is one company driver, who is fear to cause accident to hurt himself/

herself and whose staffs when who sit in whose company car together. So, who will choose to reduce to consume alcohol in possible.

In general, consumer will have choice behavior, when who needs to do decision to buy automobile among of more than one product choice or with the determinants of such consumer behavior as buying life insurance, putting money in a pension plan, using credit cards etc. actions. By comparison, questions about behaviors that involve a choice among less or more options are usually studied at a lower level of generality. Thus, consumption psychologists may be interested to know why consumers buy one second of automobile rather than another, why who choose one type of medical treatment over another, or why who fly one airline rather than another. So, consumption psychologists must clearly define the action, target, context and time elements of the behavioral alternatives to predict whose consumption behavior. For example, the decision to buy tickets on one airlines rather than another can be affected by the destination (target element): A consumer may prefer one airline for overseas flights , but another for domestic flights. Similarly , choice of insurance company may vary depending on whether who buy life insurance, automobile insurance or property insurance.

Why will decisions under uncertainty cause? In consumer choice process, who has chance to encounter decisions under uncertainty. For example, the attributes of each product were assumed to be known with certainty. Thus, the consumers knew the price, picture, quality, reliability and visual appeal of each product type. All consumers need to do was to be importance weights and subjective values to these attributes and then derive a weighted average. In many of choice alternatives are not known with certainty ahead of time. Often, the outcomes are produced by decision depend on the state of the world at the time and the decision is made. For another example, a LCD television can produce a high -definition picture only of the service providers transmit high-definition programs. To take this uncertainty into account, the consumer has to judge not only the value of a high-definition display , but also the likelihood that this attribution will be available.

Perhaps, more readily recognized are the risks and uncertainties inherent in investment decisions. The investment outcomes of a decision to invest in a fixed interest certificate of deposit or a stock market mutual fund depend on future market conditions. Whereas the CD produces a known payoff over a given time period, the amount and probability of possible gains or losses to be expected of the mutual fund can only be estimated.

Thus, advertising can reduce decision uncertainty to consumers‘ choices. If the product advertising can attract to consumer’s consideration , it will persuade the consumer to choose to buy the brand of product. Clearly, information about the decision making process, in general, as well as about decisions of particular relevance to consumer behavior. Thus, it seems advertising information can reduce consumers’ choices processes under uncertainty to decide to buy the brand of product preference choice.

Why businessmen need to divide customer segment(s) to decide who is target customer group to predict consumer behavior. Nowadays, consumers are unique in themselves. A comprehensive knowledge of consumers and their consumption behavior is essential for a firm to succeed. In order to understand and predict consumption patterns and behaviors within segment(s), market research becomes essential.

Why businessmen need to concern market research with consumer behavior. Each individual is unique himself/herself and needs and wants vary from person to person. Markets identify segments and target one or few of these segments and target one or few of these segments and thereby fulfil the qualifications of the marketing concept. First, marketers need to identify customer needs and wants and then, deliver product and service offering, so as to satisfy the customers more efficiently and effectively, than the competitors.

In order to understand and predict consumption pattern and behavior within segment(s), market research becomes essential. Market research defines to gather information about market and the customers. The environment of a firm may be grouped as the micro and macro environment both. The micro environment firm comprises forces to close affect the firm directly. For example, the firm's internal environment, the founder/leader and whose vision and mission, clients, competitors, suppliers and channel intermediaries. The macro environment, on the other hand, companies forces in the environment that first affect the micro environment and thought that which affect the firm, in other words, which affect the firm indirectly, including the demographic factors, socio-economic factors, political factors, technological factors, cultural factors, natural factors etc. The micro environment is studied in terms of strength(s) and weakness and when the macro environment is studied in terms of opportunities and threat(s) analysis of both comprises the SWOT analysis.

Thus, market research can help firms to understand the specific marketing situation facing a firm. Identifies the needs and wants of client segment(s), identifies variables target segment(s), serves them better through formulation of appropriate marketing strategies a mix of the 4(p)s. It's goal is to achieve maximum efficiency and effectiveness to meet customer needs and wants and client satisfaction . Thus is obtained through a conscious attempt at understanding " what" the client buy(s), "why" who buys, "when" who buy, from "where" who buys, "how" much who buys and "how" often who buys. Thus, the integration of market research with consumer behavior: marketing research can understand and predict consumer behavior as well as consumer research is a process and tools to be used to study consumer behavior both.

Marketing research objective is to study the marketing environment and the clients who are a part of it, as well as to study consumers as individuals as groups. It focuses to establish trends and identify opportunities and threats in the environment, to study the market and forecast potential and to predict buying patterns based on modeling and , to understand consumption behavior and consumption patterns. Besides, consumer behavior research has tradition approach and current approach has traditional approach and current approach.

Traditional approach divides positivist and interpretivist both approaches. Positivist approach refers to as modernism is the earliest approach to studying consumer behavior and trends the study as an applied science. It lays emphasis on the causes of consumer behavior, these causes are directly related to effects. Thus it treats consumer as "rational" human things, who make purchase decisions after collecting information and weighing all alternatives. The process of consumer decision making, it seems of rationality, rational decision making and problem solving is the key. It is based on certain assumption, consumer actions based on cause and effect relationship can be generalized, who can be objectively measured and tested. If researchers could identify the reasons behind consumption behavior, who would be able to predict it, and if who could predict consumer behavior, who could influence it.

The methods focus on prediction of client behavior, including surveys, observations and experiments. It aims at drawing conclusions a large samples. The positivist consumer actions can be objectively measured and tested. It focuses to predict consumer behavior, e.g. large samples of quantitative methodology. Otherwise, the interpretivist consumer action is a cause and effect relationship can't be generalized , consumption pattern and behaviors are unique, these are unpredictable. Consumer actions are unique and different both between two consumers, and/or within the same consumer at different times and situations. It can't be objectively measured, tested and generalized. It focuses the act of understanding the consumption rather than predicting the act of purchase, e.g. methodology small samples of qualitative methodology.

In consumption psychological view point, the current approach is the term " dialectics" , considers all forms of human behavior, thus the current approach to the study of consumer divided into four approaches: materialism approach implies that consumer behavior is shaped by the material environment, e.g. money, possessions etc. , change approach means consumer behavior is " dynamic" in nature, it is always in a process of continuous motion, transformation and change. Totality means consumption behavior is " interconnected" with other forms of human contradiction means views changes in consumer behavior as arising from their internal contradictions, like moods, emoting etc. The approach studies the consumer as a complex total whole and views consumer purchase as well as consumption processes.

The current approach to studying consumer behavior uses both the quantitative as well as qualitative approaches. There are three broad research perspectives in consumer behavior: they are as follows:

Decision making perspective, the experiment perspective and behavioral influence perspective. According to decision making perspective , the buying process is a sequential in nature, with the consumer perceiving that there exists a problem and that moving across a series of logical and rational steps to solve the problem; stages being problem recognition, information search, evaluation of alternatives , purchase decision and past purchase behavior, it emphasizes rational , logical and cognitive approach to consumer decision making and purchase process.

The experiential perspective believes that not all buying may be rational and logical, in some cases, buying results are from a consumers' desire for fun and fantasy, pleasures, emotions and moods. The perspective emphasizes that consumers are feelers as well as thinkers. The behavioral influence perspective holds that forces in the environment stimulate a consumer to make purchases without developing beliefs and attitudes about the product.

In general, quantitative research is used by the positivists and qualitative research is used by interpretivists. How to use quantitative research in consumer behavior? It comprises (i) research techniques that are used to gather quantitative data over large samples randomly and (ii) statistical tools and techniques, e.g. survey, observation and experiments techniques. Thus type of research is descriptive in nature. It is primarily used by the positivists when studying consumer behavior with a focus on prediction of consumer behavior and techniques are also used by " dialectics" approach.

How to use qualitative research in consumer behavior? It comprises (i) research techniques that are used to gather quantitative data over small samples techniques , e.g. depth interviews, focus group of study is subjective in nature. The focus is on understanding consumption behavior and consumption pattern . the objective is to gain an understanding of consumer behavior and the causes marketing situations are unique, and hence the finding can't be generalized to marketing situations. It is primarily used by the interpretivists when studying consumer behavior. However, the qualitative techniques are also used by " dialectics" approach.

Today, both approaches and are used to study consumer behavior. In some causes, qualitative research may act as an indicator to qualitative research through case studies and other qualitative measures. Qualitative research is very often a prelude to quantitative research are used to prepares scales for surveys and experiments.

Consumer decision making has long been of interest to research. The most prevalent model from this perspective is " utility theory" which proposes that consumers make choices based on the expected outcomes of their decisions. Some consumption psychologists view consumers are as rational decision makers and who are only concerned with self interest. However, utility theory views the consumer as a rational economic man. Consumer behavior considers a wide range of factors how to influence to change the consumer behavior , and acknowledges a board range of consumption activities beyond purchasing.

These activities commonly include need recognition, information search, evaluation of alternatives, the building of purchasing intention, the act of purchasing, consumption and final disposal. Some psychologists regard man and rational and self interested, making decisions based upon the ability to maximize utility when spending the minimum effort.

It concerns economic man theory, in order to behavior rationally in the economic sense, as consumers must aware of all the available consumption options be capable of correctly rating each alternative and be available to select the optimum course of action. Some psychologists view point, behavior is subject to biological influence through instinctive force or drives with act outside of conscious thought. So, the consumption psychological behavior is determined by biological drives, rather than individual cognition, or environmental stimuli thoughts and feelings can be regarded as consumer behaviors.

Some psychologists feel environmental variables influence consumer behaviors. However, an influential role of the environment and social experience is acknowledged with consumers activity seeking and receiving environmental and stimuli is as informational inputs aiding internal decision making . Input variables are the environmental stimuli that consumer is subjected to influence to choose either to buy or not buy the product, e.g. brand, advertisement, price, sale channel, place, salespeople service, quality, loyalty, durability etc. different elements can influence consumer final decision making.

Some investigations indicated about the changes in consumer behavior are caused by external environment influences, e.g. globalization and development of information technologies. It can help to understand the specific factors what should be taken into account in evaluation of consumer behavior.

In macroeconomic environment view point, for example, the global trend of economic liberalization, new political geography, gradual removal of international trade barriers , rapid technological advancement these environmental factors are just a few of the factors that have had major effect on the business management practices nowadays. The most obvious impact on the practical level of doing business has these macroeconomic environmental factors intensified competition. So, these factors can influence micro economical consumer behavior indirectly. Consumer behavior is mix of elements from psychology, sociology, sociopsychology, anthropology and economic. Management process will identifies, anticipates and supplies customer requirement efficiently and profitably.

Consumer decision making has long been of interest to research. The most prevalent model from this perspective is " utility theory" which proposes that consumers make choices based on the expected outcomes of their decisions. Some consumption psychologists view consumers are as rational decision makers and who are only concerned with self interest. However, utility theory views the consumer as a rational economic man. Consumer behavior considers a wide range of factors how to influence to change the consumer behavior , and acknowledges a board range of consumption activities beyond purchasing.

These activities commonly include need recognition, information search, evaluation of alternatives, the building of purchasing intention, the act of purchasing, consumption and final disposal. Some psychologists regard man and rational and self interested, making decisions based upon the ability to maximize utility when spending the minimum effort.

It concerns economic man theory, in order to behavior rationally in the economic sense, as consumers must aware of all the available consumption options be capable of correctly rating each alternative and be available to select the optimum course of action. Some psychologists view point, behavior is subject to biological influence through instinctive force or drives with act outside of conscious thought. So, the consumption psychological behavior is determined by biological drives, rather than individual cognition, or environmental stimuli thoughts and feelings can be regarded as consumer behaviors.

Some psychologists feel environmental variables influence consumer behaviors. However, an influential role of the environment and social experience is acknowledged with consumers activity seeking and receiving environmental and stimuli is as informational inputs aiding internal decision making . Input variables are the environmental stimuli that consumer is subjected to influence to choose either to buy or not buy the product, e.g. brand, advertisement, price, sale channel, place, salespeople service, quality, loyalty, durability etc. different elements can influence consumer final decision making.

Some investigations indicated about the changes in consumer behavior are caused by external environment influences, e.g. globalization and development of information technologies. It can help to understand the specific factors what should be taken into account in evaluation of consumer behavior.

In macroeconomic environment view point, for example, the global trend of economic liberalization, new political geography, gradual removal of international trade barriers , rapid technological advancement these environmental factors are just a few of the factors that have had major effect on the business management practices nowadays. The most obvious impact on the practical level of doing business has these macroeconomic environmental factors intensified competition. So, these factors can influence micro economical consumer behavior indirectly. Consumer behavior is mix of elements from psychology, sociology, sociopsychology, anthropology and economic. Management process will identifies, anticipates and supplies customer requirement efficiently and profitably.

In consumption psychological view point, technical criteria concerns the cost aspects of purchase, durability, reliability, comfort and convenience. Economic criteria concerns the cost aspects of purchase, include price, running costs and residual values, e.g. a trade in value of a car.

In conclusion, economic environmental and consumption psychological factors can influence consumer behavior changing, so businessmen can attempt to do any surveys, experiment etc. research methods to predict how consumer behavior will change to attract them to choose to buy their products more easily.

Reference

Ajzen, I (1991). The theory of planned behavior. Organizational behavior and human decision processes, 50(2), 179-211. doi: 10.1016/0749.5978 (91) 90020-7.

Alba, Joseph W. and J. Wesley Hutchinson (1987). " Dimensions Of Consumer Expertise", Journal of consumer research, 13 March, 411-454.

Baucer, R,"Consumer Bhavior As Risk Taking , In Risk Taking And Information handling In Consumer Behavior", D. Coxceds Harvard University Press, Cambridge, Mass 1976.

Bogers, R. P., Brug, J. Van Assema, P., & Dagnetie, P.C. (2004) , Explaining fruit and vegetable consumption: The theory of planned behavior and misconception of personal intake level. Appetite, 42,157-166.

Bolton, Ruth N. (1998), " A Dynamic Model Of The Duration Of The Customer's Relationship With A Continuous Service Provider: The Role Of Satisfaction", Marketing Science, 17 (1), 45-65.

B.Shiv and A. Fedorikhin, " Heart And Min In Conflict: The Interplay Of affect And Cognition In Consumer Decision Making", J. Consumer Res., vol. 26, pp. 278-292, Dec. 1999.

Brown, K.W., Ryan, R.M. Reswell , J.D. (2007). Mindfulness: Theoretical Foundatins And Evidence For Its Salutary Effects. Psychological Inquiry, 18, 211-237.

Burke, R.R. : Behavioral effects of digital signage, J. Advertising Res. 49(2), 180-185 (2009).

Conner, M. & Abraham, C. (2001). Conscientiousness and the theory of planned behavior: Toward a more complete model of the antecedents of intention and behavior. Social psychology bulletin, 27, 1547-1561.

Cooper C. Mallon, K, Leadbetter S, Pollack L, Peipins (2005) , cancer internet search activity on a major search engine, United States 2001 to 2003, J Med Internet Res. 7(3): e36.

De Visser, R.O., & McDonnell, E.J. (2013). " Man points": Masculine capital and young men's health. Health psychology, 32(

1), 5-14. doi:10. 1037/a0029045.

Eysenbach G (2006) Infodemiology: Tracking flu- related searches on the web for syndromic surveillance. American Medical Informatics Associaion Annual Symposium Proceedings , Curran Associates, Red Hook, NY, pp. 244-248.

Ettredge M, Gerdes, J. Karuga , G (2005) Using web- based search data to predict macro-economic statistics. Commun ACM 48: 87-92.

Feldman, Jack M. And John G. Lynch Jr. (1988), "Self-Generated Validity And Other Effects Of Measurement On Belife, Attitude, Intention And Behavior", Journal of applied psychology, 73(3),421-35.

Fitzsimons, Gavan, J. And Vicki G. Morwitz (1996), " The Effect Of Measuring Intent On Brand-Level Purchase Behavior", Journal of consumer research, 23 (1), 1-11.

Fiese, M, Hofmann, W., & Wanke, M (2009). The impulsive consumer. Predicting consumer behavior with implicit reaction time measurement. In M. Wanke (ed.) Social psychology of consumer behavior (pp.335-364). New York, NY: Psychology press.

Hallerman , D. (2008) video Advertising Online: Spending And Pricing , New York. E-Marketer.

Helleman, D. (2008) Video Advertising Online: Spending And Pricing , New York, E-Marketer.

Kremers, S.P. J., De Bruijn, G.J., droomers, M., Van Lenthe, F. J., & Brug, J. (2005). Environmental interventions for selected dietary behaviors in adults. In J. Brug & F. J. Van Lenthe (eds.) , Environmental determinants and interventions for physical activity, nutrition and smoking: A review pp. 282-315. Rotterdam: Erasmus Medical Center.

Mulligan, M. Banerjee, T & Thomas, N. (2008) , European Paid Content And Activity Forecast, (2008 to 2013), Jupiter Research.

Peter, J., Ryan, M, M, " An Investigation Of Perceived Risk At The Brand Level, " Journal of marketing research, 13 May 1976, pp. 184-188.

Pieters, R., & Wedel, M. (2007). Goal Control Of Visual Attention To Advertising: The Yarbus Implication. Journal Of Consumer Research, 34, 224-233 (August).

Parasuaman, and Leonard L. Berry (1985), " Problems And Strategies In Sevices Marketing", Journal of marketing, 49 (Spring), 33-46.

Jamieson, Linda F. And Frank M. Bass (1989), " Adjusting Stated Intention Measures To Predict Trial Purchase Of New Products: A Comparison Of Models And Methods," Journal of marketing research, 26 (August), 336-45.

Moschis, George p. & Roy, L. Moore (1979), " Decision making among the young. A socialization perspective " Journal of consumer research , 6 (September).

R.C. Oliver, " When is consumer loyalty?" J.Marketing. vol. 63, pp.33-44.1999.

Shostack, G. Lynn (1984), " Designing Services That Deliver", Harvard Business Review, 62 (January-February), 133-9.

Shostack, G. Lynn (1985), " Planning The Service Encounter ,in the service encounter" , John A. Czepiel, Michael R. Solomon, and Carol F. Suprenant, eds. New York: Lexington Books, 243-54.

Shostack, G. Lynn (1987), " Service Positioning Through, Structural Change", Journal of marketing, 51 (Janurary), 34-43.

Soloman, Michael R. (1985), "Packaging The Service Provider", Service Industries Journal , 5(1), 64-71.

Stevens, C.W. (1980), "K-MartStores Try New Look To Invite More Spending" The Wall Street Journal, Nov. 26, 29-35.

T. Ambler, A. Ioannides, And S. Rose, " Brand s On The Brain : Neuroimages Of Advertising ", Business Strategy rev., vol. 11, 3. pp. 17-30. 2000.

Westbrook, Robert A. (1980), " Intrapersonal affective influences on consumer satisfaction with products, " Journal of consumer research , 7 (June) 49-54.

World Health Organization (2003). Diet, nutrition and the prevention of Chronic diseases report of a joint WHO/FAO. expert consultation. Geneva: World Health Organization.

Wysocki, B. (1979), " Sight, Smell, Sound: They're all arms in retailer's arsenal" The Wall Street Journal, Nov. 17, 1979. 1-35.

CHAPTER VI

House quality influences householder electricity energy consumption behavior

Can apply artificial intelligence measure the house quality how influences the householder electricity energy consumption or useful activities to be more or less? In general, house owners have both intentions for whose property. One intention is living the house by householder himself or herself or householder with families themselves. Another intention is that renting to others to receive rent income (landlord). So, in the housing market, the housing consumer includes either the property owner intents to rent to others to live for rent income aim or the property buyers intents to buy the house to be house owner to live. Does these both different property purchase intentions, which will influence the householder's attitude to use electricity energy consumption desire to be more or less, due to the householder's demand to whose house quality factor influence? This is one interesting question concerns the householder electricity energy consumption desire change to the householder, due to house's investment or house's living intention influences to house quality factor.

How does house quality factor influence to householder electricity energy consumption desire to be more or less? Has it relationship between house quality and house investment or living intention to cause house quality demand to influence the householder electricity energy consumption desire change or demand to be more or less? Has it relationship between regional housing market living or rent investment intentions, housing quality and electricity energy consumption more or less desire? I suppose that the determinants of the residential electricity energy demand form space-heating and cooking, due to the property quality demand influence and the householder's living or rent investment intention influence both, which will influence the householder's electricity energy consumption or useful behavior when he/she/they is/are living in the house.

I argue that rent properties are not only consumer goods, but it also constitute financial market assets. It is therefore reasonable to assume that rational (rent income investment intention) investors choose to raise housing quality (e.g. thermal insulation technological installing at home, heating or cooling technology or artificial intelligent window, lighting, door opening or closing) in order to attract many people choose to rent whose house to live. The householder's aim is to achieve an acceptable return on investment (ROI) or raising rent income aim when he/she rents whose house to anyone, it is easy to attract many people to choose to pay higher rent his/her house to live in the property rent market. Moreover, the another important factor is that rents and future house sale prices of properties differ regionally (or even locally), and largely depend on housing market fundamentals, such as either the house living buyer's income levels or the house rent buyer's income levels, vacancy rates, and/or householder investor's expectations.

Thus, if the householder expects to rent whose house and raises rent to attract many people choose to rent whose house to live, who will attempt to install many new technology in order to satisfy their high quality of life need when they can pay higher rent to rent to choose to rent whose houses to live. Their aim only achieves to raise housing quality, but any new technology will lead to increase electricity energy consumption or use in the house.

Hence, any high quality of houses will influence the householder to use or consume more electricity energy at home. It means that the householder will choose to consume or use more electricity energy at home, if he/she or the family householder demands to live more comfortable house and he/she/they can have high quality of living life at home. This comfortable living demand to the householder (property renter or property buyer) view point can explain why the better quality of house factor will influence the electricity energy consumption desire to the householder also to be more daily.

I shall indicate one home electricity energy consumption experiment, it indicated that utilizing aggregate data on regional space-heating energy consumption form over 300,000 apartment buildings in 97 German planning regions. The study applies structural equation modelling to estimate the influence of housing market fundamentals on the level of housing quality, and subsequently on regional electricity energy consumption. Consequently, it suggests that housing market fundamental explain regional differences in the housing quality.

In particular, findings show that the level of per capita income, investor' expectations about future housing market development as well as vacancy all explain regional differences in housing quality has a significant impact on electricity energy consumption.

In the way, this experiment can indicate evidence that regional housing market fundamental have a substantial influence on regional levels of housing quality and energy consumption desires to the German regional householders.

This Germany regional householder experiment found important implications for high or low housing quality of the regional property building and householders either property living or property rent intention of comfortable living feeling need factor which will influence the regional property householder electricity energy consumption desire to be raised or reduced. These factors will influence the consequence of electricity energy demand to be increased or decreased needs every day for the regional householder as well as the country's electricity energy supplier(s) can gather the regional properties whether they are high or low quality to predict the regional properties householders' electricity energy consumption supply budget more accurate. It implies that an important determinant of residential housing quality will have possible to influence electricity energy demand to be more or less for long term. IN particular, this Germany regional residential experiment can explain and find an important role in formulating assumptions about the quality factor has chance to influence the regional residential future levels of electricity energy efficiency and consumption in the country. Hence, housing developments and electricity energy firms can follow this regional residential housing quality factor to evaluate whether the regional housing market is the corresponding investment patterns as well as the energy researchers can follow the regional residential housing quality whether it is high or low housing quality factor to evaluate the more accurate models of regional electricity energy demand to any regional residential householders' houses in the country.

In consumer behavioral view point, it explains that if the country government expected many householders feel to need to spend much electricity energy or have much electricity energy useful demand or desire at home. The country government ought to encourage the country residential property or house developers choose to build many houses which have technological product installed to satisfy the regional householders' residential comfortable living need when they choose the regions to build the high quality houses to let them to live. Then, the regional householders will be influenced to consume or use much electricity energy at homes, due to they feel that they are living at high quality and comfortable and high building technological installed apartments in the country's regions. Then, the country's government and electricity energy provider(s) may be raise much electricity energy efficiency and supply and profit , due to the regional residential householders' electricity energy consumption or useful desire need is therefore influenced to be more by the regional high quality of residential houses factor. So, the regional high quality of residential house factor will have relationship to the regional electricity energy consumption and efficiency to the regional householder's houses.

Otherwise, if the country government felt electricity energy is shortage, it ought encourage the property developers build many low quality and low building technological houses to let householders to live themselves or rent to others to live in the country's different regional residential development market. Due to the low quality of properties and low technological installed to properties factor which will influence any these different regional residential householders to choose method to solve shortage of electricity energy challenge to the country.

In conclusion, to apply consumer behavioral economic theory to property development market, if property quality factor can really influence the householder's electricity energy consumption desire to be used more or less at home daily. The country's property developers can apply this factor to predict property consumer individual property buying consumption behaviors more accurate. For example, if the US property developer planned to build low quality and low technological design buildings and lesser comfortable residential houses in the region in US. Then, its residential householder target will be trended the less acceptable of electricity energy consumption property buyers to choose to buy these regional properties to live in the US region because they can only accept to spend less electricity energy to use when they are living in the houses in order to save money daily. SO, the low quality , less comfortable and low technological installed design residential houses will satisfy their living needs. Otherwise, if the US property developer planned to build high quality and high technological installed design buildings and more comfortable residential houses in the region in US. Then, its residential householder target will be trended to the more acceptable of electricity energy consumption property buyers to choose to buy these regional properties to live in the US region because they can accept to spend more electricity energy to use when they are living in the houses in order to improve their living of quality. So, they wont's consider to spend more expenditure to use electricity energy for any technological products are installed in their properties in order to satisfy their comfortable living needs at their homes every day.

Consequently, property developers can attempt to gather marketing research concerns whether how many people who accept to use more electricity energy or use less electricity energy in order to predict they ought build how many high quality or low quality houses number in different regions more accurate in themselves countries or overseas countries property development market.

Environmental impacts of householder greenhouse gas electricity energy consumption activities

Can artificial intelligence measure whether what environment factors influence householder electricity energy consumption activities? Has environment factor relationship to influence householder electricity energy consumption behaviors? Socially, householder electricity energy consumption provides us with sources of living satisfaction , but if any sudden environment factor changes, whether it will influence householder consume or use more or less electricity energy decision at home. However, I assume householder electricity energy consumption will have a considerable proportion of the environmental impacts be influenced by our way of life and our economic decision of electricity energy consumption behavior.

What different environmental factors will influence householder electricity energy consumption decision? The external environmental factors include, for example, the country's electricity firms or government changes to electricity energy regulations, electricity energy production technologies change and business practices and government policies changing etc. different external environmental factors will influence any country's electricity energy consumption to householders' consumption desire to be more or less. It will also require changes to influence the householders to consume which kinds of electric products which are needed to be used in different electricity energy natural manufacturing resources.

Why does these external environmental factors impact householders' any behaviors to influence them to concern to use more or less electricity energy power or which kinds of electricity energy products choice at homes. How any why environmental factors impact will influence householder activities at home, such as electricity energy consumption and choice? What are the key components of external environmental factors influence householders' electricity energy consumption behaviors. I shall explain as below:

Firstly, we need to know whether what external environments are which can influence why and how householders need to change their activities to choose more or less or which kinds of energy power to be provided to them to use at home. Who is householder? Householder is an individual, family, or group of individuals living together as unit in a home. Consumption of electricity energy at home may be cooking food needs, needing have colder feeling to turn on fan or air condition at home in summer or needing have warm feeling to turn on heater at home in winter, watching television programs or listening music , playing computer games or used computers activities , reading activities and applying artificial intelligent technological tools to help householders to open or close homes' windows, doors etc. different home equipment which need to use electricity energy provisions. SO, their home activities need to turn on lighting electric tools , televisions, music machines, radios etc. different equipment which need to use electricity energy provision at home. SO, the purpose of householder consumption means consumption by individuals living in a household and it includes consumption both in and outside the home. Why does environmental impacts link to householders' electricity energy consumption? I shall focus on discussing of greenhouse gases (GHGS) energy product how any why it can influenced to householders to use.

The environmental impacts will influence this kind of greenhouse gases (GHGS) energy in the product lifecycle or delivery of the service to link the householder's energy consumption at home such as these several aspects:

Extraction and greenhouse gases production (supply number), physical distribution (delivery far long or close near short distance between the greenhouse gases manufacturing factory and the greenhouse gases supplier), resources consumed by marketing and retail activities (householder's needs to use the quantity of the greenhouse gases energy product), the greenhouse gases consumers search and purchasing activities(e.g. travel to shops, internet purchasing channel, , finding the which kinds of greenhouse gases products from internet, magazines, newspapers, radio advertisements etc. different medias,) , post-use greenhouse gases energy disposal (resale, reused or rubbish). The householder's physical behavioral impact environmental factor will influence how and why he/she chooses to consume greenhouse gases energy daily , e.g. impacts of a housing development, or a wind –farm that supplies greenhouse gases with power. So, the householder's greenhouse gases energy consumption behavior which will depend upon individual personal and subjective perspectives and value.

So, the householder's useful behavior or attitude of greenhouse gases energy product which will influence how he/she/ the family use or consume greenhouse gases energy, such as the householder individual environmental protection attitude which can impact how he/she/the family spends the quantity of greenhouse gases energy every day at home, if the householder does not expect our air or water or land is polluted , due to extraction of any natural gas resources to be manufactured any kinds of greenhouse gases products. Then, this environmental pollution issue will influence some householders choose to reduce to use more quantity of greenhouse gases products every day. Another environmental factors include the bio relates the (unsustainable) use of resources to avoid wasting much greenhouse gases energy to cause greenhouse gases energy supply shortage, avoiding the cause negative impacts of quality life , e.g. noise causing when the extraction of any natural resource from lands to the householder's house is near to the natural resource extraction land and health impacts, e.g. when the greenhouse gas householder user who often use the kind of greenhouse gas product when it is used to cook or heat any equipment to cause they to breathe dirty air at home often. These impacts can be measured in different ways include: monetary costs or loss, physical quantities of resources used or waste or pollution produced and the burden the greenhouse gases energy place on environmental resources. All of these external environment factors will impact the householder individual attitude or behavior how to use or consume greenhouse gases energy product at home.

All these environmental factors concern householder greenhouse gases energy consumer individual consumption attitude is influenced by environment pollution, greenhouse resource supply shortage challenge, greenhouse gases influence the householder's negative quality of life, negative health impacts, noise, waste money , raising economic cost to the householder which will impact whether how the householder choose to use the quantity of greenhouse gases product or the kinds of greenhouse gases products or other kinds of electricity energy products.

However, these are other external environmental factors which can impact how the householder decides to use greenhouse gas product at home. They include: the changes of energy regulation, e.g. the country government has quota number implementation to prohibit to import above the limited quantities of any kinds of greenhouse gas products to any countries. So, when the greenhouse gas energy supplying quantity is decreased, but if the country has may householders who need to buy different kinds of greenhouse gases products to be used at home. Then, the different kinds of import greenhouse gases energy products prices will be raised in possible, due to demand is more than supply in the country's greenhouse gas energy product market. Consequently, if the greenhouse gas energy price us risen above the general social acceptable level to the home greenhouse gas energy product householder consumers. Finally, it will influence them to choose to buy other kinds of gas energy products to replace the greenhouse gas energy product to use at home.

Another side, if the country's greenhouse gas energy manufacturing supplier sudden changes its greenhouse gas energy production technologies to choose to concentrate on manufacturing other kinds of energy products. Then, the greenhouse gas energy supply quantities will be only decreased, even future one day , it will cause greenhouse gas supply shortage challenge to let the country's home greenhouse gas householder consumers who can not buy enough quantity of any kinds of greenhouse gas energy products to satisfy their electricity needs at home every day. Consequently, when future on day , the country greenhouse gas energy manufacturer has none any quantity of greenhouse energy products to supply to the country's greenhouse energy householders to use at home. The, they must only choose other kinds of new energy products to replace the traditional useful greenhouse gas energy products to be used at homes.

In conclusions, these non-controlled external environmental factors can impact and influence the country's every householder consumer individual attitude or consumption behavioral change to how any why the country's householders either choose to buy much or less quantity of greenhouse gas products to use at home.

The effect of house space occupancy
and building characteristics on
householder electricity energy use

Can artificial intelligence mesaure how much space occupancy is the suitable size as well as what the most suitable building characteristics influence each householder electricity energy useful activities or behavious? In general, society believes large space size occupancy house building characteristics factor which will influence householder use more energy at home, e.g. in summer, when the householder is living at the large space size occupancy house, who ought turn on all air conditions or fans at sleeping rooms or eating room or studying room. So, if the householder's house has two to three or more sleeping rooms. Then, he / she needs to buy more air conditions or fans in order to let all rooms' temperature to be fallen down to let he /she feel more cool comfortable feeling when the temperature is above 30 degree or more extreme hot in summer weather. Otherwise, when the temperature is low, e.g. between 0 degree to 10 degree or below 0 degree in winter weather. When the householder is living in

one large space size occupancy appartment, which has thee to five sleeping rooms , even more and two studying rooms and one eating room, even more as well as every room has one heater. Then, he / she must turn on all heaters to let who to feel warm feeling when he / she is staying in the house. It brings these interesting questions.
Will large or small size space occupancy housing characteristics influence any householder often turn on heater or air condition or fan in whole house space occupancy area in order to the householder feels warmer or cooler feeling when he /she is staying in the house?
Has any space occupancy housing characteristics relationship to influence any householder to turn on heater or air condition or fan in whole house space occupancy area in order to the householder feels warmer or cooler feeling when he /she is staying in the house?
Does it bring positive relationship between turning on long time fan or air condition or heater and the house occupancy space characteristics is large or small size?
I shall attempt to give psychological evidences to explain the householder's house space occupancy area large or small size factor whether it can influence the householder choose to do long time or short time turning on heater or air condition or fan behavior in order to let he/she/the family to feel more cooler or warmer comfortable feeling when he/she/the family is staying in the house in summer or winter weather.
Does the house occupancy space size characteristics factor is the only one or important factor to influence the householder choose to turn on long or short time fan or air condition or heater in the house to let him/her/the family to feel more cooler or warmer comfortablc fccling in summcr or winter weather?
I feel that it is not exact right , due to the householder's house space occupancy size whether it is large or small characteristics to influence the householder choose to turn on long time or short time fan or air condition or heater time to let him /her/ the family to feel more cooler or warmer when he / she / the family is staying at home in summer or winter weather. The reason is because that

the lifestyle of living quality need is different between developed countries and developing countries. The lifestyle of living quality factor will change the country's householder's expectation about the quality of living life. For example, for Africa, Korea, China , Japan, Hong Kong etc. developing countries. On the lifestyle of living quality need to these developing countries' householders aspect, that will cause a high environmental burden when they need to often turn on air conditions to satisfy more cooler feeling when they are staying at homes in summer or they need often to turn on heaters to satisfy more warmer feeling when they are staying at home in winter. Due to if their houses are large size space occupancy characteristics and they have more than at least two sleeping rooms and studying rooms and eating rooms and toilets number. Then, these householders who are developing countries' large space occupancy size characteristics houses, they won't like often turn on heaters long time to keep more warmer in their indoor whole space area in winter or they won't like often turn on air conditions or fans long time to keep more cooler in the their indoor whole space area house environment in summer .

The reason is possible because that the developing countries' householder chooses often to turn on their heaters or air conditions or fans long time in their houses when they are staying long time in their houses and their houses space occupancy sizes are very large, it will bring the electricity energy to be used more to these developing countries' householders' large space occupancy size characteristic houses. It means that the electricity fee will be also increased due to they often turn on heaters or air conditions or fans long time to keep their indoor temperature to be more cooler in summer or more warmer in winter. So, it seems that the developing countries' householders are living in the house whose space occupancy have very large size characteristics and more than two rooms house characteristics in the developing countries as above. Then, they won't often choose to turn on heaters or air conditions or fans long time to keep more cooler or warmer feeling in their house whole indoor space occupancy environment when they are often staying at home long time.

Their lifestyle of living comfortable feeling are lesser than the developed countries householders. Consequently, their lesser cooling or warming comfortable demand of living lifestyle factor will change their attitudes to use air conditions or fans or heaters turning on time in order to limit heaters or air conditions or fans turning on time to be shorter than the developed countries houeholders' heaters or air conditions or fans turning on time at homes. Due to the long time turnong on air conditions, fans , heaters at the developing countries' householders' homes, it will cause to spend much electricity energy to lead electricity fee charges to be raised to the developing countries' householders ' homes when they are often staying at homes in summer or winter weather. Hence, the house space occupancy large size characteristics ought not influence the developing countries householders choose to turn on air conditions , fans or heaters long time in order to let them to feel more cooler or warmer at homes in summer or winter weather.

So, the developing countries' house space occupancy large size characteristics householders won't be more acceptable to pay higher electricity energy fee when they are staying at homes at summer or winter weather. Due to they do not often choose to turn on heaters, air conditions or fans long time during they are staying at homes. Otherwise, the developed countries, e.g. UK, UK , France, Germany, Swiss, Singapore, Italy etc. countries. In general, these developed countries' householders' living lifestyle quality needs are higher than the developing countries. So, when the summer or winter weather is coming, if the temperature is extreme cold, e.g. below than 0 degree or it is extreme hot, e.g. higher than 30 degee.

Then these developed countries' householders will easy accept to turn on air conditions or fans or heaters long time at home in order to keep their appartment in door temperature to be more cooler in extreme hot in door environment or more warmer in extreme cold in door environment when these developed countries' householders are often staying at homes long time at night after their day time working time or schooling time. Because these developed counties' householders' quality of living lifestyle needs or demands are higher than the developing countries' householders. So, they won't consider that they will pay more electricity fee , due to they often turn on air conditions, fans or heaters long time to let them to feel more comfortable in cooler or warmer indoor large size space occupancy environment. So, it seems that the electricity energy efficiency will be raised to the developed countries' householders who are living in the house space occupancy large size characteristics and they will be possible to pay more electricity fees during they are often staying at home in extreme hot summer or extreme cold winter weather.

In conclusion, due to the living lifestyle quality need (demand) is different between the developed countries' householders and the developing countries' householders. It will influence the householders' long time or short time spending time on air conditions or fans or heaters indoor space occupancy size characteristics environment in order to achieve more cooler or more warmer feeling in their houses. Consequently, the long or short time of turning on air conditions, fans, heaters for the developed or developing countries householders' activities factor will be more influential to compare the house space occupancy large or small size characteristics factor to influence their cooler or warmer feeling in their houses. SO, the house indoor environment electricity energy consumption efficiency degree to the developing or developed countries' every householder house in summer or winter to the developing or developed householders in summer or winter weather , which is more influenced by the living lifestyle qualty factor to the either developed countries or developing countries householders. Hence, any developed or developing countries' electricity suppliers need to consider the building areas of property development market buyers their living style quality demands (needs) whether their living style quality demands are higher or lesser than the other building areas of property development market, they ought not consider whether the building locations of the houses' space occupation sizes whether they are large or small sizes in order to evaluate the householders will live at the building areas of property development locations ,whose electricty energy spending efficiency more accurate.

How to help low income household earners to reduce not essential electricity energy expenditure spending at homes

Can artificial intelligence measure whether which income level influences low income household accept to use the much electricity energy at home? Has it relationship between the householder income and the electricity energy needs? How to evaluate the subsidies and social tariffs to assist lower income earners to analyze household energy consumption more accurate?

Electricity energy is essential needs for every householder at home, e.g. lighting, cooking power, healthcare, sanitation, cooler or warmer temperature indoor control at home. However, for lower income household earners, it its burden when they need often to use electricity energy to supply power to any home electricity tools to do any acticities at homes. If any these countries' lower income householder earner target can not get the reasonable subsidies to assist them to solve any electricity energy tools' electricity energy poer needs. Due to their lower income leve, it is possible that to knfluence them have enough electricity supply to help them to use to cook rice and food and vegatabe to eat, boil water to drink, turning on light tools to help them to read, watch TV, listen radio, music any entertainment or essential needs at homes at night or morning afternoon time. These lower income household earners will be easy to sick , due to they have no enough electricity supply to help them to use use electric bottles to boil water or cook food to eat. Then they only drink not boiled water or not cooked food to eat at homes in possible, due to they have no enough income to pay electricity fees every month.

Hence, how to evaluate the lower income household earners'

electricity fee need (demand) level in order to provide the reasonable subsidies amount to assist every country's low income household earner to help them to pay the reasonable electricity fee which is one important issue to every country's government today. It brings this question: How to evaluate or analyze or predict every lower income household individual or family earner's every month electricity energy demand (need) more accurate?

It is one essential issue to be value to consider to every country's government. Moreover, to the estent that energy subsidies must be essential to be provided by public sources to all low income household earners or that a social tariff may be designed for improving access to energy for certain low income social earner groups. Hence, how to structure the energy subsidies between energy and income levels to be better target, such public mechanisms, and to avoid regressive subsidies unfairly. For example, India and China these both countries ' income poverty and energy poverty population are the large number. So , these both countries' governments need to focuse on more aggregated effects and analyze the effects of rural electrification at the local level on the decrease in energy poverty in rural low income poverty and energy poverty householders. Therefore, every country government needs to point regressivity of the subsidy for electricity. There is room to analyze to what extent low income household earners along the income distribution demand some forms of energy, and to suggest better and fair low income targeting household earners energy subsidies supply policies.

Each government does not only consider energy issues from a social point of view, it also needs have a manner to consider a possible link between energy, hunger reduction, and food security for each country's low income household earners group. So, every government has responsibility to calculate the determinants of different sources of energy consumption at the low income houehold earner level for urban and rural both populations in order to evaluate the electricity subsidies and to test whether every low income householder earner characteristics plays a role in determining energy consumption.

In general, in the use of energy measured as that for cooking, such as LPG reduces the exposure of households to hazardous, increases the consumption of different types of foods and medicines, improves the distribution of time between household memners, enables studys with more light, reduces the use of digital computer entertainment tools at home, and moderates the use of wood as fuel, preventing deforestation. These methods are the best suggestions to help low income householder earner groups to reduce time to use electricity at homes. When they spend less time to use electricity to do any not essential activities, e.g. watching television, playing electric games from home computers, listening music. They only use electricity to turn on light read, to turn on rice cooker to cook, when they feel hungey to eat. Then, I believe that these social low income household earner groups will reduce to pay much not essential electricity energy expenditure at homes. Hence, every country government ought need to persuade low income household earners to avoid to use electricity to do any not essential activities in order to raise electricity energy consumption in long term time.

It will bring less amount of energy subsidies expenditure benefits to every country's government. Hence, the success to persuade any countries' low income household earners to reduce to spend much time to do any electric entertainment activities of consumption behaviors at homes often. This is the most efficient and the most successful energy subsidiary method to help them to reduce electricity energy expenditure when they are staying at homes. Hence, if any country government expected the low income household earners can continue really reduce electricity energy expenditure, they need to learn to do the meaning essential activities which are needed to use electricity at home habitally. Then, they can change their electricity useful entertainment living habit, e.g. using computers to play games, listening music, watching television entertainment habits at homes to cause essential daily needs of electricity useful living habit, e.f. using cookers to cook rice or cook food to eat, turning on lights to read , turning on heaters to bath, turning on air conditions to keep cool temperature or turning on heaters to keep warm temperature at homes. Consequently, they won't need to pay much electricity expenditure at home, due to their waste useful electricity entetainment living habits have changed to do any essential useful electricity activities at homes.

Another kind of method to reduce the determinants of energy demand to the low income householder earners. The governments can persuade them to consider the variation factor can influence their electricity energy expenditure are increased or decreased at homes. It is not the electricity or gas price is increased from the electricity suppliers. It is that their bad living habits of waste electricity or gas to do any not essential activities at homes. e.g. the householder often turn on light tools to read or listen music or watch television in whole night, he/she ought need to sleep at night, but he/she does not go to bed to sleep in whole night. He/she chooses to turn on light to do these activities. Then, he/she will waste much electricity at whole night. Also, some householders like to bath more than half hour, even one hour, when it is winter, they need to turn on heaters to provide electricity to cause the bath room has warm water to provide to them to bath, Their long time bathing behaviors will be also waste electricity or gas energy from long time heating in bath rooms. So, they need to change their waste electricity consumption living behaviors at homes.

So, I suggest that some low income household earners will need to be taught to change their bad using electricity enery living habits from governments' public relation promotion in order to change the low income household earners' bad or incorrected useful electricity or gas living attitude to achieve and to avoid them often to do electricity or gas energy waste behaviors at homes. So, different countries' governments need to teach them how to do the correct or right electricty or gas useful activities (living habits) or let them know or feel how to use their electricity or gas which can help them to reduce to waste the not essential extra electricity or gas energy.

Consequently, they must reduce electricity or gas expenditure as well as electricity or gas shortage challenge won't be caused by their electricity or gas useful waste behaviors (activities) at homes.
In conclusion, energy subsidies method is not the best solution to help low income household earners to reduce to use electricity or gas energy. Because it is only short term benefit to reduce their electricity or gas expenditure at homes. The best solution is that to let them to know or feel why and how they have responsibilities to change their incorrent or wrong electricity or gas consumption bad habits in order to avoid global electricity or gas energy is waste to be used, even it is caused shortage from householders' energy waste behaviors.

Factors influence householder energy
efficient consumption behaviors
at homes

Can artificial intelligence measure how householder uses energy level at home ? What factors can influence householders how to use energy in efficient way at homes. It depends on different countries householders' living habits to cause their choices to use energy efficiently at homes. In general, global householders energy every day consumption or use aims include cooking, heating, and cooling or warming rooms, lighting , water-boiled use and computer playing games entertainment etc. activities at homes every day. Some activities are often essential at homes, e.g. cooking, cooling or warming temperature in rooms, lighting , water-boiled use. So, their activities must not avoid to use energy at homes often. Otherwise, some activities are not essential at homes, e.g. playing entertainment games from computers, cooling rooms in summer, listening music, watching television etc. these activities. The householder can choose either to use energy to turn on these equipment tools or not to do these non essential activities at homes often. In general, householders rely on energy to make ourselves lives comfortable, productive and enjoyable. However, global householders need to learn how we can use energy resources wisely because global every householder has responsibility to manage resources includes: reducing total energy use and using energy more efficiently in order to avoid energy shortage crise occurrence. The choices are make about how we use energy, e.g. turning machines off when not in use of choosing to buy energy efficieny appliances will have increasing impacts on the quality of our environment and lives.

Energy conservation includes any behavior that results in the use of less energy. Energy efficiency involves the use of technology that requires less energy to perform the same function. For example, a compact fluorescent light buld that uses less energy to produce the same amount of light as an incandescent light buib is an example of energy efficiency. So, a householder's decision to place an incanadescent light bulb with compact fluorescent is an example of energy conservation. So, as individuals, every countries' householder choices and actions can result in a significant reduction in the amount of energy used in each sector of the economy.

So, I bring this interesting question: What factors can influence householder to choose to do any efficient energy consumption or useful behaviors at homes? I believe every countries' householders will have their different living attitudes and their living attitudes can influence their behaviors or activities to choose hoe to use energy at home. I shall indicate some countries' householders' living attitudes to explain the factors can influence them to use energy efficiency at homes as below:

Is the low income and rising price of modern fuels both factors best to influence Nigeria householders choose to use energy efficiently?

Firstly, for Nigeria householders energy consumption habit at homes example, it is richly with natural resources, modern energy resources which provide many householders with biomass (mostly firewood) and some other householders modern energy sources, such as kevosene, liquefied, petroleum, gas and electricity for their use. So, it is one country which can manufacture to provide energy for itself to use. It doesn't need to depend on other countries to import any kinds of energy to householders to buy to use at homes. But, it has social challenge, the poverty problem in Nigeria goes beyond low income, savings and growth rate, due to its low level of education, poor governamce, high level of unemployment factors influence.

It is important to know how Nigeria householders meet their basic energy needs between poverty and energy can bde described in terms of quality and quantity of energy used. Generally, most poor householders use biomass fuels because of affordability and they (householders) do not have energy equipment (such as, gas cookers, electric cookers etc.) . So, it seems Nigeria householders won't demand their living quality to be improved. It implies that they will use any kinds of energy efficiently at homes, e.g. gas, electricity, due to they find themselves in energy poverty. Although, this country has enough nature resources to manufacture energy to provide to householders to use, but due to many people are low income group, so they won't spend too much expenditure to buy much energy to use at homes. So, the rising prices of modern fuels, such as liquefied, petroleum , gas (LPG) and electricity and their erratic supply have made many householders revert to the use of traditional fuel, such as firewood and charcoal.

It brings this questions: Is the low income and rising price of modern fuels both factors best to influence Nigeria householders choose to use energy efficiently?

The hypothes is predicated on the economic theory of consumer behavior. However, when income increases, householders not only consume more of the same goods, they also need higher quality . So, it applies economic theory to householder's energy consumption behavior at home. It explains why low living standards induce greater dependence on firewood and other biomass fuels owing to a combination of income and substitution effects, such as Nigeria low income household energy home users case. it explains why Nigeria householders can accept to use firewood and charaval traditional energy to replace liquefied, petroleum , gas (LPG) and electricity modern energy . So, economic theory explains the Nigeria household energy users why they can accept to use traditional energy to replace modern energy and their energy useful or consumption behaviors are efficient at homes. Although, Nigeria has enough natural resource to manufacture modern energy to supply to householders to use at homes. But, due to these modern energy products prices are raised to the price level of householders who can not accept. it causes to Nigeria householders only choose to buy the cheap biomass, firewoods to replace high price of modern energy products to use at home often. So, they can accept their quality of living to be fallen down. So, expensive modern energy product price is one factor to influence some countries' householders to choose to buy cheap traditional poor quality of nature energy, e.g. firewood or biomass, to use at homes. Hence, they can raise energy efficiency to use when they choose to use traditional nature energy to replace modern nature energy at homes.

Does season factor influence New Zealand householders' energy consumption behaviors at homes

Secondly, for New Zealand householders energy consumption habits at homes , for example, their living quality needs are general comfortable need feeling. Their countries' houses of space heating was found to average 34% of total housholder energy use. The relation to space heating includes low indirect temperature are associated with persistent under-heating , whether some space heating sources tend to be higher or lower in winter indoor temperature than others and winter indoor temperatures are compared to international benchmarks and established healthy temperature ranges. So, New Zealand occupant's perceptions of winter indoor temperature conditions are presented and explored in relation to heating patterns and household energy consumption. So, it seems that NZ winter temperature is low. Moreover, it will influence householders need to turn on heaters to keep more warmer feeling indoor. Then, they will use more electricity energy. In special, if the householders' houses spaces are large sizes . Hence, their heaters need long time to keep whole houses' areas or spaces or rooms temperature to be rised up in order to let they do not feel very cold in winter. So, NZ's winter extreme cold weather will influence householders' energy use or consumption to be increased in winter.

The electricity efficiency to every NZ householder is very high in winter to compare spring, summer, autumn seasons. Hence, if NZ electricity suppliers expected to forecast electricity consumption more accurate in NZ. In order to ease the life for both electric net designers and electricity suppliers, it was decided to find out, how the NZ weather conditions and every householder's house space size factors to influence the power consumption to NZ householders. If there is a clear trend observed , then this relation can be used for power consumption forecasts to NZ householders.

Why does NZ weather condition factor and householder's house space size factor can predict householders' electricity consumption at homes. Due to geographic location on the global the lowest south sets specific conditions for weather, such as NZ's south island geographic location is near to south ocean in our earth. It is a country where average annual temperatures are well between 10 degree to below 10 degree at NZ south island special geographic location to near to the sourth ocean in our earth at the same time.

However, large part of mankind is living in the conditions where there are four different seasons in NZ geographic location, dark winter, which is cold and snowy, spring with rising temperature and high precipitation, sunny , dry and rather hot summer, and windy and wet autumn. These conditions lead to different patterns in electric appliances use in NZ householders, in special, in NZ south island householders. If trends in electric energy use have substantial correlation with weather conditions, this can help NZ electric energy suppliers and producers to forecast electricity consumption and thus organize and manage production of electric energy.

Consequently, it will lead to much more stability in energy supply to NZ every householder. For example, when the NZ energy supplier gathers data concerns every householder's house space size data, e.g. the house has how many sleeping rooms, toilets, bath rooms, eating rooms and reading rooms number, even the house has how many family members are living in every NZ geographical location. Then if it can follow different location of NZ houses spaces sizes whether they are large or small space size as well as whethe every house has how many family members are living to evaluate whether how much electricity efficiency can satisfy their comfortable living needs in winter. Then, it can evaluate whether they will use how much electricity efficiency for their needs in different seasons. If in winter, many householders are living in the large space size house in the geographic location. Then, it is possible that the geographic location is householders will use much electricity efficiency and where geographic location hosueholders who will be possible to pay the most highest electricity fee to compare the other geographic location of small space size of house householders. Hence, weather factor is the most influential to change NZ householders ' electricity energy consumption behaviors at homes.

Urbanization level and income per capita both tangible factors as well as temperature (weather variation factor) will have close relationship to influence China householder energy consumption or useful needs at home every day

For China householder energy consumption habit example, what factors can determine to impact this country's householders energy useful behavior at homes? Can the impacts of these factors be quntified? What are China householder energy consumption trends and characteristics? I shall explan as below:

I believe the influential factors include these three aspects to China householder energy users: Income per capita, urbanization level an annual average temperature (weather). These factors will influence any China householder energy useful or consumption behavior at homes.

Temperature (weather variation factor) is intangible from eastern region to western region of Chin, variances largely depend upon economic level and the provincial level. So, some regions were warmer and cooler temperature will influence the regional China householder how to use electricity. In addition, th influence of urbanization level varies according to income level as well as the urbanization level has more significant impact on the structure and efficiency of China householder energy consumption thatn on its quantity. So, the urbanization level and income per capita both tangible factors will have close relationship to influence China householder energy consumption or useful needs at home every day. Moreover, these two tangible factors (urbanization level and income per capita both factors) have the more influential to impact China any one of household family energy consumption or useful habit to compare temperature factor at home. Because temperature can only influence than to choose to turn on heaters to keep more cooler in summer or turn on air conditions (fans) to keep more warmer in winter.

The electricity energy needs for these equopment tools which will be influenced less. Otherwise, the urbanization level and income per family householder how to choose to spend more or less electricity or gas etc. energy at homes. Because in behavioral economy view point, when individual householder has more income and the urban in the China geographic location is lising many high income and high household families memebrs to every house. Then, the urbanization household energy household enery useful or consumption level will be raised. Such as China household electricity users case, e.g. large cities have many high income and many houses have more than four families members to live on one house together. Then, the electricity or gas energy efficiency will be influenced to rise. The city urbanization and per capita income level is high to these large cities have high to income population, who are living in these cities in China.

Moreover, the impact of lifestyle on energy use mainly reflects types and purposes of fuels are chosen by different China households factor which will influence the urbanization level of energy choice use. China is a country with typical binary economics and social diversity and these is significant difference in the consumption pattern between urban and rural regions. Urban residents consume high-quality energy, such as electricity, natural gas , heating power, solar energy and gasoline. For rural residents, usually use coal, and bismass energy because they are cheaper price energy products which requires much time and labor and are heavy indoor pollutants . The difference in energy consumption pattern between urban and rural China residents is closely related related to living of quality needs, building structure, e.g. steel or stone etc. different materials, manufacture, easily access clean and effective feels through the electric grid, natural gas network and district heating systems.

Therefore, it explains why urbanization level is as an integrated variable reflecting social progress situation to influence urban and rural regions, such as large cities , small cities and rural countryside regions' household energy consumption or useful behaviors which have differnet kinds of fuel useful demands and energy efficiencies qualify and quantity demand, or needs at homes. Consequently, it explains, urbanization level and income per captia level both factors are more influential to China household energy consumption at home to compare temperature (weather , seasonal) factor.

Employment rates or gross domestic product macro economic variation factor, residential space size factor, and the government's implementation of energy labeling schemes provide significant impacts on Taiwan residential electricity consumption .

For Taiwan householder electricity consumption characteristics in the residential sector, which has different factors and pattern to compare China householder electricity householder electricity consumption habit at home. Although, they are the same Asia country. I shall explain these reasons as below:

For Taiwan electricity householder factors influence their energy useful or consumption behaviors at homes. The main factors can influence their electricity energy useful patterns include:

employment rates or gross domestic product macro economic variation factor, residential space size factor, and the government's implementation of energy labeling schemes provide significant impacts on Taiwan residential electricity consumption . However, the impacts of electricity raising price and the energy supply reducing shortage efficiency standards do not significant to influence the Taiwan residential electricity consumption behavior at sources.

It means that it won't influence Taiwan householders to use electricity or gas or any kinds of energy number to be reduced, even the Taiwan government energy suppliers sudden raise, any kinds of energy price and reduce to supply energy to satisfy Taiwan householders daily essential needs at homes.

In fact, Taiwan had improved gross domestic product (GDP) and it had raised employment rates recently. So, many Taiwanese has jobs to work, due to Taiwan economy had improved to be better. So, growth had also raised. The economy improvement causes many Taiwanese had enough jobs to work, due to new businesses are set up. Many consumers excit any kinds of businesses are invested to Taiwan from overseas or local investors. So, consumption is grown, the electricity consuming applicances are selected, as the household consumer focus grousp number if also influenced to be increased. So, Taiwan economy had improved to be better, it will encourage many electricity consuming applicances products are encouraged to excited to be selected to seel in Taiwan. Due to many different kinds of electricity consuming appliances are supplied to attract Taiwanese to choose to buy to bring to their homes for cooking, boiling water, or keeping rooms to be cooler or warmer temperature confortable feeling intention in winter or summer seasons. So, these electricity consuming appliances, e.g. rice cookers, heaters, air conditions, fans, bathing gas heaters etc. different home electricity consuming appliances will be increased to supply to satisfy Taiwan householders' needs. When they decide to buy any news electricity consuming applicances to bring to homes to use.

Environment scientists' education message how to influence Greece householders home energy consumption behaviors from primary energy to change secondary energy

Finally , I shall indicate Greece, this western which will influence this country's householders have desires to do household energy conservation patterns or conservation energy consumption behaviors or energy conservation activities at homes. I shall explain the social economic variable, such as consumers' income and family size variation factor which can influence the different Greece family household members differences towards energy conservation preferences. IN addition, the variable, such as environmental information feedback and consciousness of energy problems are characteristics of the energy saver consumer.

Why and how can environmental pollution , environmental protection, energy conservation information message can influence Greece householders to choose to do energy use consumption conservation or less energy useful behaviors at homes. It is one interesting energy efficient use behaviors , due to Greece householders are influenced by energy conservation or environmental protection message.

In fact, scientists agree overconsumption of natural resources is a major threat to oue lives in earth. Environmental problems like greenhouse effect, ozone layer depletion, and acid rain effect are not any more problems of a specific region or environmental problem. Also, economic theory is indicated that in order to gain comfort and time households are becoming excessive energy users, neglecting the environmental impact of their choices.

Environment scientists bring these environment pollution message to influence Greeks (Greece householders) to change their energy consumption behaviors at homes. The environment scientists' message indicate that we are facing global warmth and natural resource and energy shortage challenges. Due to our Earth have limited natural resource numbers to supply to us to manufacture energy, but global population has been increasing every year. Thus, it is possible that we have energy shortage crisis. Also, manufactures are spending too much energy to waste to manufacture any products, the energy will cause air or water pollution in manufacturing process or drivers are driving their vehicles to pollute air on the roads.

Hence, environment scientists' message influence Greece householders began to consider these questions concern to reduce fossil fuel energy. Why do we need to Safety in using fuel and handle gas leaks? Why do we feel town gas smell? How is electricity located at electric station far away from town area? How to solve problems caused by the use of fossil fuels? How to reduce the use of fossil fuels?

Greece householders consider to solve the problems, the best way is to reduce thir used of fossil fuel. This helps prevent fossil fuels form being used up too quickly. Also, it helps them to reduce environmental problems because fewer pollutants are given out when less fossil fuels are used. Can human help to reduce the use of fossil fuels? Fossil fuels are mainly in power station. Although they use some fossil fuels for our gas cooker and car, it won't make much difference if I use less. Fossil fuel is not used renew primary energy. Most of energy Greece householders use come from fossil fuels, for example, the electricity we use is generated in power stations by burning fossil fuels. The buses they ride use diesel oil. Therefore, they can help reduce the use of fossil fuels by saving energy in Greece daily lives.

The actions that Greece householders can take such as: setting the air-conditioner to a higher temperature, walking instead of using lift, taking a short shower instead of a bath. This reduces the use of the hot water and thus the energy needed to heat the water. Thus, many people can help a lot to reduce our use of fossil fuels to avoid fossil fuel shortage risk occurrence.

Greeks (Greece householders) had been beginning to conern that they will face energy shortage challenge if they can not adopt more energy conservation actions. Because the Greece government began to bring negative environmental pollution and energy shortage challenge message if they often waste to use any kinds of energy, e.g. electricity , gas excessive number efficiency at homes. Then, they will be possible to fac energy shortage and environmental pollution challenge to their country in future one day. So, this energy shortage and environment pollution message has bring predictive negative worries to influence many Greece householder energy home users choose to reduce to avoid the waste of any kinds of energy use at homes.

So, their reducing energy use actions that had encouraged them to cause habits to avoid to waste excess energy to do any non essential electric appliances useful or consumption activities at homes often. Moreover, the environment protection and energy conservation message has changed many Greece householder to make decision and activities to change their lifestyle to b low living quality from high living quality. So, the environment protection and energy conservation message factor has much influential to change Greece household energy users' daily energy conservation or less energy use consumption activities at homes.

Greeks feel greenhouse energy can be environmental protection enegy. A greenhouse can trap heat in the sunlight and keeps the air inside the greenhouse warm enough for plants to grow. The glass roof and walls of a greenhouse let in sunlight but prevent heat from escape, this makes the greenhouse warm inside. Similarly, some gases in the Earth's atmosphere can trap heat from the sun and keep the Earth warm. This is called the greenhouse effect. The gases energy that can trap heat from the sun are called greenhouse gases. It is future one kind of potential primary energy to reduce environmental pollution new energy products for human consuming. So, environmental protection message influence them to consume greenhouse enegy at homes.

So, environment scientists‘ environment pollution message had influence Greece householders concern to apply seconday energy (environment protection) to replace electricity energy to use at home. They will change energy to use at home. The scientists' messages have more influential Greece householders energy change consumption behaviors at homes. The messages are as below:

There are different forms of energy, e.g. light, heat, sound, wind, water, electrical kinetic, chemical and potential energy. Some form energy is primary energy and it can not renew to use, e.g. light, sound, wind, water, fossil fuel etc. Some form energy is secondary energy and it can renew to use in possible, e.g. nuclear, electric charge battery etc. Why does human need to concern how to manufacture secondary energy? Because it is possible that our natural resource will be consumed all, thus we will face primary energy shortage risk. If human can invent any new form of man-made secondary energy to renew to use in order to avoid primary energy shortage to supply to use to use, then human won't only depend on our Earth natural resource energy supply numbers. We can invent any new secondary energy to renew to use again either replaces primary energy or instead of primary energy limit number supply.

What is energy change? For television energy change power case. Firstly, electrical energy changes to television power to be used by television itself, then it changes to light power, next it changes to light power. How to choose fuel form to use? Due to energy can change to different form of powers to supply different form of power advantages to supply to human to use, so it is possible that we can also invent any secondary man made renew used energy to change different form powers to supply us to use, e.g. nuclear energy changes to light or sound or heat form of powers ; electrical charge batteries changes to light or sound or heat form powers to satisfy our daily life needs.

The environment scientists' energy consumption education influence Greece householders concern how to change to use secondary energy to replace primary energy at homes as below:

For primary natural resource fuel energy example, different fuel has different feature, e.g. easy to burn, safe to use, gives out a lot of energy, inexpensive, produces little air pollution, easy to transport and store. How can we use in different channels, such as heating food, hot pat, driving vehicles.

For example, although coal is not expensive to cause electricity energy for past transportation tool, e.g. traditional coal energy train or our daily home cooking, but it has negative influence to environment air pollution. Hence, we ought to follow the primary natural resource energy's feature to decide how to apply what aspects of our life needs.

For example, if the country's people hope to reduce pollution when who use any kind of energy, e.g. US , Europe energy markets. The energy entrepreneur ought concentrate on manufacturing the kind of energy which can reduce environment pollution to be the least level to supply the country people to use, e.g. electric charge battery supplies to these countries' drivers to drive their vehicles on the roads, wind energy or water energy to manufacture electricity power supply to reduce air or water pollution ; or if the country people hope to buy the inexpensive energy to use, even the energy's quality and performance is worse, e.g. China, India, Hong Kong markets. The energy entrepreneur ought concentrate on manufacturing the lowest cost and enough supply of natural resource to manufacture the kind of energy to sell cheap price to these countries to use, e.g. China, Africa can accept to use e.g. gas, coal, fuel energy to use to compare developed countries people, e.g. UK, US; or if the countries people who hope to use energy which can easy to transport and store, e.g. light coal. The energy entrepreneur can choose to concentrate on manufacturing much coal to supply to the countries people to use, e.g. China, Arica Thus, to choose to manufacture which kinds of energy supply to the countries market people to use, the energy entrepreneur how decides to manufacture which kind of energy, it depends on which kinds of fuel advantages of the countries people most concerning.

What is energy meaning? It is defined a dynamic quality, it is a fundamental entity of nature that is transferred between parts of a system in the production of physical change within the system, and it is usually regarded as the capacity for doing work, and it is usable power (such as heat or electricity) or the resources for producing such power.

Why does secondary energy own investment worth? Because the different forms of primary natural resource energy will have supply shortage crisis, such as natural resources coal, gas, solar, wind, water, geothermal, biomass(organic material) etc. However, human can attempt to explore any undiscovered Earth or Space resource to manufacture any kinds of secondary energies, e.g. nuclear energy, electric recharge battery energy to supply to electric vehicle or space robots transportation tools to use or satisfy our daily life needs in future one day. So any kind of undiscovered secondary man-made renewed used energy resources have potential commercial worth to any energy entrepreneurs, it is possible that they can replace traditional primary energy to supply to human to use for our different aspects of life needs. In the future, the secondary energy demand will increase, when primary energy supply number has decreased form natural exploration. So, it will cause the effect of any demand of secondary energy product to be raised and prices to be increased in possible. Due to global population has been growing up, considerably China and India both countries populations have been increasing rapidly. Scientists predict there are more than 1.2 billion people worldwide will lack access to electricity, and more than 2.5 billion still use wood, charcoal to cook and heat in the future when primary energy has no enough number to supply to us to use. Hence, the fact that demand is this much greater than supply to make energy a prime market for further growth.

Although, secondary energy will have much investment worth, but energy like all other investments will carry risks. The internal and external risk factors include such as: policy is always changing to prohibit which do energy trading more easily between the energy exporting and importing countries, the secondary energy manufacturer itself own abilities to invent and to manufacture any kinds of secondary energy, improved technology can quickly make an technology obsolete, geopolitical rifts can happen overnight, the country's energy consumer (user)'s preferable choice to use which either kinds of secondary energy or secondary energy. So, it seems that (man-made) renewed used secondary energy industry can provide above-average returns, but it can also bring high risk commercial investment.

Traditionally, energy supply companies will apply those methods to operate energy providing businesses. For Shell,. Exxon examples, which had own gas stations, explore and drill for gas on their own. Other companies specialize in a part of the energy market, e.g. leasing oil rigs for example, or operating a pipeline. Energy supplying companies can choose to manufacture any kinds of energy to supply, e.g. trade oil, gas, coal, uranium, electricity etc. Any energy price and supply is demanded on the countries energy users' which kinds of energy most choice need or certain energy commodities to be chose to use popularly. For example, if US most people prefer to use secondary man-made renew used energy more than primary energy. Then, US energy manufacturers ought concentrate on manufacturing much different kinds of secondary man-made renew used energy to prepare to supply to its domestic US market in order to raise secondary energy price to sell in its country. So, the energy manufacturer's energy manufacturing choice, it is depend on which the country's people prefer to use which kinds of energy for their daily life needs.

However, scientists predict secondary energy market will have large market share, due to primary energy will have shortage to explore to supply in our earth and future energy consumers(users) prefer to choose to use more efficiency, less energy consumption, none environment pollution cause, cost effectiveness, renew to use of any kinds of energy. For example, the electricity recharge battery secondary man-made renew used energy is one kind of reducing air pollution power to push any electric battery vehicles to be driven to compare gas energy during drivers are driving their cars on the roads. They can reduce noise and air pollution and drivers can drive safely, who only need to buy one electric recharge battery to recharge in any electric recharge battery stations on streets when the electric recharge battery has no enough power to push their cars and they need to recharge their electric recharge battery drive when they had driven between one to two days. Due to primary energy, e.g. fuel , gas, the kinds of primary energies will have shortage to supply to global drivers to drive their traditional cars. Thus, the electric recharge battery or any undiscovered secondary energy will be future driving market needs. So, man-made renew used secondary energy, e.g. biofuel, hydro-electric, nuclear, will be one kind of efficient, clean, less pollution cause, cost-effective of energy to supply to our global vehicle market, even any other undiscovered new markets. Supposing they are popular to be used for electric vehicle market globally in future one day, then their prices will be decreased and constructed to average car requires up to 1,700 gallons of oil. Also supposing that making average computer requires more than ten times or weight to fossil fuels, every calories of food eaten in the US requires roughly then calories of fossil fuels. Hence, cheap energy will be one successful factor to influence future potential energy consumer (user) individual choice needs. Conversely, ion good economic times, people are more willing to travel, to buy products, and all of which success demand and low process for energy.

In the future, secondary energy will be the best choice to food production market. The modern food production system is essentially a success of changing fossil fuels into food. So, raising energy prices are almost higher food costs and even shortage for fossil fuels energy. If one day, one kind of discovered secondary man-made renew used energy can supply to any restaurants or homes to be used to cook at the cheap price, then the profit is very high for this kind of food production energy. Thus, future food production secondary energy consumption market is large and because the primary energy inputs for agriculture are higher than the energy outputs of the food. However, future secondary man-made renew used energy for food production system is only one part of whole energy consumer in food industry. The food production is related to whole food consumption market which includes: household cooking energy market, agriculture or vegetable, rice, fruit etc. foods farming machines energy market, food manufacturing factories market, food machine package market, transportation food delivery market, supermarket or fruit/ food sale stores market. They must need any energy inputs to achieve the food production or food transportation or warehouse / stores electricity supply or cooking energy needs. Hence, these food suppliers relate to any whole food factory manufacturers, food retailers, food wholesalers, farmers and home/restaurant cookers, all of them must need to use energy to carry on their food producing or food cooking or food transportation activities every day in overall food industry. Thus, it seems that undiscovered any second energy demand will be increased, when the primary energy supply number is decreasing. Also, when people can accept to use secondary energy to replace primary energy to be used for any cooking, transporting food, manufacturing food, food retail stores or warehouse food delivery energy need activities. Then, the secondary energy price will be fall down to attract many food energy consumers.

Nowadays, the food industry energy may includes primary nature resource gas energy or electricity energy for house house families or restaurants cooking needs, food delivering lorry drivers driving needs usually. If future second man made renew used energy is invented successful popular to be used, e.g. hydrogen, electric recharged battery energy for electric vehicles or restaurant/home families cooking needs or food factories machine maufacturing energy needs. Then, the seconday energy will have possible to replace primary energy to be food industry energy market.

Wiley, composition services graphics indicated that global primary energy consumption had been increasing 30 billion tons from 1830 year to 510 billion tons in 2010 year as well as global population size had been increasing from 70 billion 1830 yeat to 510 billion in 2010 year. Thus, it seems that global primary energy consumption will be needed largely after 2010 year. If future global nature resource primary energy is explored full number and it had not enough energy number to supply global human to use. Then, it will being many people feel uncomfortable and inconvenient,e.g. Some countries won't have enough energy to supply transportion tools to be driven, some homes and restaurants won't have enough energy to supply to cook to eat or to provide restaurant clients to eat etc. daily activies, due to human's much activities which are needs energy supply. Thus, it seems that global primary energy comsumption will be needed largely after 2010 year.

Wiley, composition services graphics also explianed that why the primary energy consumption demand can be needed to achieve the same level to the global population size increasing in 2010 year. The graph showed these reasons why cause the same level of global population size and global primary energy consumpion demand which may include: The graph showed that after a nation is developed, its per-person energy use hegins to level off. In North Ameruca and Europe, where energy demand has remained flat, or fallen dightly, in each of the past few years. But the 1.3 billion people on those two continents are far outweighted by the 5 billion people in Asia and Africa, e.g. Chinese and Indian. who currently have more energy need to comapre average per man to North America and Europe per man, ensuring that overall energy demand will rise for years to come.

Wiley, composition services graphics also predicted that the growth in primary energy demand. China will have 4,500 million tons in 2035 year. India will have 3,000 million tons in 2035 year. Other developing Asia will have 2,000 million tons in 2035 year. Russia will have 1,500 million tons in 2035, Middle East will have 1,300 million tons in 2035, other rest of world will have 1,000 million tons in 2035. Hence, it implied that China will be the largest primary energy need country in the future.

China will be future the primary potential energy consumer market. The primary energy includes water, coal, wind, fossil oil, gas ,solar, geothermal energy, biomass (organiz material) etc. different natural resource primary energy. Otherwise, US, UK, Europe will be secondary energy potential need market. For example, electrical recharge battery energy will be raised demand to supply to any future new design electrical charge battery vehicles in US, Europe, UK markets.

Due to US, Europe, UK people concern environment protection, so they will invent many electric charge battery vehicles to consume electrical charge battery to replace polluted gas energy to avoid air pollution when the drivers are driving cars on themselve countries' roads. For example, second man-made renew used nuclear energy can be applied to rockets to pusch them to leave our earth to fly to other space far away and consuming nuclear energy will be cost efficient, and nuclear energy saving will be more when nuclear to spend long time to be used in any long time space journey. Hence, nuclear energy and electric charge battery secondary energy will be popular to be applied to vehicles and rockets energy needs in US, Europe, potential marketss, even our daily energy needs in global second energy market.

Who are your energy business's competitors (peers)? How do they compare? How have your energy business company performed cyclically? How to choose to manufacture to sell which kinds of primary or secondary energy product(s), either manufactures only primary energy product(s) or manufactures only secondary energy products or both? Which countries do you plan to sell your energy product?

Illustration by Wilsey, composition services graphiss showed that these natural resources to energy product the world's electricity percentage, such as below:

41% of coal, 5% of oil, 21% of gas, 13% of nuclear, 16% of Hydro, 3% other renewable secondary man-made energy.

Hence, coal will be future the major natural resource to produce electricity. The energy entrepreneur ought attempt to explore any coal resources, when who choose to supply electricity power to consumers for future energy consumption country markets.

Wiley, composition services also predicted that the expectation is that North America coal will supply the expectation is that North America coal will supply Asian demand, Us export terminals have a total capacity of 173 million tommes output. China will drive 16%

of the nations total output. China will drive the sea-born demand for coal over for the forcessable future. Chinese energy consumption will grow more than 12 % between 1980 and 2009 years. Though, China heads global demand, India is growing faster in terms of coal imports. Much of the global coal demand will be supplied by Indonesia and Australia. Colombia, Russia, South Africa and Mongolia are also players in global export coal energy resources.

Hence, environment scientists‘ education messages influence Greece householders believe that secondary energy will be one kind of new energy product to replace traditional primary energy product for human energy consumption market global needs. Hence, it is right time any energy entrepreneur needs to research how to explore any undiscovered man-made renew used secondary energy products to avoid primary energy shortage crisis occurrence. Greece householders will be the highest population number to choose secondary energy to replace primary energy to use at homes. it means that environment scientists had changed Greece householders' energy consumption behaviors at homes.

In conclusion, different countries will have different factors influence how the country's householders energy consumption behavioral changes. Hence, it seems that any country's householders‘ energy use of consumption behaviors will be possible influenced by extermal environment factors influence. Also, every country's energy providers can attempt to find whether the country has what kinds of unique factors to influence its householders' energy consumption efficiency to increase or decrease in order to find the methods to solve the energy efficiency demand reducing challenges successfully.

CHAPTER VII

Social factor influences household renting Behavioral choice

Can artificial intelligence find what social factor influences household renting behavior ? Can rent subsidies assistance social behavioral factor influence the country's householders' housing needs in society? Why and how will the impact of social information factor influence on willingness to householders to pay rent in the country? The housing rent decisions will be determined by objective factors as well as housing market renting decision will be depended by future housing consumption desire beneficial influence as well as it is relative to current housing investment and consumption. If the householder expected or predicted future housing choice to pay rent to live because he / she feels future housing price will fall down in possible.

Hence, if the country's government can provide rent subsidiaries assistance to its householders. Also is the country has many householders feel the housing price will be fall down within five years for example. Then, it will be possible encourage that many householders choose to pay rent to live within five years. So, they country government's tent subsidiaries assistance will encourage the country's renting house market to be grown up rapidly within five years. It means that the social expectancy factor will have indirect influence to impact household housing buyers or renters' housing consumption behaviors.

However, in addition, the above householder expected or predicted future housing choice social information factor influence , other social factor influences can also influence housing activity, they include such as : When conditions are favorable in terms of house price, property taxes, fiscal incentives etc. factors. These social factors will impact how many household property consumers how to make house renting or buying decisions. SO, property buyers and property sellers both will have incentives to wait for more information about the state of the housing market before deciding to buy or rent house to live. However, the property buyers and sellers have limited information about the real intentions of transacting parties, the probabilities of renting or buying property decision will have possible increase the riskiness of housing decision.

A behavioral housing model is constructed which allows that the country householders' housing decisions of owner occupies are the outcome of interactions between objective analysis and subjective behavioral factors (social factors) of the householder himself / herself decision factor.

The social factors, such as objective process of social learning or / and the more subjective influence of social pressure, which will influence the householder's renting or buying house decision when he / she feels have living need in society. For social learning expectations, the impact of uncertainty and judgements about future benefits and costs of housing. So, every householder will usually gather information from social medias to attempt to predict when the country's houses prices will be fallen down or risen up. SO, it explains why some householders who have enough money to buy houses to live, but they choose to rent houses to live in themselves countries. Because their judgements let them to feel that there is possible to reduce housing price in society, e.g. after one year. Hence, this " after one year, the houses prices reducing information or message in society will influence the country's many householders choose to rent houses in the year. Because they feel that it is possible the society's houses prices will be decreased after this year. This " after one year housing prices reducing social information or message factor" will influence the country's many householders choose to rent houses to live in this year. They expect the social houses prices to be fallen down after one year, then they will choose to buy the falling down prices of houses to live.

After aspect of social influence to the country's householders to choose either house renting or buying behaviors it normative influence , such as housing renting or buying case, when an householder's renting or buying one house decision is affected by social media perception of information as well as the householder individual's attitude and response of others. The householder individual's renting or buying one house's decision which will be influenced by the social media information influence. SO, it makes sense to judge that the crowd is thinking in the very short-term and moving housing renting or buying markets in the country.

The information that is important that other many people are prepared to pay rent to rent the houses in the country, when the householder (either renting or buying house) consumer thinks that housing market valuations of house assets are going to increase in value, even though the householder may privately think the future house sale prices are over-priced.

These external housing market valuations information may influence the householder (either renting or buying house) consumer to make decision when he/she feels that it is the right time , he/she ought choose to buy one house or rent one house to live in the country. So, at this moment, he /she will prefer to pay long-term rent expenditure to rent one house to live, due to the housing market information indicates the future housing market valuation will decrease in order to influence he/she can pay lower housing price to compare to buy one house today. So, at this moment, it is the right time that the country can implement rent subsidiaries assistance to support the low income working age group to have effort to rent low quality of houses in society.

Consequently, it explains why social housing media factor and the country's government 's rent subsidiaries assistance implement will influence when the country's householder planners who choose to buy or rent houses to live in the country. For example, if the country's government encouraged people to rent houses to live , when the country's government predicts that the country's any houses prices are raising to above the society's houses purchase burden effort in society. Then, the country's government can provide rent subsidiaries assistance to excite or encourage many low income working age group people to choose to rent houses to live. Otherwise, when the country's government predicts that the country's houses prices will decrease in future day. The country government can choose not provide rent subsidiaries assistance to attract or encourage them to rent houses in society. Then, it will encourage many people to choose to buy low price houses to live.

In conclusion, this rent subsidiaries assistance strategy can help the country's housing market to achieve the more housing supply and demand balance between house renters and house buyers both. It is beneficial to develop the property renting and property purchase market development in the country.

Can the government rent subsidiaries
assistance bring housing benefit
for landlords in society

Can artificial intelligence estimate how much rent subsidiaries is the most right level to attract householders to choose to rent houses in preference ? When one country provide rent subsidiaries assistance to support people to pay lesser rents in the country. Can this country housing benefit bring advantages for landlords in society? Although, in the country's society, it is possible to encourage many people to choose to rent houses in the country. It seems that the country's landlords will increase tenants number and they can earn more renting income in short term benefit. But, in long term , it will bring negative influences to landlords. I shall explain the reasons as below:

When, the country provides long term rent subsidiaries assistance to its people, e.g. five years rent subsidiaries assistance. Although, it can encourage many people (tenants) choose to pay lesser rent expenditure into accommodation in the social rented sector. However, in this five years, it means that the properties buyers number will also decrease. Even, their properties prices will be fallen down to attract new tenants to rent the property developers' houses to live.

I believe the property purchase demand won't be raised, due to the rent subsidiaries assistance benefit to this country' people in this five years period. Hence, many people will choose to rent houses to live in this country. Even, their salaries are increased. It is not easy to influence their rent choices. Hence, the properties sold number must be decreased.

In fact, this country's properties or providers must not earn more profit from properties selling in this five years. Hence, long term rent subsidiaries assistance housing benefit to the country's people, it can help the low income working age group people who can have enough money to rant the better quality houses to live to improve their housing and living qualities. But, it also influence the middle or high income working age group people . When they have effort to buy houses, the rent subsidiaries assistance implementation will influence their mind to choose to rent houses to live in this five years, because they can pay lesser rent amount form government's rent subsidiaries assistance. It will reduce the middle or high income working age group property buyers number to the landlords in society. Hence, rent subsidiaries assistance will decrease the society's house buyers number, but , it also increases the tenants number in the rent subsidiaries assistance period. It will bring negative impact to reduce the house buyers number and the property developers will reduce houses selling profit, due to the house tenants number rises to influence the choice or house buyers number decreases in the country's house renting or buying markets.

However, rent subsidiaries assistance can also bring these benefits to the country's society, such as it encourages greater mobility within the social rented sector, because the properties developers will increase the small, medium, large different sizes space apartment number to let them to choose to rent, e.g. one small or large bedroom, or two small or large bedrooms, or more than two small or large bedrooms of apartment to let the tenants to choose to occupy. So, the property market will increase many different occupying space size of bedrooms number to let the country's tenants to choose to rent to satisfy their living needs. Moreover, it can make better use of available social housing stock, when there are many houses to used to be rented intention only. It can improve work-incentives for working age group tenants in the society, due to many people choose to rent houses to live in the country, they won't need to pay long term installment payment to buy the house in long term installment period, e.g. they won't need to pay twenty to forty years , even more installment housing payment to the housing developers. Hence, the tenants will reduce finance burden when they choose to pay cheaper rents from their government's rent subsidiaries assistance long-term. It will influence the working age tenant group 's saving habit to be better any more, due to they will have more extra money to save to banks when they pay lesser rent from government's long term rent subsidiaries assistance per month. Because of the high proportion of tenants in respect of rent subsidiaries assistance housing benefit may have a sizable positive influence to encourage their saving habits on the saving behaviors or work-incentive behaviors both.

So, the rent subsidiaries assistance housing long-term fixed amount paid benefit will continue to provide support where apartment is suitable for the needs of the tenants, and it will provide an economic incentive for working age tenants to move out from smaller space size properties to their apartment is consider larger space size apartment than necessary. When rent subsidiaries assistance can support the working age tenants to rent larger space size apartment to live to bring both working and economic incentive to improve their living of quality needs.

As a result, working age rent subsidiaries assistance housing benefit in the social rented sector will face similar choices in the private houses rented sector, instead of public houses rented sector. Rent subsidiaries assistance can also encourage the working age tenants either to occupy appropriately sized accommodation , when they had paid cheaper rent in a period, then they expect to buy the accommodation to live or they pay towards another accommodation which is larger than the needs of their long-term rent accommodation choice.

Hence, if the working age tenant still chooses to live cheaper rent accommodation , the choice is to move and a lower rent is payable. This will help to provide an additional work incentive. Because the working age tenant does not choose to pay higher rent to rent large space size or more bedrooms or better quality of apartment to live, then he / she will have more extra money to save to bank, even, the working age tenant can earn rent subsidiaries assistance housing benefit at lower income level when he / she still chooses to pay less rent amount to live poor quality and / or small space size of lesser bedrooms number houses to live.

Hence, rent subsidiaries assistance seems that it can bring work and economic incentive both benefits to the low income level of working age tenants when they still choose to pay lesser rents to live small space size or lesser bedrooms number or poor quality of houses to live in their countries. It can encourage them to hard to work to save more money at bank to prepare to have enough money to buy another new or second house to live. Moreover, rent subsidiaries assistance will bring social attribution benefit from these young working age workers (tenants) in any countries' societies.

In conclusion, rent subsidiaries assistance implement can bring benefits to the low income working age tenants, but it can also bring low housing selling profit to the country's property developers. Hence, it depends on the country's policy implement whether it is beneficial to economic growth or improving low income working age living beneficial aims. If it felt that economic growth is more important to compare low income young working age living improving benefit in the year. The, rent subsidiaries assistance implementation is not right time to implement in this year. Otherwise, if it felt that low income young working age living improving benefit is more important, then rent subsidiaries assistance policy is right time to implement in this year. Hence, every country's government need to consider when is the right time to implement rent subsidiaries assistance policy in order to keep it's country house market's renting and house buying supply and demand number more balance between the house buyers or tenants and the house developers. It is beneficial to the country's long term economic and improving of living quality development.

How to attract young age homeowners
to choose to rent appartments by rent subsidiary assistance

Can artificial intelligence estimate how much rent is the most attractive level to influence you age house renters to choose rent in preferable? Can rent subdisiary assistanc attract householders to choose to rent appartments to live easily? Some country governments indicate that rates of residentil mobility tend to be lower among homeowners than renters. It is possibly reflecting the higher moving costs to owner, occupied housing, which my cause the the old house owners won't change their old houses to move to new houses to live easily, if the higher moving costs are charged to them higher costs . So, it seems that it is not easy to attract the homeowners to choose to pay rent to live when they are borrowing mortage loan to pay installment to live the houses, even the country government has rent subsidiary assistance to persuade or attract them to sell their houses to choose to py cheaper rent expenditure from rent subsidiary assistance support. When, the country has many homeowners who are not easily to move to another new appartment to choose rent payment, even the country government can provide rent subsidiary assistance to them.

So, it can explain that the country has the increase in homeownership rates, it mens the tendency for homeownership rates rise with young age, it implies that th country's unemployment rate is reducing, due to there has young population ageing group who is working in society. So, it can also explain that why the homeowners who borrowing house mortage loans (debts) to pay installment to live the houses, they won't easy to choose to change to pay rent to live. Although, they have government rent subsidiary assistance to support them to pay the lower housing market rent for long term.

It brings this question: How to attract the young working age population homeowners to choose to pay rent to live from their countries' government rent subsidiary assistance, when they are borrowing housing mortgage loan to pay installment to live their houses?

A significant proportion of the changes in aggregate homeownership rates is. However, not explained by changes in the characteristic of the population , a possible chnge in the relative attractiveness of owner-occupied housing has possible influenced to attract the young working age homeworkers to choose to borrow housing mortage loans to pay installment to buy the houses to live for long times, e.g. ten to twenty years installment time, even more than twenty years installment time. It is possible that the appartment location has many transportation tools to provide them to choose any kinds of transportation tools to go to work conveniently, or the appartment location has many shopping centers or entertainment facilities, e.g. public hospitals , public swimming pools, public libraries, cinemas, public gardens, restaurants etc. facilities to attract them to choose to live the location. So, even the country government can provide rent subsidiary assistance to support them to rent high quality of provide houses to live. This rent subsidiary assistance policy can not influence the young working age population homeowners to change their mortgage loan installment houses to move to another better quality of houses to pay lower market rent to live, even their government has rent subsidiary assistance to persuade them to live another housing location. So, the attractive old housing location and natural environment factor and low young age unemployment factor both will influence the young age homeowners (borrowing mortgage loan installment homeowners) still choose to live their old house locations. Even, their government implement rent subsidiary assistance to attract them to pay low rent market valuation to rent another higher quality of houses to live.

Hence, if the country government can provide the rent subsidiary assistance house locations which can be close to the shopping centers, transportation tools, public facilities, restaurants etc. service facilities to satisfy the working young age population homeowners (borrowing mortage loan installment homeowners). Then, it is possible to attract them to choose these renting subsidiary assistance houses to live as well as the rent subsidiary assistance houses locations can be close to the locations (places) which have more offices, factories etc. working buildings to let them to walk to work conveniently. Then, the unemploymwnt young age homeowners can also be influenced to change their present borrowing mortage loan appartments to move out to rent these houses which are close to these working places more easily. The reason is due to they need to spend less time to go to work every time for the unemployment young age homeowners, if the country government can provide the rent subsidiary assistance houses which are built to close to th working places. Then, these renting house locations are close to the working places, it can influence them to choose to rent these houses to live more easily if their present borrowing mortage loan installment of house locations are far away from any working places.

The final factor to attract working young age homeowners to move out to rent another rent subsidiary assistance appartments to live more easily. It is the rental income maximisation strategy. What is the income maximisation strategy benefits to working young age homeowners (borrowing mortage loan installment payment homeowners)? Why does this strategy can attract them to choose to rent?

This strategy benefits include as below:

The working young age homeowner is intended to be revenue self financing, when he / she is chosen to rent another new appartment by government's rent subsidiary assistance. Consequently, combination of significant additional rental income and borrowing will be required for stock investment and to finance other activity. The rental income to various sources and it can be adversely impacted by non-payment of charges. So, low market rent payments or rent subsidiary assistances are supplemented by recovered from current tenants (the working young age population), and subsidiary assistance planning can let the working young age population to pay lower market rent payment to the country's government for either (public houses) or lanlords (private houses) in arrears rent payment later. Hence, they do not need to pay the lower market rent of this rent subsidiary assistance support immediately.

They can pay lower market rent in arrear to maximize longer arrear rent payment due to the maximisation three years period. So, the working young age tenants can save income, when they pay lower market rent (rent subsidiary assistance) in whole lating arrears whole amout is up to three years rent payment strategy. When they choose to leave their borrowing mortage lown installment payment present houses and move out to choose pay cheaper rent to rent another new renting appartment to live from their country' government rent subsidiary assistance support.

Hence, this three year arrear lower rent market subsidiary assistance strategy can reduce the working young age tenants significant financial pressures, due to the impact of welfare reform measures (allowing them to pay lower market rent maximisation in arrear up to three years period later) by this rent subidiary assistance strategy. Consequently, I believe that this rent subsidiary assistance maximisation three year rent in arrear payment strategy can attract them to choose to move out to choose to rent another new appartments to live more easily.

Can rent subsidiary assistance influence renters behave like homeowners

Can artificial intelligence analyze rent subsidiary method can increase renters number ? If the country government implemented rent subsidiary assistance to attract its resident to pay lower rent market valuation to attract them to live. For long time, when they will live the renting appartment for one year, even more time, whether the renters will change their behaviours to feel the renting appartmentd are similar to homeowning apprtment to live in order to decide to live th renting houses long time.

In fact, rent subsidiary assistance implementation has benefits to solve the housing raising prices challenge, such as Hong Kong has many people re living in this small city. But, the housing prices are continue rising. Hong Kong property developers aim to earn more profits when they can sell many houses. Although, these property developers feel Hong Kong has many people who will need to buy houses to live. When Hong Kong has many people demand houses to live. But, the private houses are limited to build to supply to satisfy their living needs.

So, the Hong Kong property developers will raise housing sale prices or housing rent prices in order to sell or rent to them to earn more profits. As this Hong Kong housing case, if Hong Kong government can implement rent subsidiary assistance policy to let many Hong Kong resident to pay lower market rent valuation to rent any private houses or public houses to live. Then, it can possible encourage many Hong Kong people to choos to rent appartments to live in Hong Kong. The housing welfare to Hong Kong people which will cause many Hong Kong resident do not choose to buy houses to live in Hong Kong. They will be possible to choose to pay lower rent subsidiary expenditure to rent to rent either low quality of public houses (HK government owning) or high quality of private houses (private property developers owning) to live in Hong Kong in possible.

If rent subsidiary assistance can change Hong Kong resident to choose to rent houses to live, it can also bring renting housing shortage challenge in Hong Kong. Because Hong Kong resident only hope to pay long term rent to rent any appartment to live in Hong Kong. When the renter feels the appartment is old or another reasons cause the renter expects to find another new appartment to rent to live. Due to Hong Kong government can provide rent subsidiay assistance, then it is possible to encourage the Hong Kong renters only choose to rent any appartment to live in Hong Kong long time. Hence, many Hong Kong resident won't need to borrow mortage loan to pay installment to buy any houses to live, if they choose to pay long term low market rent valuation to the landlords (private house owners) or the Hong Kong government (public house owner) to live in Hong Kong.

It brings this question: Can rent subsidiary assistance change renters behave like homeowners?

I shall give evidences to explain as below:
Many countries, e.g. UK, US developed countries have restrictions expanded to majority, center central cities, where high house prices threatn the well being of not only most residents, but the nation's economy as a whole. So, all US, UK have restrictions housing sale prices limited to manage th property sellers‘ house sale prices to avoid householders feel burden when they choose to buy any houses or mortgage loans to pay installments to any houses in US or UK both property markets.

Why do the US, UK housing become to hard to build in these traditionally development, friendly cities, Such as New York, Washington, London big cities? The reason is because that despite supporting houses supply citywide in UK, US residents individually have an incentive to defect and block new housing proposed for their own neighborhood. So, it implies many UK, US residents do not hope to live their houses which are close or near to neighborhood.

As this reason, it explains that why many Uk, US residents do not expect to live in big cities, because big cities have built many tall appartment and every appartment is built to close or near to another or other appartment. Otherwise, US, UK country side, there are many one to three floors independent self built wood houses and private car parks at homes which are built on every independent private land as well as the distance between every independent seld build wood house which is so far awary from each others on the countryside roads. So, UK, US city side houses are very attractive to UK, US residents to choose to live. Such as this reason, it explains why it can encourage UK, US residents choose to pay long term low rent market valuation to rent these kind self built or send hand wood made houses to live in UK, US countryside if UK, UK can provide rent subsidiary assistance to support them to live long time.

When, these both US, UK countryside residents who decide to pay long term low rent market valuation to live these countriesside wood made houses. Also , when they are living one year at least in here. They will possible feel that they are UK, US the country side independent wood made houses homeowners more than renter role. So, these UK, US countryside independent renting house lands and renting private car parks and renting private wood houses which all will let them to feel that they are these renting wood houses; homeowners. So, they will not feel that they are renters in these both countries' countryside independent housesholders. Moreover, when these UK, US countryside wood house renters choose to pay rent more than ten years or twenty years low rent subsidiary assistance market valuation to rent these countryside independent wood houses to live. It is possible to influence them living behaviors are like to homeowners, and are not like to renters.

Hence it also explain why HongKong residents can pay low rent subsidiary assistance to rent low rent market valuation of either high quality of private houses or low quality of public houses to live long time. Then, their living behaviors will be influenced to do any similir homeowners' behaviors at homes, because Hong Kong long time housing renters won't feel that they are renters role to their houses, they will feel that they are homeowners to their houses in Hong Kong city.

Hence, rent subsidiary assistance policy can help any countries residents to feel that they are like homeowners more than renters when they are renting the houses to live long time. It also explains why they do not need to move out to another new house to rent or buy to live, due to the renters feel that they are the houseowners actually. So, rent subsidiary assistance policy can lead ot influence householders' minds to choose to pay long term rents to rent high of low quality of houses to live in the country. Then, it will influence the country's houses prices can not be increased more easily , because the property buyer number will be influenced to reduce in the country. Due to the country has many residents choose to rent long term houses to live in the country.

When do renters behave like homeowners? I believe that renters will feel their behaviors like homeowners when themselves country can provide rent subsidiary assistance to support them to pay lower rent market valuation to choose to rent public houses or private houses to live in long term period. For US housing prices case example, its houses prices are experienced to change dramatically. In New York and Los Angeles cities when nearly tripling in San Francisco. Driving this appreciation is an inability of new housing supply to keep up with housing rent or purchase demand, causing the price of existing units to increase. So, if US government can provide rent subsidiary assistance to let residents to pay lower rent market valuation to rent any US public housing (poor quality) or private housing (better quality) houses to live in US these cities for long term. Then, the low wage of US workers are no longer migrating to high wage cities, due to they have afford to pay lower rent market valuation rent to rent any public houses (poor quality) or private houses (high quality) houses to live in low wage cities long tim from US goverment rent subsidiary assistance support.

Consequently, US government will reduce many societal and housing problem, when many low wage workers have afford to pay rent to live either high quality of houses (private houses) or low quality of houses (public houses) in any low wage cities in US for long time. So, they do not need to forgive their jobs to migrate to high wage cities to work in order to raise their wage effort to pay high rent to rent houses in low wage cities in US more long, because they won't need to rent any houses to migrate to high wage cities to live in US. Otherwise, if US government can implement rent subsidiary assistance to share these low wage workers' rent burden to help them to rise effort to rent any public houses or private houses to live long time in low wage cities. Then , these low wage workers won't need to migrate to high wage cities to find new jobs to work. They can have enough effort to pay long time rent, even these low wage cities ' employers can only provide lower wage jobs to them to work.

Hence, rent subsidiary assistance can solve low wage workers' social competition challenge in US low wage and high wage cities' both job markets in US, because they do not need to migrate to high wage cities to find jobs to work and they need to pay higher rent to rent houses to live in high wage cities in US. Moreover, they will encounter difficulties to seek jobs in high wage cities because there are many high wage similiar skillful workers who will also need to find any kinds of similiar skillful jobs to compete to the low wage migrating workers from low wage cities. So, it will raise the competition to high wage cities workers when the low wage cities workers choose to migrate to the high wage cities to find jobs to work as well as they also need to live in high wage cities to pay higher rent when they need to live here in US.

Hence, US government can help the low wage workers to avoid to migrate to high wage cities to find jobs and live, if it can provide long term rent subsidiary assistance to support them to pay lower rent market valuation to rent either public or private houses to live in lower wage cities in US. Hence, it is one good housing welfare to US low wage residents or workers if US government can implement rent subsidiary assistance to help the lo wag workers do not ned to migrate to higher wage cities to find any jobs to work and live in US. Then, they can feel living security to live in low wage cities in US long time, when they are assisted to pay the rent subsidiary expenditure to let them to pay lower market rent valuation to live in these low wage cities in US long time. So , although, these low wage cities employers pay lower wage to compare the other higher wage cities in US. It won't influence them have no enough income to pay rent to live in these low wage cities in US. Due to US government can provide rent subsidiary assistance to reduce their rent burden to live in these low wage cities . So, the rent subsidiary assistance policy can encourage the US low wage workers to choose to pay long term rent to live any public or private houses in any one of US low wage cities long time. They will be influenced to feel that their behaviors like homeowners when they are living in any one of low wage cities long time. Although , in fact, they are payin rents to live these any one of low wage cities in US long time.

Finally, regional scientists, land economists and transportation planners have confirmed that a householder's location decision depends to a large degree , on access to opportunities sities. Subject to budget, time and otehr constraints, it is a common assumption that householders maximize their utility by locating in a desirable a home or long term renting appartments as need to necessary and desired activities. Such as work, shopping, and recreation as possible. Also, they indicate that the utility maximization is profoundly complex, dependent on far more environmental attributes than those that can be observed and quantified, for example, people often care about neighborhood qualities, public services, proximity to relatives and natural environment offer factor.

Hence, when the country government expected to implement its rent subsidary assistance policy to attract residents to choose to pay low rent market valuation to rent public houses long time successfully. They need to consider whether the location can have above any one of these services provision in order to satisfy the future public housing renters‘ living needs daily. The country government's rent subsidiary assistance policy whether which can attract many residents to rent houses or not. It depends on whether the location is chosen to build public or private houses where it can provide above services to satisfy future renters' living needs , if it expected many residents can choose to pay low market rent valuation to live the location long time and let these renters to feel that they are like homeowners more than renters when they are paying low market rent valuation to rent public or private houses at the location long time in order to threaten the property developers can not raise their houses prices to sell easily. So, location factor is an important factor to influence the country residents choose to pay lower market rent valuation from rent subsidiary assistance.

Consequently, rent subsidiary assistance policy can influence some countries or cities ,such as Hong Kong, US, UK, etc. their residents feel their behaviors are like to homeowners more than renters, although, in fact, they are paying rents to live. However, rent subsidiary assistance can attempt to explain that why this housing welfare policy can threaten the property developers' houses prices can have effort to be raised easily, due to this housing welfare policy will influence the housing renter number to be increased.

CHAPTER VIII

Why environmental factor can influence food shortage

Can artifical intelligence measure which the lowest environment pollution level influences food consumers' good wastage behavior rises ? What are objective indicators of standard of living and quality of life? Objective circumstances refer to the economic and material conditions which are important aspects of the standard of living and quality of life. In the assessment, eight different indicators were used: CPI, GDP per capita, shopping basket, household's expenditures, GFIC basket, poverty rate, income inequality and HDI. However, these indicators is one number measure. It can't measure anyone's psychological feeling, such as health, safe emotion. The challenge concerns whether environmental pollution factor, such as air pollution, water pollution can cause human's health to be poor, even goes down human's quality of life and economy loss. I shall indicate some evidences to give reasons to support my conclusion why I believe that environment pollution is a factor to cause human quality of life to be poor , even it can also cause economy will encounter loss too.

In general, measure of quality of life need include human's psychological feeling indicator. I shall indicate, Hong Kong, China countries air and water environmental pollution challenges how to influence these two countries' people quality of life to be poor, even, it will cause their economy loss. Nowadays, China and Hong Kong and India and Afria are encountering health problems arising from damage to lungs, heart and blood vessels. Hong Kong and India and Afria and China e.g. Shanghai city pollution is a significant cause of premature death from cardiopulmonary disorders. Present level of pollution cause injury to the immature developing lings of children and adolescents. This damage will lead to life-long health problems in many and a reduction in life-expectancy. Although, there is no evidence from analyses of trends in pollutants that pollution measures in recent years have reduced pollutant concentrations in a way which will benefits public health.

There are clear indicators that for some pollutants. The problem is worsening. In fact, air and water pollution is Hong Kong and China and Afria etc. developing countries' the biggest cause of social and environmental injustice. It harms not only citizens today, but because its transquenerational effects on the urborn and youngest members of the society, it will cause its will health effects well into the later years of this century, even environmental pollution challenge will cause these countries will encounter economy loss.

Human activities have created forms of air and water pollution, such as gases from fuels, uncontrolled emissons from fossil fuels and other chemical sources have long been recognized as a cause of ill health and premature death. For example, in December, 1930 year, a dense fog affected the Meuse Valley in Belgium. Beginning on December, 3 date, the fog intensified over three days and was associated with laryngeal symptoms, chest pain, coughing, and breathlessness. Some patients showed signs of pulmonary oedema. Overall 60 deaths were attributed to the episode. After a long investigation, the cause was considered to be emissions from high sulphur fuels, including suplhur dioxide and sulphuric acid.

What is the current threat to health? the migigration of air polluton following the introduction of clear air has been followed by a period of unprecedented economic development creating new forms of pollution from the combustion of fossil fuels. For example, in constrast to the relatively large tar laden particulates from burning dirty coal which caused episodes like the London city, UK. Smog , traffic pollution now genertes fine with a different size and composition and gases,such as which may cause injury to the respiratory system and the effects of other pollutants. Such as particulates and drive the formation of the secondary pollutant ozone. The effects of pollution will therefore to some extent reflect genetic, environmental lifestyle and behavioral factors to develop these distance in a population together with the existing prevalence of diseases which may be polluted.

Hence, living in polluted urban environments is associated with increased levels of biological markers of inflammation compared with residence in a clean air environment. The damage is caused by air pollution manifests itself through a variety of common and recognized health problems, such as upper complaints heart and lung disease. Because of this, we can use statistical methods as well as clinical studies to detect the signal of changes in health problems and increased health care demands in the population. However, doctors had proved air or water pollution can cause these both curdiovscular or respiratory disease indirectly. Curdiovscular disease includes formation of arterial plaques, coronary artery, heart attacks, irregular heart rhythm, loss of heart rate variability, high blood pressure, stroke etc. disease. Respiratory disease includes inflammation of nasal, throat and tracheal airways with acute, lower respiratory tract inflammation and infection causing bronchitis, reduction long growth and function in young people. So, it seems environmental pollution can influence quality of life to human as well as environmental pollution and illness and poor health problem has close relationship.

On the other side, envionmental pollution can bring health risk, over it will influence social inequalities. Some researchers had found that the evidence has been compiled for six envionmental health challenges, such as air quality, housing and residential location, unintentional injuries in children, work related health risks, waste management and climate change. It seems human need to concern air and drinking water quality, waste management and climate change how to influence our environmental pollution challenge. Although, the evidence base on social inequalities and environmental risk is fragmented and data are often available for few countries only, it indicates that inequalities are a major challenge for environmental health policies. Irrespective of development status, environmental inequalities can be found in any country for which data are available. The valid for the exposure to environmental risk factor is also unequally distributed, and this unequal distribution is often related to social characteristics, such as income, social status, employment and education, even environment risk factor can influence human's quality of life.

(i) How environmental risk factor can influence different groups
However, human need to concern how environmental risk factor can influence inequally health outcomes to different groups. Such as, the first group is social determinants affect the environmental conditions of an individual and may contribute to the fact that specific individuals or population groups more often experience loss adequate or potentially harmful environmental conditions. The second group is the affected population groups could still be more exposed through e.g. the mechanism of education and health behavior. The third group is given socially disadvantaged groups could show more severe health effects of the social disadvantage is associated. The final group is social determinants affect health (what remains unclear is the relative importance of socially determined exposure to environmental risk factors). Thus, human need to concern our behavior can lead environmental pollution to influence poor health to alive. Even, we can not neglect how to protect our natural environment to be clean issue. Due to environmental unhealth poor issue can lead our bodies to be unhealth and to be ill and we have no health to work to influence our job inefficiency and low productivity if we often need to see doctor to raise workload to my staffs often. Then, our employers will be probable to dismiss and many unhealth employee will lose jobs and unemployment ratio will raise and DP will reduce, it will influence our economic growth . Hence, we can not neglect environmental justice and environmental inequity issue, e.g. indoor air pollution and occupational or exposure to environmental tobacco smoke pollution exposure to high traffic roads or to industrial plants pollution in our society.

(ii) How Afria country environmental pollution influences Surprisingly, most of above countries , among of them, although Africa is a green and natural environmental country, but Africa has encounted poor natural environmental quality to influence it has poor quality of life to its citizen and poor economy growth to its society both. Why does Africa encounter this natural environmental pollution challenge? Afican have now two potential sources of pollution: consumption and production . This looks reasonable to Africa, since maintenance is completely dedicated to improving the environment, when production generates pollution only as a " by product". Capital implies the possibility of a country being trappical in an economent poverty trap by both a bad environment and low longevity. Some countries (or regions) may even experience other time, both environmental degradation and decay in expectancy. The fact that, in some cases, environmental degradation doesn't imply lower longevity may be due to the fact that economic growth might , at the same time, worsen environmental quality, but generate additional resources that can help increasing (or preserving) longevity. However, these is also evidence of countries where environmental degradation is associated with a reduction in life expectancy. It seems worsen environmental quality will influence any country's economic growth and poor quality of life both. For example, McMichael et al. (2004) identify 40 countries that experienced a loss in longevity between 1990 year and 2001 year (26 between 1980 year and 2001), they also support that the resulting world divergence in terms of life expectancy might be explained by ".... (the growing) health risks consequent on large-scale environmental changes is caused by human pressur, by both bad environment and low longevity, biodiversity and sustainable energy".

(iii) How human adult consumption and environmental quality influences future environment for human survival probability of life expectancy.

I shall assure human adult consumption and environmental quality has relationship to influence the future environment (green preferences) to provide human survival probability, it depends on inherited environmental quality. Thus, human will increase or decrease in the survival probability when we need a higher or lower life expectancy. In general, we depend on these environmental conditions to live, which include quality of water, air and soils etc. and resource availability, biodiversity, forestry, fisheries etc.

It is interesting to analyze different possible strategies to escape from the environmental poverty trap as well as factors that could push some economies back to a low equilibrium characterized. To research whether environment factor has relationship to influence human quality of life. We need to give idea of explaining whether environmental care has relationship to an uncertain lifetime. However, I suppose that an environmental kind of factor can be instead of being defined in terms of GDP per capita, capital accumulation etc. economic factors. Poverty is now related to environmental quality. It should be clear, however, I focus only on one specific mechanism lying behind environmental traps. Just as under development traps may be related to a wide variety of factors, ranging from financial to technological ones, including human capital accumulation and life expectancy. So, I should use this assumption to explain why it has relatively between environmental quality and life expectancy.

This " synthetic" indicator (YCELP, 2006) indicated environmental health is defined by child morality, indoor air polluton, drinking water, adequate sanitation and urban particulates and ecosystem vitality that includes factors like air quality, water and productive natural resources, A key ingredient of our setting is that survival until the last period is probabilistic and depends on the inherited quality of the environments. This survival probability affects the weight of the future environmental quality in human's utility function to achieve interest aim. Final stage, human will have optimal choices depend on life expectancy: in particular, a higher probability to be alive in the third period boosts investment in the environment and reduces consumption. In this case, a given country may be caught in a high morality/poo environment if low income is associated with a deteriorated environment.

John and Pecchenino (1994) were the first to introduce the possibility of multiple identifying, case for a poverty cause characteristic by poor economic performance and environmental degradation, however, life expectancy is assumed to be exogenous and plays no role in their model. Such as soils deterioration are the like, are all susceptible of increasing human morality (thus reducing longevity). So, the existence of both environmental performance and longevity, with countries being concentrated around two levels of environmental quality and life expectancy respectively. The two-way causes are between the environment and longevity. If the causal relationship between environmental quality and life expectancy involves the existence of an environmental poverty, characterized by both bad environmental conditions and short life expectancy.

Human life stage will encounter generations of three periods to get utility from consumption and environmental quality. During adulthood, when all relevant decisions are taken, adult can work and allocate their income between consumption and investment in environmental maintenance: consumption involves deterioration of the future quality of the environment (through pollution and/ or resource depletion) when maintenance helps to improve it. The dynamics of environmental quality may also be affected by external factors on more resourced communities. The most importance, unhealthy physical environments across the region adversely affect everyone, ever though who are likely to be most concentrated in more burdened community which also have less social power to change those environments.

Why life expectancy and the environment has close relationship to influence quality of life? Life expectancy and environmental quality dynamics are jointly determined. Human may invest in environmental quality, depending on how much , we expect to live. However, environmental conditions affects life expectancy. In particular, some countries may encounter in a low life expectancy / low environmental quality. This outcome is consistent with stylized facts relating life expectancy and environmental performance measures. Some expects to live longer, who would be willing to invest more in environmental quality, because who feel which have causal link between life expectancy and environmental quality. However, environmental quality is a very important factor affecting health and morbidity: air and water pollution, depletion of natural resources and quality of life.

(iv) Why social and physical environmental factors have close relationship to influence economic growth or
food shortage causing

I shall indicate reasons to explain why social and physical environmental factors have close relationship to influence economic growth, even human health of quality of life. The social and economic burdens of poor education, lack of affordable housing and less than self sufficient income affect, not just those individuals and families who have the fewest resources. The social gradient means that not only do whose in the bottom worse health outcomes to bottom of income group and the top income group whose will have poor quality of life influence. The higher rates of disease and disability and lesser productivity among many communities means a higher public and private burden of life years, particularly life expectancy once one reaches age 65. In recent decades, research and has increasingly shown how powerfully social and economic conditions determine population health and differences in health among subgroups, much more so than medical care. It seems that environmental factor can influence human's quality of life.

Los Angeles Country Department Of public Health (2016) indicated a country health rankings model, this department explained these three health factors can cause this health outcomes. These health factors include health behaviors (30%), it includes tobacco use, diet and exercise, alcohol use, unsafe sex; clinical care

(20%), it includes access to care, quality of care; social and economic factors (40%), it includes education, employment, income, family and social support, community safety; physical environmental factor (10%) , includes natural environmental quality, built environmental quality. Then these factors can cause this health outcomes, such as morality (length of life):50% and morbidity (quality of life) :50%. SO, it implies that physical environmental factor can influence human's length of life. So, on our social environmental problems result is from a complex interplay of a number of forces. An individual's health –related behaviors , particularly diet, exercise and smoking, surrounding physical environment and health care (both access and quality) all contribute significantly to how long and how well human love. However , none of these factors is as important to population health as are the social and economic environments in which human live, learn, work and play. We refer to these factors can be as the social determinants of health to influence our quality of life. How do social determinants affect our quality of life? In the late 19th and early 20th centuries, public health concentrated particularly on the physical environment. Improvements in, for example, clean water supplies, healthier housing, sanitation, workplace safety and safe food lead to sharp increases in average life expectancy . Also our quality of life needed to be concentrated on expanded access to medical care, resulting in further expansion. So, the poverty tap is now characterized by those elements, such as low levels of : (i) environmental quality, (ii) life expectancy and (iii) human capital.

In fact, environmental degradation can have a significant impact on human health. De Hollander et. al (1999) & Melse & De Hollander (2001) showed that estimates of the share of environment, related human health loss are as high 5% for high income countries, 8% for middle income countries and 13% for low income countries. Air pollution and exposure to hazardous chemicals are important causes of the related burden of disease in countries. The transport and energy sectors are major contributors to air pollution, when important sources of chemical pollution are agriculture industry and waste disposal. Opportunities for reducing environment-related health risks are considerable. The benefits of many environment policies in terms of reduced health care costs and increased productivity significant exceed the costs of implementing those policies. So, the impact of environmental risk factors on health are extremely varied and complex. For example, the effects of environmental degradation on human health can range from death caused by cancer, due to air pollution to psychological problems resulting from noise. So it implies environmental factor can influence our quality of life in our societies. However, many factors can also influence human's health of a population, including diet, sanitation, socio-economic status, literacy and lifestyle.

De Hollander et. al. (1999) & Melse and De Hollander (2001) showed that total burden of disease, with estimated environment-related share expenditure, mid-1990 year. The average income group has 15 daily/1000 capita, the middle income group has 20 daily/1000 capita, the high income group has 10 daily/1000 capita. As regards both total burden of disease and the health conditions related to environmental; degradation. The result indicates the environment –related share of the burden of disease is greatly dependent on income, with higher-environmental shares generally occurring in lower-income countries.

On the one hand, it seems the large environmental share of health problems is primarily, due to factors related to poverty, such as limited to access to proper food, housing, health care and drinking water. Environmental determinants of human health in developing or developed countries are related. On the other hand, those to the exposure to air pollutants (particularly in urban areas and chemicals in the environment than to poor living conditions. Also sources of human exposure to chemicals are many and varied. Chemicals can reach the environments, for example, through emissions from industries, anti-fouling paints on marine vessels, pesticides in agriculture, waste incineration and leakage from waste disposal sites. When emissions of chemicals from industries and other point sources of pollution have lead to poor quality of life, source of chemical exposure. Intensive agricultural production uses chemicals in pesticides and fertilizer and in feed additives and medication for livestock. Residues remain in fruit, grains, vegetables, meats and daily products, all of which can reach the consumer.

Other sources of chemicals in food include bio-accumulative chemicals in the environment, such as heavy metals and persistent organic pollutants, which can be found in fish, meat and dairy products. So, environment pollution can influence human need to eat bad or unhealthy food to cause we have poor quality of life to live, such as the high income group or middle income group or low income group of families in our societies fairly. Other human health risks that have recently received considerable attention include unsafe livestock feeding practices through which toxins reach the food chain unintentionally. Dioxins that have accidentally contaminated poultry feeds that contain diseased animal remains can cause the so-called " mad cow disease" in livestock which has been linked to a new form of disease. The effects on health from exposure to chemicals and air pollutants vary from allergies to cancer. Although, the link between exposure and disease is often not clear, Even at low exposure levels, urban are pollutants can cause, asthma, allergies, respiratory diseases and cardiovascular disease if the exposure is continuous or long term. Heavy metals have been shown to cause neurological disorders and various cancers. In addition to , physical diseases, environmental contamination can also cause psychological problems. Noise, one of the determinants of the quality of urban life can have an impact on human health, decreasing the quality of life and potentially contributing to depression.

For Ireland, UK country example, this country politicians and policy makers believe the role of environment can be used to measure quality of life, concerning on either in its own right or relative to economic and social aspects of quality of life. Agreement on what measures quality of life and how it can be measured by the role of environment, not just in Ireland, but everywhere. The conventional approach is used for policy has been to use measure of gross domestic product(GDP) or regional valued added. However, it is acknowledged that such conventional economic measures have only a partial relationship with societal wellbeing. To the extent that economic measures are related to public products and consumption, there are also pressing issues in relation to public products and the sustainability of economic growth. However, the role of environmental factor can influence resource use and human's behavioral consumption.

Aspects to quality of life other than income include the environment, freedom, health, working condition, leisure, social and family relationship. Economists don't deny that these factors do play a role in quality of life. However, environment factor can be one role to influence other factors to influence our quality of life to be good or bad effect. For example, locations which might be desirable as paces to life (in terms of income earning opportunities or other factors) were also likely to have higher costs of living, particularly with regard to house prices or health or unhealthy air/ water pollution of environment situation of the place to provide human to live. Alternatively, social indicators are based on normative ideals of literacy, low rates of premature mortality or a quality environment. Other measurement of people's personal evaluation of their quality of life, much depends on personal expectations and experience.

(v) How environmental factor can influence any country's house price and food shortage causing

I shall indicate that why environmental factor will influence any country's house price. For Ireland example, citizen average incomes and higher in the east of the country, house prices are lower in the west, who are also more able to afford a property of choices. There are more opportunities to purchase houses, where people own their own houses, who are more likely to have benefits from an appreciation is its value and to consequently perceive a higher degree of health. Generally, levels of property appreciation have been higher in the east. Unfortunately, young people and the more economically active segment of the population are more likely to be faced with rising entry level house prices and the prospect of large borrowings. So, the quality of life, such as education, crime and access to healthcare and living environment are not uniformly better in the west or the east regions. Indeed, many measures of social disadvantage are at their worst in the west regions. Some indicators of environmental quality are , indeed better in the west regions, but there are others, such as drinking-water quality or recreational access that are often worse.

Comparisons can often be reduced to an urban-rural dimension rather than a regional one. Factors such as incomes, house prices, crime levels, air pollution and congestion are all likely to be higher in urban areas in Ireland city, UK country. Why environment and housing price has relationship in Ireland to influence quality of life to its citizen? If Ireland's regional development policy is successful , it will bring with it greater competition in the housing market and greater pressures on the environment in Ireland. Because the forest will be decreased to build house, the natural environment will become wood and steel and stone of housing built environment. In fact, it appears that there is a fair of amount of agreement on the relative rating of factors influencing quality of life. Ability to own one's home and security of income were needed, but respondents also placed almost equal important on clean air and drinking water, low crime were differences. The Ireland's rural respondents appeared to place a slightly greater emphasis on key natural environmental attributes, when urban residents valued absolute incomes and social or leisure activity rather more.

In this respect, the analysis identifies three components to Ireland people of quality of life, each of which was evident in all three locations. There components can be broadly described as domestic security, social/leisure and aspects of the planned environment. The first of these includes indicators, such as security of income, absolute income, house ownership and low crime. As this component includes air and drinking-water quality, it suggests that these indicators may be associated with personal health and well-being. When the planned environment component includes those attributes that affect quality of life over which the authorities have a direct influence, for instance, a clean environment, traffic and reducing vehicle numbers on the roads in busy time.

(vi) How environmental pollution can influence social welfare and cause food shortage

Environmental quality has an undefined impact on quality of life and various indicators are used to show regional variations in aspects, such as water quality . There are many measures of environmental quality , but is only for quality of life. Moreover, the measurement of societal welfare is important. Societal welfare is not simply , the sum of the parts, but varies depending on the individual in which people find themselves at any time in their life. In principle, it should be possible to apply weights to each element of societal welfare, but as preferences for each of these vary within the population. In the absence of a method with which everybody is satisfied, GNP and GDP are typically the most popular used measures for quality of life or standard of life. But, these are problems with the data itself to measure quality of life because quality of life is feeling or satisfaction of level to the country's citizen and it can not be seen by numbers or statistic method. For example, GDP ignores household production, such as the effort that goes into the rearing of children, the benefits that this provides for society and the public expenditure that is avoided. Neither are costs treated equally with the benefits. GDP counts all economical activities irrespective on pollution appears to increase. GDP even through it is a degree of double counting. Otherwise, environmental products are good to be measured to quality of life. For example, many environmental products are unpriced. Consequently, environmental products that people value, or which are critical to the sustainability of development, are abused or depleted because of their public products have good characteristics and the absence of a market price signal.

Environmental economists try to work within the economic model to measure quality of life. Rather than questioning the link between utility and consumption or choice, the preferred approach is to add an element into the utility function that represents the value of environmental products or the stock of natural capital. By one means or another , the preservation value of these environmental products is estimated in terms of willingness to pay to protect the environment or as willingness to forego other products in return. It seems the quality of people's environment can be represented by objective indicators. At another, their interpretation will vary and can be represented by subjective indicators.

Objective indicators come in two forms: (i) economic indicators and (ii) social indicators. The former depends on an ability to select the products and services that are desires, in other words, the satisfaction of preferences . The economic argument is that people select the best quality of life, who can obtain commensurate with their resources and personal desires. By comparison, social indicators are based on normative ideals on what could be considered the food life. For example, would be infant morality, literacy, crime rates and social indicators are objective measures. Both have guided, much of the research on quality of life, particularly concerning with the urban environment. Quality of life can include natural a significant influence on local quality of life, for instance, natural beauty spots used for recreation.

Whether environmental factor is the main factor to influence food consumers to waste food

Can artificial intelligence find what the main environmental factor influences food consumers food wasting behavior rising ? For environmental quality concept, it concerns with health, safety, wellbeing, residential satisfaction and the physical sustainability can be considered to result from an when live ability can be considered to represent the interaction between the physical and the social domains. As with expenditure on the environment, investment in social capital contributes to quality of life. However, the benefits will again vary amongst individuals, depending largely on the security of their individual circumstance. As with the environment, the government can certainly adopt strategies that provide for public security by taking measures to reduce crime, a measure likely to be appreciated by everybody (except criminal) , at least to one degree or another. In other necessary to enhance social interaction, namely community centers or sports facilities. Furthermore, the creation of social capital has an statement which responds to general social trends to raise Ireland citizen's quality of life.

I shall indicate Ireland to explain whether environmental factor is the main factor to influence our quality of life and economic growth as well as to cause food wastage. Is environmental quality higher in the Ireland west regions? And if so, does this compensate for lower incomes in these regions? Is it bad that rural areas are characterized by higher costs of living in areas other than housing by environmental factor? In fact, in Ireland , UK country, population increase has a direct impact on the environment by placing demands on local natural resources, particularly open space and water. It also leads to a sense of crowding that reduces the utility associated with access to the environment. How can environment factor influence economy growth in Ireland? In Ireland, agriculture has gone through a period of significant change that has been accelerated reductions in the amount of mixed cropping and traditional land management. Indeed, changes in the expectations of young farmers will ensure that further change is likely to be characterized by increases in farm size and greater specialization with implications for landscape and wildlife. These characteristics of farm holdings are more familiar in the east regions of Ireland , UK country. As with likely to extend to the west regions as the older generation of farmers retires, although this will probably be accompanied by a trend to more farming of production needs to young farmers. So, good natural environment can provide Ireland young farmers to produce more agriculture to earn income, even who can export more rice, fruits, vegetable etc. agriculture foods to overseas. Hence, Ireland GDP will be raise if it can have good natural resource environment to provide Ireland young farmers to grow foods to sell to domestic and /or foreign agricultural market. Given the rate of economic growth, and its concentration in the east of the Ireland, UK country, it would be easy to presume that the quality of the environment is higher the further away from the mid east one goes. Thus, good natural environment is an important factor to influence the farming industry development in Ireland , UK county to satisfy their needs and to raise their quality of life nowadays.

I shall indicate New Zealand and America two developed countries to explain why which are facing environmental pollution challenge to influence their citizen's quality of life and economic growth and cause food wastage nowadays. The first country is NZ, although, New Zealand is a developed and natural environmental country, but it had been envountering air pollution annouance and noise annoyance to influence it's citizen's health-related quality of life. I shall indicate why which has this relationship between of them in New Zealand. Nowadays, New zealand population growth is an increasing demand for consumer products and urbanization have lead to concerns over the lived environments in many of the world's cities, such as Auckland, wellington cities in New Zealand.

However, environmental quality is an important determinant of health, such as the bad influence of traffic-related air and noise pollution on health outcomes, specially with respect to at risk groups, both in relation to long term exposure as well as acute effect, from brief exposures. For example, cholesterol levels and in relation to myocardial infaction. Nowadays, New Zealand is encountering the high degree of air pollution and noise annoyance to influence it's citizen's quality of life. Air pollutants can be detected either visually, such as witnessing smoke emanating from a vehicles's exhaust, or by smell, such as when odorants stimulate olfactory receptors. The evidence linking air pollution to adverse impacts on human health.

Many air impacts on human health. Many air pollution health studies have focused specifically on urban area, and vehicle generated pollution in particular, as road vehicles are one of the major sources of pollution across much of the world. Elemental carbon, Nox and ultrafine particles an considered to be pollutants most strongly associated with road traffic emissions. In Auckland and Wellington cities, New Zealand , it has been estimated that 71% of summer and 21% of winter concentrations of fine particulate matter is attributable to motor vehicles. Moreover, poor town planning decisions in Auckland (and in New Zealand in general) over many decedes has meant that may people live in very close proximity to busy road and motorways within " road corridors" and so are the adverse effects of road traffic, including noise and air pollution as well as experiencing on potential for degradation in their quality of life. Such as, New Zealand is highly suitable for studies investigating the impact of roads on the health of its residents. For example, NZ, road traffic noise and aviation noist has been linked to cardiovascular disease, hypertension and ischemic heart disease. It influences NZ resident personal psychological and physical both health challenges. In fact, NZ noise increases morbidity and mortality independently of air pollution exposure, though air pollution constituted a greater burden of disease when arise exposure had a greater impac on quality of life, e.g. NZ road traffic noise and air pollution will be caused from drivers in busy time. Specially in Auckland and Wellington cities. It will influence urban and rural environmental pollution. Some retired old people who will feel annoyance when this road traffic occurs in Auckland or Wellington cities to close to their houses in transportation busy time every day.

Next developed country is America, this country's air pollution is also serious nowadays. Because traffic jam often occurs in New York, Washington, Boston etc. big cities in US. So, U.S. cities' parks and its trees have significant influence to produce fresh air to provide U.S. residents who are living in cities to breach for their body health. David J. & Gordon , M. (2016) indicated " In U.S. these urban parks are estimated to contain about 370 million trees with a structural value of approximately $300 billion." The number of park trees varies by region of the country, but which can produce significant air quality effects in and near parks, related to air temperatures, air pollution, ultraviolet indication and carbon dioxide (a dominant greenhouse gas related to global climate change). Additional open space and other vacant lands in cities, which may contain trees and other vegatation. Contribute significant additional benefits, effects of parks and open space at the city scale can vary significantly depending on the amount of parkland and amount of tree cover within the parkland.

The reasons why parks can reduce air pollution. Parks generally have lower air temperature than surrounding areas. Temperatures are usually cooler toward the center of a park than around its edges. At night, the center of a large park may be 13 degree cooler than surrounding city areas. The cooler air from parks often moves out into adjacent developed neighborhoods. This cooling of surrounding areas tends to increase with park size and percentage of the park covered by trees. So, cooler air temperature is provided by urban parks can have significant impacts on human health. During heat wave events, which can kill hundreds of people, park areas may provide city dwellers with some respite from high air temperture, particularly in the evening, during hot, sunny days tree shade can greatly increase human comfort. Because park influences on air temperature extend to developed areas outside of parks, local energy use for heating and cooling buildings is also effected. Although, the net around effect of parks on energy costs has been by reducing temperature is difficult to estimate at least in the southern United States the effect will usually be a net annual benefit. Futhermore, large park trees will reduce winds and may provide a benefit of winter heating of buildings near the park. Although, the overall economic effect of urban trees and parks on air temperature reduction is not fully billions of dollars annually at the national scale in terms of improved environmental quality and human health.

In fact, trees and vegetation in parks can help reduce air pollution both by directly removing pollutants and by reducing air temperatures and building energy use in and near parks. There tree effects can reduce pollutant emissions and formation. However, park vegetation can increase some pollutants by either directly emitting volatile orgnic compounds that can contribute to ocone and carbon monoxide formation or indirectly by the emission of air pollutants through vegetation maintenance practices, such as operation of chain and use of transportation fuels. David J. & Gordon , M. (2016) showed "Annual pollution removal and economic benefits by U.S. urbank park trees is estimated at about 75,000 tones ($500 million) or 80 pounds per acre of tree cover ($300 per acre of tree cover). Carton storage and annual removal by urban park trees and soils in the United States is estimated at about: carton storage trees: 75 million tons ($1.6 billion), carton storage (soils) : $102 million tons of carbon removal (trees): 2.4 million tons ($50 million)". Park management is recommended by U.S. environment protection department: considering that most of the effects of trees on microclimate and air quality are beneficial for park users and nearby residents; park designs that include a variety of land cover, areas of dense trees, scattered trees and lawn are likely to provide the greatest opportunities for optimum physical comfort of visitors; increase the number of healthy trees (increase pollution removal and carbon storage); sustain existing tree cover (maintains pollution removal levels) and (carbon storage); maximize use of low volatile organic compound emitting trees reduces ozove and carbon monoxide formation; sustain large, healthy trees (large trees have greatest per tree effcts on pollution and carbon removal); using long-lived trees (reduces long term pollutant emissions from removal; reducing fossil fuel in maintaining vegetation reduces pollutant ans carbon emissions)." So, if US had many green parks, then which can reduce air pollution, also it can assist many travellers who prefer to travel to US to raise GDP travelling income growth generally.

(i) Why environmental pollution and human right abuses has close relationship to influence quality of life and economic growth as well as bring food wastage ?

In fact, environment pollution and human right abuses has close relationship. It is clear that poverty situations and human rights abuses are worsened by environmental degradation. The result can influence poor human quality of life to the developing countries' people unfairly. There are these several abvious reasons: firstly, the exhaustion of natural resources leads to unemployment and emigration to cities; secondly, this affects the enjoyment and exercise of basic human rights. Environmental conditions contribute to a large extents to the spread of infections diseases. From the 4,400 million of people who live in developing countries, almost 60% lack basis health care services, a almost a third of these people have no access to safe water supply; thirdly, degradation poses new problems, such as environmental refugees. Environmental refugees suffer from significant economic, socio-cultural and political consequences. And fourthly, environmental degradation worsens existing problems suffered by developing and developed countries. David J. Nowak & Gordon M. Melsler (2016) showed" Air pollution , for example, accounts for 2.7 million to 3.0 million of deaths annually and of these 90% are from developing countries. " Hence, our societies need to concern human right law to protect unfair treatment to developing countries people. Firstly, both disciplines have deep social root, even though human rights law is more rooted within the collective consciousness, the accelerated process of environmental degradation is generating a new " environmental consciousness". Secondly, both disciplines have become internationalized . The international community has assumed the commitment to observe the realization at human rights and respect for the environment. Thirdly, both areas of law tend to universalize their object of protection. Human rights are presented as universal and the protection of the environment appears as everyone is responsibility.

Human right and environment law can raise our quality of life because the first approach is one where environmental protection is described as a possible means of fulfulling human rights standards. Here, environmental law is conceptualized as giving a protection that would help ensure the well-being of future generations as well as the survival of those who depend immediately upon natural resources for their livelihood. So, the end is fulfulling human rights, and the route is though environmental law, the second approach places the two sphere in inverted positions, it states that the legal protection of human rights is an effective means to achieving the ends of conservation and environmental protection. Therefore, the presently existing human right is as a route to environmental protection. The focus is on the connection to influence any economy: health, food supply , housing, fresh natural air supply etc. aspects of quality of life issues. Hence, human right and environment law and human quality of life and economic growth has close relationship . We can not neglect to concern how to achieve human right law to protect our nature environment existing in our societies.

What are environmental factors affect human health in important way, both positive and negative? On positive environmental factor aspect, which can sustain health, and promoting them is preventive medicine. They include : sources of nutrition (farming, oil quality, water availability, bio diversity/bio integrity, genetically modified organisms ; hurting, fishing: wildlife, fish populations; water (drinking, cooking, cleaning,sanitation); air quality; ozone layer (protection from cancers disease etc).; space for exercise and recreation, sanitation/waste recycling and disposal. On negative environmental factors aspect, which are threats to health, and controlling them is public environmental health. They include: environmental conditions favouring disease sectors (endemic and exotic sectors); invasive biota (visuses, bacteria etc.), their hosts and sectors; environmental disruptions: floods, droughts, storms, fires earthquakes, volcanoes; air quality: pollution landing to respiratory disease or cancers; water quality: biotic and abiotic contaminants ; integrity of water transport and intrastructure; monitoring and management of municipal, agricutural, industrial outflows to the environment (gases, liquids, solid waste), human changes of the environment that: create conditions that favour disease; disturb and release noxious levels of previously bound chemicals (e.g. mercury released becomes poison) or bioto (e.g. methane released from thawed peat contributes to climate changes, create temporary, intense, life threatening heat islands (e.g. urban heat waves exacerbated by climate change); result from nuclear; biological or chemical welfare or terrorism, disruption cased by other war and violense.

(ii) What is space and environmental technology to avoid food wastage?

For example, Cananda is a developed country and it begins to concern environmental pollution challenge to announced $3 million to support the initiative strengthening health and environment linkages: from knowledge to action. The initiative will bring together scientific, technical and socio-economic information on environment and health linkages, and transfer that knowledge to inform decision-making at the local, regional and national levels. Also, Canada is principally concerned with the health of Canadians. This involves health factors in Canada and in biologically shared health regions (shared geography or exposure through trade and travel). Supports international health initiatives, such as determining health risks throught environmental analysis of disease vectors in Africa or Asia.

How can the space and environmental factors affecting health? Environmental information and environmental management contribution to the maintenance and restoration of health. Space based environmental management factors and communications can play roles in: Environmental information is for optimising use of health resources; distribution of and access to health advice and treatment (i.e. to health staff treatment facilities; short range environmental prediction for avoidance of high risk, situations and to guide immediate health system responses. Managing acute risks, adopting to them (e.g. temporary moving of vulnerable elderly monitored; modeling of health impact of environmental parameters; prediction of long term health resource needs and environmental planning and mitigation and adaptation to global changes. Large benefits are possible from attention to environmental factors, e.g. asthma prevention, disease and epidemiology. Benefits need to be quantified. This is of particular interest and relevance to pandemics , such as malasia in underdeveloped countries, potentially saving thousands of lives.

What is space and environmental technology? It can contribute to and keep abreast of environmental health forecasts (using existing models and known parameters); prepare and deliver prospectuses for what space can do in anticipation or response; steer space programs according to real risks and real accumulative health benefits, as long technical investment, don't focus primarily on threats that may have high emotional impact , but are of low actual risk; position space technology and the canadian space program in people's winds, aggressively and realistically, as a first line contributor to foresight and preduction, long term maintenance of well-being and prevention of factors of ill-health ; ongoing delivery of health services and management of current health factors and potentially capable and ready to respond in health emergencies. Finally, making the full business case for investment in space technology and space program contributions relative to the full and public and private cost of health programs. This connects not only to GDP raising, but to indicators of quality of life to any countries.

Reference

Cornelia, B.F. (1999) Rural development news, the North Central Regional Center For Rural Development vol. no 24 , IOWA.

David J. Nowak & Gordon M. Melsler (2016) " Air quality effects of urban trees and parks." National recreation and park association, USA.

De Hollander, A. E. M., J.M. Melse, Elebret & P. G.N. Kramers (1999), " An Aggregate public health indicator to represent the impact of multiple environmental exposures" Epidemiology: 606-617.

Felce, D. and Perry, J. (1995). Quality of life: A contribution to its definition and measurement, vol. 16, no.1 pp: 51-74.

Los Angeles Country Department Of public Health (2016), Country Health Ranking Model, Retrieved From www.countryhealthrankgings.org/our-approach. USA.

Melse, J.M. & A.E. M. De Hollander (2001). " Human Health And The Environment", background document for the OECD Environmental Outlook, OECD, Paris.

McGregor, S.L. T., & Goldsmith, E.B. (1998). Expanding our understanding of quality of life, standard of living and well-being. Journal of family and consumer science, 90(2), 2-6, 22.

McMichael, A.J. M. Mckee, J. Shkolnikov and T. Valkanen (2004), " Morality trends and setbacks, global convergence or divergence?", Lancet 363, 1155-1159.

Yale Center For Environmental Law And Policy (2006). Environmental Performance Index. Data available on-line at http://epi.yale.edu

The failure of human education method influences consumers to change food and energy waste behaviours

Can artificial intelligence analyze human education method is the main factor to influence consumers to change food and energy waste behaviors ? I shall indicate the reasons to explain why human education method can not persuade to change consumers and manufacturers to do food and energy waste or loss behaviour easily.

The first reason is that , food waste is a serious ethical, environmental and economic problem of excessive consumerism. Usually, food waste occurs in all phases of the food supply chain, starting with producers and ending with consumers. There are several factors which contribute to excessive qualities of wasted foods. Some are related to current quantities of wasted foods . Some are related to current production systems and product commercialization, including food quality and security norms, others are more personal like people's food habits, awareness, values and consumer attitude in regards to consumption and food waste.

So, changing consumers and manufacturers whose wrong food consumption and excessive quantities of wasted food behaviours. It is difficult to avoid from only education method , because human's eating habits or food habits are very difficult to change to reduce to do food waste behaviours in their eating processes easily. Education is only teaching how to avoid food waste knowledge promotion or persuasive method. It can not provide useful food waste methods to assist food manufacturers how to present to avoid excessive food quantities waste in food manufacturing processes , e.g. efficient operative production as well as it can not assist consumers to understand how and why the reasons for food waste, why to do the right food consumption behaviours, eating attitudes, the most reason level of consumer knowledge and opinions with respect to food waste as well as perception about the quantities of wasted food in the consumer's household. Otherwise, future (AI) technology can assist food manufacturers how to avoid and to cause food losses in food manufacturing process as well as it can assist food consumers understand they ought how to do to change wrong food habits to right food habits in order to do the right daily eating behaviours daily more influentially.

The second reason is that, in order to reduce consumer individual food waste in developed countries, there is a need to understand the factors which shape consumer behaviours. Future (AI) technology can be used to research and analysis of customer behaviours, knowledge and attitudes of people including analysis of different developed countries' consumer behaviours for food. The objective of (AI) technology research is to determine food waste attributes, daily food routines, shopping routines, planning as a predictor of food waste and policies varied in terms of household characteristics in each country.

The (AI) data gathering results can give qualitative information about food waste including data on frequency of wasting food and reasons for wasting it, which can be based on each country's consumers' food habits or eating behaviours analysis. The (AI) gathering data concerns consumers play a crucial role to combat food waste via their own households. It is important to find solutions that are relevant to food habits more easily.

Hence, (AI) technology can gather data to understand food waste problem to household level by picturing main causes affecting food waste giving deeper insight into consume behaviour throughout the every time of right food purchasing number, storage, preparation, consumption toll disposals. So, future (AI) technology (big data gathering tool) can analyse origins and quantities of food waste quantifying the scale of the problem, including all causes and food waste influence as well as to understand the variety of factors which can cause influence food waste behaviours more accurately.

The third reason is that, future (AI) technology can also be applied to solve food loss challenge. Food loss is considered to be food that gets spilled before it reaches its final product or retail chains, which occurs at production, post-harvest, and at the food manufacturing or transportation processing stages. It is also caused by poor infrastructure , and logistics, lack of technology , inefficient skills, knowledge and management capacity , it may be accidental or intentional , ultimately leads to less food available. So, it seems that education method is difficult to avoid food losses for food manufacturers. However, future (AI) technology can be applied to assist farming agriculture to grow crops to avoid food loss easily in good climate or food growing environment.

Instead of (AI) technology can be applied to avoid humans do food waste or food loss behaviours easily. It can also be applied to avoid energy waste aspect. I shall explain why (AI) technology can change or influence householders and manufacturers' energy using or consumption behaviours to save more electricity, gas energy at homes, offices or plants or shopping centres etc. working or entertainment places more easily or effectively to compare energy waste educational or learning method. I shall indicate the reasons as below:

(AI) technology is the more quality training data to a (AI) data gathering energy sector, which has access to the better , the (AI) can be integrated into its everyday operations. The energy sector is one of those industries with a wealth of data that is for machine learning and its comparison technologies to assist humans to avoid to do energy waste behaviours.

The commercial opportunities from using (AI) in this energy industry come from the technology's real-time optimisation, predictive analysis and forecasting power. For example, a number of New Zealand energy distribution companies are working with postgraduate students in big data and machine learning to analyse information gathered from both their networks and smart meters. Between 75 and 85 per cent of data in this sector is structured and machine learning can be used to analyse it, platforms using unsupervised learning techniques are well-suited for energy detections which can boost the efficiency of utility operations to reduce optimising energy cost. Machine learning algorithms are being used to understand vast amounts of data to predict mining, drilling and power generation failures and then to recommend tailored maintenance based on the potential issues.

SO, (AI) systems can monitor the emission of nitrogen oxides from gas turbines and vary the distribution of fuel to maintain the required levels of energy generation. Scaled across the network, this is a genuine opportunity to better control energy useful cost to avoid energy waste. Moreover, machine learning can also manage energy to use within complex systems. For example, Goggle's deep mind (AI) achieved a 40 per cent reduction in energy used to cool the company's data centres, even after human engineers had supported optimised the facility's energy use. ON a bigger scale, machine learning can be employed to manage the use of resources, such as water energy in " smart cities" to avoid to cause water natural energy power is excessive waste.

On benefits to energy end-users, based on real-time usage data, machine learning algorithms and supervised learning can improve energy management , even in power plants. This in turn optimises total pricing for energy consumers and provides opportunities to offer promotions based on energy customer demographics. SO, machine learning is used in some of these products as part of a deeper effort to provide customers with more choices about how to produce, consume and store energy and encourage them to do in many energy saving right behaviours.

(AI) has the ability to transform resources distribution and compensate for drastic fluctuations in energy demand. The technology will also go beyond just pricing and distribution to respond directly to the dynamic needs for energy, water power and natural drinking water and waste management. Through an ecosystem of " smart city", water and electricity can be distributed from many small energy producers and be personalised to specific regions and time frames. Each energy producers could use techniques which are particularly suited to time series data . This network would take in and learn energy user behaviours and use the information to manage the energy or water power or drinking water supply . A energy producer can then sell excess energy capacity back to the grid, maximising efficiency and reducing energy wastage to energy consumers.

SO, in the future, the key (AI) technologies in energy sector, they will bring high impact on machine learning, natural language programming, chat bots which will be applied to machine learning technology in energy saving sector to avoid energy wastage when energy consumers use energy daily. With the high volume of data available, global energy businesses can readily continue develop their (AI) technologies. Better resource allocation, improved customer satisfaction are obvious benefits as well as the most important influence is that (AI) energy saving consumption or using technology can impact energy end –users to avoid to waste too much excessive energy when they are using energy at homes or any public places or private factories or offices manufacturing places for every day necessities. So, it can explain why (AI) technology can impact energy end-users energy saving and using behaviours to be improved.

Next, two chapter, I shall explain how (AI) technology big data gathering tool how it can help energy end-users and food consumers how to impact to avoid to do wastage behaviours more influentially every day.

How (AI) technology impacts food consumers
and food manufacturers food eating habits
or attitudes to avoid wastage

Can artificial intelligence impact food consumers' eating habits to be influenced to change ? Future (AI) technology (big data gathering tool) can be used to gather data concerns to supervise or manage or control these below food consumers and food manufacturers' food waste or food loss behaviours in order to find the main reasons to cause their food waste or loss wastage behaviours in order to achieve to prevent or avoid their wastage behaviours occurrence again more easily. I shall explain to these aspects as below, they include :

On (AI) auto-supervised food consumer individual food waste behavioural aspect:

Firstly, for the original food wastage supervised, the original food which included food in unopened packages behaviours, which was thrown away because it passed the expiration date including products to like cheese, yogurts and other daily products, loose fruits and vegetables which became rotten and was never used. (AI) technology can follow these waste food gather number from different countries' supermarkets, food stores to gather waste food number in order to carry statistic analysis to find the reasons why these kinds of original food, cheese, yogurts, fruit and vegetable wastage number has increase to every month in order to attempt to find the reasons to cause wastage food behaviours , it is either caused by either food manufacturers' food losses (good manufacturing process negligent factor) cause or food consumers' food eating habits cause in order to find the solution methods to change their wrong food loss or waste influential behaviours to the food manufacturers as well as the wrong food habits or attitudes to the food household consumers more easily and accurately.

Secondly, for another kind of wastage food is partly used food supervised, the food which could have been opened or started, but was never finished. (AI) data gathering tool can attempt to follow different countries' food rubbish to gather the number data to find how much rubbish number is belonged to the country's wastage food is partly used food or the food which could have been opened or started, but was never finished to find the main reasons (factors) why they caused those kind of food wastage number is increased from food consumers; eating habits or what the reasons (factors) caused their number is decreased the country's food consumers' eating habits in order to find the most effective or accurate methods to solve this kind of food wastage behaviours from the country's food consumers.

Thirdly, for the another kind of food wastage is leftover supervised, which consist of food left or the plates or were cooked in big amounts which ended is not being eaten. (AI) technology big data gathering tool can gather global these kind of food waste number concerns every householder's food left on plates or were cooked in big amounts to every country, but not being eaten number from their rubbish.

TO attempt to find what factors(reasons) influence their food habits to do food left on the plates or were cooked in big amounts , which are nor being eaten food habits. SO, it can follow this kind of global food wastage increasing or decreasing number every month statist data to attempt find what factors influence this kind of food wastage to household food consumers to be either decreased or what factors influence this kind of food wastage number to be increased to conclude the more accurate food behavioural wastage judgement for this kind of food wastage habits to every country household food consumers, e.g. life habitual factor, food price factor, food perishable factor, climate influence factor etc. different kinds of external factors to cause every country's household food wastage behaviours.

Finally, the final kind of food wastage is that preparation residues, (vegetable peels, egg shells) supervised, this kind of food wastage could potentially be still used and not known away by global every householder food consumers, they can not be avoided to waste before cooling, due to the householder feels these foods are not fresh to eat. So, the householder chooses not to cook it to eat.

However, (AI) technology can gather data concerns different countries' householder fresh food purchasing habits ,e.g. per week or per twice week or per day fresh food purchasing frequently and fresh food purchasing number, such as vegetable peels etc. fresh food wastage rubbish number in order to find what the main factors (reasons) is (are) to cause the next month fresh food wastage number to be increased or decreased to every country householders in order to conclude the more accurate or reasonable wrong fresh food wastage habitual behaviours to cause different countries' fresh food householders' fresh food wastage behaviours habitually.

In conclusion, basing on above evidences, I can explain why future (AI) technological big data gathering tool can be applied to find solutions to avoid that food consumers to do food wastage behaviours habitually. It also explain why food wastage education method is only knowledge concept to educate to let public to know. In fact, food consumers can choose either do or not do to avoid food wastage in their eating habits daily. Otherwise, (AI) big data fathering tool can be applied to attempt to gather global householders (food consumers) their daily eating habitual data in order to achieve the more accurate and predictive householders (food consumers) their eating habits or eating behaviours analysis and concludes the most efficient and effective solutions to avoid global food wastage number to be raised to every country household food consumers. So, (AI) technology can impact global householders (food consumers) eating or food habits to be improved more better to compare education method.

On (AI) auto-supervised food manufacturer individual food loss behavioural aspect:

How (AI) technology changes food manufacturers cause food loss in their food manufacturing processes, I shall indicate as below:

How to apply (AI) technology to avoid vegetable, fresh fruit loss to global farmers' fresh vegetable , fruit excessive wastage loss increasing number when their crops growth process in global agricultural sector? (AI) will enable significant and valuable new solutions to avoid fresh crops, fruit, rice, vegetable food loss in their growing or irrigation process.

The internet of things (OIT) will assist (IA) in future intelligent agricultural systems, fuelled by large volumes of data acquired from images, videos and IOT sensors. For example, it be applied to water and sprays in agricultural sector. (AI) is smoothing the way for new levels of optimisation on our farms and across all horticultural activities. The automated irrigation systems are getting and the transporting of water to specific places. It is based on the real-time needs of plants. Moreover, (AI) techniques using IOT and sensors to analyse what's happening across many hectares of farming land in real time will enable improvements in predictive modelling.

Farmers will be able to check the advantages of specific phenotypes , or traits in certain growing over time . Predictive modelling will also help them forecast pest resurgences, dramatically preventing yield losses and reducing farmers' dependence on chemical pesticides to let vegetable, fruit, crop can be grown healthy.

For the university of Waikoto , NZ example, researchers are applying machine learning to near infra-red images of soil, meaning the soil does not have to be sent to the lab. This will enable farmers to apply fertilisers much more efficiently. Moreover, robots will be developed to roam between strains of needs. These bots are high enough that do not damage the soil, and because they release herbicides only onto the weeds. They are also doing more environmental protection behaviours. Many uses of (AI) in agriculture are focused on reducing the biological and ecological damage caused by inefficient use of pesticides.

For meet waste loss reducing aspect, (AI) technology can be applied to animal health monitoring . It can also be used to improve efficiencies in livestock management by optimising feeding and dispensing of medication. The (AI) technology can constantly monitor livestock , e.g. pigs, cows sheep animals movements, eating patterns and health and immediately flag animals that are showing unusual behaviour or reduced welling. They can then be treated quickly before they spread infection. So, farmers benefit is from cost reduction through more targeted use of antibiotics when also improving the treatment of livestock.

In the simplest terms, images are constantly captured and pre-processed through detection for frequency and density to livestock eating animals' eating behaviours and living and health conditions in order to provide health pork, beef, sheep meet to consumers to eat.

However, (AI) can be applied to crop seed or fruit improved growing or better irrigation aspect, for New Zealand kiwifruit agricultural irrigation case, yield well ahead of scheduled harvests. New Zealand kiwifruit growers have had to manually count fruit over certain areas and then to achieve the more accurate kiwifruit supplying number of consumers' demanding number scheduled harvests to satisfy New Zealand itself country's kiwifruit consumers' needs , even overseas kiwifruit consumers' needs. The agricultural sector would not know until the kiwifruit product hit supermarket shelves whether its spot sampling had been correct. Any miscalculation could cause kiwifruit waste loss. For example, if NZ kiwifruit farmers predict China kiwifruit consumer number will be on million kiwifruit consumer number in this year. However, they miscalculate the wrong kiwifruit supplying number either their needs are lesser. Then, it will occur shortage kiwifruit number to export to Chinese kiwifruit consumers in this year or their supplying export number are more, then it will occur excess kiwifruit number to Chinese kiwifruit consumers. So, (AI) technology can help NZ kiwifruit farmers to predict every country's kiwifruit needs in order to supply the enough kiwifruit number to every countries' supermarkets or fruit stores to sell. SO, it won't cause NZ kiwifruit excessive or shortage challenges occur more easily.

Hence, (AI) enabled technological tools can observant or supervise every countries' fruit consumers' eating habits to predict whether how many fruit number that they will need to eat every year more accurate. It is as simple as a smartphone to video along on trailers can help provide better estimates. The device videos , the orchard on –the-go and can then produce global fruit consumers' fruit eating habits to predict their fruit consumption behaviours more accurately in every year. From these video-based machine learning systems can detect more better and therefore count seeds and fruit months in advance. So, having these (AI) predictive crop or seeds growing number technology to predict whether is enough insights in advance would also enable harvesters to undertake section-based optimisation, improve food safety and direct fertiliser to specific locations. Global faming suppliers can better manage their crop , fruit seeds, vegetable seeds growing process and time to control or predict when they can be grown to sell when it can reaches the mature stage , even meat pricing and revenue forecasting with supermarkets or food or fruit store retailers accurately book shipping logistics and storage and reducing waste.

So, key (AI) technologies will extreme impact agriculture to change farmers' vegetable, fruit, tomato, potato, crop, and livestock animals feeding methods or behaviours to be improved better by machine learning, drones, computer vision. IOT robotics, satellite , data influence.

How to putting (AI) work in the vineyard for grape fruit growing better? For Lincoln Agri. Tech. a research and development company owned by Lincoln university , NZ case example, it is developing an (AI) solution which can make early season predictions of vineyard harvests. (AI) technology can help NZ grape growers and wineries to predict their grape yield each year. SO, (AI) technology can help them to do grape yield prediction work. A large number of manual workers do sample grape bunches work. SO, (AI) technology is working on creating a system that instead uses electronic sensors to accurately count grapes for NZ grape fruit farmers. The sensors will capture and analyse grape bunches within individual rows, and access the number, sizes and distribution, feeding these different kinds of grape number data into computer algorithms in order to predict grape yield at harvest time to calculate the different kinds of grape yield to different countries grape consumers' needs more accurately. New date will also be added to the (AI) computer system each year, leading to continuous improvements in the model's accuracy as more information is gathered under different conditions. Hence, (AI) system will enable NZ grape growers to accurately access differences in yield , not only between regions or vineyards, but also blocks and rows. Over the long term, site-specific grape yield prediction will help reduce costs by enabling better planning both in the vineyard and in NZ grape market, even overseas grape market both. This (AI) technology will benefit the agricultural industry by supporting better crop or seed management, smoother processing and fruit , vegetable, crop market based on capacity to supply the more accurate number.

Global farmers can apply (AI) technology to improve agricultural water system to let crop, fruit, vegetable to grow more easily to avoid waste loss number rises. Applying on farming sensors and other data to provide farmers with daily recommendations around nitrogen application and water and effluent irrigation . It can be accessed via smartphone, take the guess-work out of interpreting the large amounts of data farmers need to consider before making an irrigation decision.

(AI) agricultural water irrigation computer system can expand into nitrogen application management and water irrigation scheduling. Optimising the amount and timing of effluent are key components of ensuring farm sustainability and resource consent compliance, minimising leaching and optimising pasture growth.

Future (AI) technology just-in-time water management can provide enough water supply to satisfy agricultural fruit, vegetable, crop etc. food irrigation need to global different farming lands more easily. In farming industry, enough fresh water irrigation need is very important to influence any fruit , vegetable, crop etc. food growing process successfully. (AI) technology can be applied to this farming land water supply aspect. It can measure when the farming land needs how much water supply to provide to the farming land's fruit, vegetable, crop growth more easily. Either when the farming land does not need water supply, or when the farming land has still have enough water in the farming underground land. For example, a Florida water company is using artificial intelligence to reduce withdrawal of water from the area aquifer in Jacksonville, USA. Tis (AI) water supply measurement system can forecast water consumption , then monitors, regulates and adjusts supply in real-time , providing a just-in0time water supply to the farming underground lane. This minimises wall production during peak hours, optimises reservoir storage, and reduces the number of pump starts required, lowering energy consumption and maintenance costs.

The (AI) water supply management system can meet the fruit, vegetable crop growing demands of these food consumers needs and reduce the need to big new wells and preserve for un-predictive water supplying need for any fruit, vegetable, crop water need on any farming lands. So, every farming land will have accurate water supplying , it won't have excessive or shortage water supply challenge to every farming lands, if the country's farmers chose to use this (AI) water supply management system.

In the future, (AI) technology advantages to be applied to food waste aspect, it can influence: assisted farming to provide enough water supply to irrigate the most accurate and measured water to every farming underground lands to let any fruit, vegetable, crops' seeds to have enough water supply to grown rapidly, reducing open-sea fishing, considered use of farming land energy supply or affordable and clean energy supply.

In the future, artificial intelligence has the potential to let any fruit vegetable, crop seeds grow up successfully. It can be used to analyse seed genetic data to create crops that can thrive and adapt in any sudden changing environment or weather in order to keep the fruit, vegetable, crop seeds can still have large adapting effort to grow up in any bad conditions. It can increase effectiveness of food supply chains through the use of (AI) technologies to drive insights that improve any fruit, vegetable, crop growing up efficiency and reduce waste in any farm. It can also give recommendations to support for farmers to choose the best decision making in order to increase in productivity. Instead of these , it can reduce the food loss in growing or manufacturing process. It can also help human to choose the healthcare diets. It includes to mine health care records to improve quality of treatments and provide better and faster health diets. It can analyse of large scale genetic data sets to help create new types of treatment and precision medicines customised for individuals, providing expert assistance in diagnosis especially in repetitive tasks, such as analysis of images and large bodies of research information, providing immediate first line consultation to improve waiting times to see a doctor, reducing pressure on frontline staff by using robots in healthcare, speeding up the development of new drugs allowing treatments to reach whose who need them more quickly, improving learning outcomes through the analysis of data about individual learning, social and learning contexts, and personal interests, providing virtual monitors for learning by integrating modelling, social simulation and knowledge representation, providing lifelong learning companions that help the learner to adapt and build new skills throughout their lifetime. Hence, it can bring the actual life knowledge to let food manufacturers, farmers and food consumers to learn how to avoid to do food wastage or food loss behaviours in our daily life experiences. Moreover, it can help farmers , food manufacturers to learn how to optimize energy generation and reduce environmental impact through analysis of operational and environment data as well as helping food consumers or food manufacturers to find the most affordable and clean energy in efficient ways od deals when they are cooking or manufacturing foods by using (AI) agents. Even, it can improve actions to fight climate change through better modelling and analysis of large or complex data sets in order to generate better insight to help to improve the sustainable management of land resources, e.g. soils, forest, biodiversity and allow greater understanding of the impact of better farming land use choices for fruit, vegetable, crops ‘ seeds growth through global agricultural industry development predictive analytic and machine learning.

In conclusion, based on above different (AI) technology predictive function s, so it explains why it can replace education method to avoid or reduce future good or energy shortage challenge more easily. It is due to food consumers or food manufacturers' food waste or loss behaviours which can not be controlled to avoided to cause easily in their food manufacturing or crop growing processes as well as food consumption processes. (AI) green data revolution will create a smarter, more flexible food waste controlling system as more data is created and shared between food supply chain partners and food consumers. It can bring positive benefits to agricultural industry, such as food factory manufacturing automation, intelligent food packaging, food waste or loss risk analytics in manufacturing processes , food supply chain number forecasting, food product personalisation and new avoiding food waste or loss ways of engaging with food consumers.

Finally, I shall discuss how (AI) technology can gather data to bring food waste or food loss threat consequent message to let humans (food consumers or food manufacturers) to understand how to change their eating waste habits or food manufacturing loss behaviours more easily as below:

Future (AI) technology can gather global food manufacturing and food consumption data to conclude one accurate food system trend model to let us to influence our negative or wrong eating habits or food manufacturing behaviours to improve to more positive in order to avoid food loss or food wastage causes easily.. The food eating or manufacturing behavioural system trends model can be as below:

It includes how to consider a number of trends that will influence the food system over the coming decade, focusing on small number of " key trends" in agricultural industry and supermarket, food stores, food grocery and food manufacturing industry, fishing industry, restaurant and hotel food supply industry, these trends which focus on a number of issues across the natural environmental, social and economic influences , due to future food waste or food loss consequent causes.

Changing social norms and working practices continue to influence the frequencey and format of food consumption. Predicting how the soical media influences to the way householders make food purchasing and dining decisions to influence food consumers' food waste behaviors from online. Predicting how the widening wealth gap and aging population are altering household food shopping and eating behaviours changes. Predicting explosion of data enabled technology concerns how the amount of data is growing at an predictive rate. The offers potential for a smarter, more responsive reducing or avoiding food waste behavioral system to food consumers or food manufacturers. Predictinv how the positive changes or influences of tackling major public health and environmental challenges are caused from humans (food consumers and food manufacturers) whose food waste or food loss behaviours. Predicting food system (big data gathering method) concerns food consumers or food manufacturers' frequency of food waste or food loss behavioural data to adatp to an uncertain operating environment as well as to find the methods how to fight the risks of climate related shocks to the food shortge challenge.

Hence, the (AI) data gathering aims to achieve these missions as below:

Learning how to grow in most technology is driven a revolution in how the entire food system operates from a better understanding of land resources to automated factories and kitchens. To bring data enabled technology that will be become cheaper and more accessible all the time, but the avoiding food waste system will fully capitalise on the benefits over tehe next ten years. This avoiding food waste system will be explored to companies, households and food waste policymakers seek to make better use of data. They include as below:

(1) Increasing number of devices connected to the internet and number of social media users to learn how to avoid to do food waste or food loss behaviours daily.

(2) Decreasing the cost of data storage technology and the size od data enabled devices.

(3) The food waste avoiding system can deal with th increasing complexity and sudden changing environmental , social and economic systems to avoid the failure to respond proactively to these new challenges to bring energy, water and food shortages consequences.

(4) Increaing efforts to fight the impacts of extreme weather events, agricultural pest ranges to the food avoiding waste system interconnectedness.

(5) Understanding how to increase soil health, crop diversity, global nutrition and quality and availability of water resources.

(6) Understanding how to fight climate change, it brings significantly affect the fruit, vegetable, crop's seed growth to the improved better in agricultural industry through its impact agricultural yields, agricultural food changing prices influence, reliability of supply, food quality and food safety for ensuring long term food security and supply chain (food transportation process).

(7) Developments of the use of advanced monitoring agricultural systems to increase input efficiencies and anticipate food production risks, such as adverse weather.

(8) Skills for future food wastage or shortage challenges, learning how to fight climate change challenges.

In conclusion, (AI) preventive food wastage or shortage technological system will need to gather the data concerns when global climate and environement sudden change and finding anywhere the global most suitable farming lands are located in order to provide the right agricultural farming lands to let fruit, vegetable, crops' seed which can grow rapidly, finding anywhere the lands are located which have enough natural water supply in order to help us to solve food shortage challenge in order to irrigate enough water to farming lands to let agricultural foods grow more rapidly, and finding anywhere have enough weeds or food for pigs, cows, sheeps livestocks on the land to eat. So, above these are future (AI) preventive food wastage or shortage technological system will be invented to solve any one of these agricultural seeds growth and livestocks feeding challenges.

CHAPTER IX

House quality influences householder electricity energy consumption behavior

Can artificial intelligence influence householder energy consumption behavior changing ? Can the house quality influence the householder electricity energy consumption or useful activities to be more or less. In general, house owners have both intentions for whose property. One intention is living the house by householder himself or herself or householder with families themselves. Another intention is that renting to others to receive rent income (landlord). So, in the housing market, the housing consumer includes either the property owner intents to rent to others to live for rent income aim or the property buyers intents to buy the house to be house owner to live. Does these both different property purchase intentions, which will influence the householder's attitude to use electricity energy consumption desire to be more or less, due to the householder's demand to whose house quality factor influence? This is one interesting question concerns the householder electricity energy consumption desire change to the householder, due to house's investment or house's living intention influences to house quality factor.

How does house quality factor influence to householder electricity energy consumption desire to be more or less? Has it relationship between house quality and house investment or living intention to cause house quality demand to influence the householder electricity energy consumption desire change or demand to be more or less? Has it relationship between regional housing market living or rent investment intentions, housing quality and electricity energy consumption more or less desire? I suppose that the determinants of the residential electricity energy demand form space-heating and cooking, due to the property quality demand influence and the householder's living or rent investment intention influence both, which will influence the householder's electricity energy consumption or useful behavior when he/she/they is/are living in the house.

I argue that rent properties are not only consumer goods, but it also constitute financial market assets. It is therefore reasonable to assume that rational (rent income investment intention) investors choose to raise housing quality (e.g. thermal insulation technological installing at home, heating or cooling technology or artificial intelligent window, lighting, door opening or closing) in order to attract many people choose to rent whose house to live. The householder's aim is to achieve an acceptable return on investment (ROI) or raising rent income aim when he/she rents whose house to anyone, it is easy to attract many people to choose to pay higher rent his/her house to live in the property rent market. Moreover, the another important factor is that rents and future house sale prices of properties differ regionally (or even locally), and largely depend on housing market fundamentals, such as either the house living buyer's income levels or the house rent buyer's income levels, vacancy rates, and/or householder investor's expectations.

Thus, if the householder expects to rent whose house and raises rent to attract many people choose to rent whose house to live, who will attempt to install many new technology in order to satisfy their high quality of life need when they can pay higher rent to rent to choose to rent whose houses to live. Their aim only achieves to raise housing quality, but any new technology will lead to increase electricity energy consumption or use in the house.

Hence, any high quality of houses will influence the householder to use or consume more electricity energy at home. It means that the householder will choose to consume or use more electricity energy at home, if he/she or the family householder demands to live more comfortable house and he/she/they can have high quality of living life at home. This comfortable living demand to the householder (property renter or property buyer) view point can explain why the

better quality of house factor will influence the electricity energy consumption desire to the householder also to be more daily.
I shall indicate one home electricity energy consumption experiment, it indicated that utilizing aggregate data on regional space-heating energy consumption form over 300,000 apartment buildings in 97 German planning regions. The study applies structural equation modelling to estimate the influence of housing market fundamentals on the level of housing quality, and subsequently on regional electricity energy consumption. Consequently, it suggests that housing market fundamental explain regional differences in the housing quality.
In particular, findings show that the level of per capita income, investor' expectations about future housing market development as well as vacancy all explain regional differences in housing quality has a significant impact on electricity energy consumption.
In the way, this experiment can indicate evidence that regional housing market fundamental have a substantial influence on regional levels of housing quality and energy consumption desires to the German regional householders.
This Germany regional householder experiment found important implications for high or low housing quality of the regional property building and householders either property living or property rent intention of comfortable living feeling need factor which will influence the regional property householder electricity energy consumption desire to be raised or reduced. These factors will influence the consequence of electricity energy demand to be increased or decreased needs every day for the regional householder as well as the country's electricity energy supplier(s) can gather the regional properties whether they are high or low quality to predict the regional properties householders' electricity energy consumption supply budget more accurate. It implies that an important determinant of residential housing quality will have possible to influence electricity energy demand to be more or less for long term. IN particular, this Germany regional residential experiment can explain and find an important role in formulating

assumptions about the quality factor has chance to influence the regional residential future levels of electricity energy efficiency and consumption in the country. Hence, housing developments and electricity energy firms can follow this regional residential housing quality factor to evaluate whether the regional housing market is the corresponding investment patterns as well as the energy researchers can follow the regional residential housing quality whether it is high or low housing quality factor to evaluate the more accurate models of regional electricity energy demand to any regional residential householders' houses in the country.

In consumer behavioral view point, it explains that if the country government expected many householders feel to need to spend much electricity energy or have much electricity energy useful demand or desire at home. The country government ought to encourage the country residential property or house developers choose to build many houses which have technological product installed to satisfy the regional householders' residential comfortable living need when they choose the regions to build the high quality houses to let them to live. Then, the regional householders will be influenced to consume or use much electricity energy at homes, due to they feel that they are living at high quality and comfortable and high building technological installed apartments in the country's regions. Then, the country's government and electricity energy provider(s) may be raise much electricity energy efficiency and supply and profit , due to the regional residential householders' electricity energy consumption or useful desire need is therefore influenced to be more by the regional high quality of residential houses factor. So, the regional high quality of residential house factor will have relationship to the regional electricity energy consumption and efficiency to the regional householder's houses.

Otherwise, if the country government felt electricity energy is shortage, it ought encourage the property developers build many low quality and low building technological houses to let householders to live themselves or rent to others to live in the country's different regional residential development market. Due to the low quality of properties and low technological installed to properties factor which will influence any these different regional residential householders to choose method to solve shortage of electricity energy challenge to the country.

In conclusion, to apply consumer behavioral economic theory to property development market, if property quality factor can really influence the householder's electricity energy consumption desire to be used more or less at home daily. The country's property developers can apply this factor to predict property consumer individual property buying consumption behaviors more accurate. For example, if the US property developer planned to build low quality and low technological design buildings and lesser comfortable residential houses in the region in US. Then, its residential householder target will be trended the less acceptable of electricity energy consumption property buyers to choose to buy these regional properties to live in the US region because they can only accept to spend less electricity energy to use when they are living in the houses in order to save money daily. SO, the low quality , less comfortable and low technological installed design residential houses will satisfy their living needs. Otherwise, if the US property developer planned to build high quality and high technological installed design buildings and more comfortable residential houses in the region in US. Then, its residential householder target will be trended to the more acceptable of electricity energy consumption property buyers to choose to buy these regional properties to live in the US region because they can accept to spend more electricity energy to use when they are living in the houses in order to improve their living of quality. So, they wont's consider to spend more expenditure to use electricity energy for any technological products are installed in their properties in order to satisfy their comfortable living needs at their homes every day.

Consequently, property developers can attempt to gather marketing research concerns whether how many people who accept to use more electricity energy or use less electricity energy in order to predict they ought build how many high quality or low quality houses number in different regions more accurate in themselves countries or overseas countries property development market.

Environmental impacts of householder greenhouse gas electricity energy consumption activities

Can artificial intelligence influence householders accept to use greenhouse gas electrcity energy in preference? Can environment factor influence householder electricity energy consumption activities? Has environment factor relationship to influence householder electricity energy consumption behaviors? Socially, householder electricity energy consumption provides us with sources of living satisfaction , but if any sudden environment factor changes, whether it will influence householder consume or use more or less electricity energy decision at home. However, I assume householder electricity energy consumption will have a considerable proportion of the environmental impacts be influenced by our way of life and our economic decision of electricity energy consumption behavior.

What different environmental factors will influence householder electricity energy consumption decision? The external environmental factors include, for example, the country's electricity firms or government changes to electricity energy regulations, electricity energy production technologies change and business practices and government policies changing etc. different external environmental factors will influence any country's electricity energy consumption to householders' consumption desire to be more or less. It will also require changes to influence the householders to consume which kinds of electric products which are needed to be used in different electricity energy natural manufacturing resources.

Why does these external environmental factors impact householders' any behaviors to influence them to concern to use more or less electricity energy power or which kinds of electricity energy products choice at homes. How any why environmental factors impact will influence householder activities at home, such as electricity energy consumption and choice? What are the key components of external environmental factors influence householders' electricity energy consumption behaviors. I shall explain as below:

Firstly, we need to know whether what external environments are which can influence why and how householders need to change their activities to choose more or less or which kinds of energy power to be provided to them to use at home. Who is householder? Householder is an individual, family, or group of individuals living together as unit in a home. Consumption of electricity energy at home may be cooking food needs, needing have colder feeling to turn on fan or air condition at home in summer or needing have warm feeling to turn on heater at home in winter, watching television programs or listening music , playing computer games or used computers activities , reading activities and applying artificial intelligent technological tools to help householders to open or close homes' windows, doors etc. different home equipment which need to use electricity energy provisions. SO, their home activities need to turn on lighting electric tools , televisions, music machines, radios etc. different equipment which need to use electricity energy provision at home. SO, the purpose of householder consumption means consumption by individuals living in a household and it includes consumption both in and outside the home. Why does environmental impacts link to householders' electricity energy consumption? I shall focus on discussing of greenhouse gases (GHGS) energy product how any why it can influenced to householders to use.

The environmental impacts will influence this kind of greenhouse gases (GHGS) energy in the product lifecycle or delivery of the service to link the householder's energy consumption at home such as these several aspects:

Extraction and greenhouse gases production (supply number), physical distribution (delivery far long or close near short distance between the greenhouse gases manufacturing factory and the greenhouse gases supplier), resources consumed by marketing and retail activities (householder's needs to use the quantity of the greenhouse gases energy product), the greenhouse gases consumers search and purchasing activities(e.g. travel to shops, internet purchasing channel, , finding the which kinds of greenhouse gases products from internet, magazines, newspapers, radio advertisements etc. different medias,) , post-use greenhouse gases energy disposal (resale, reused or rubbish). The householder's physical behavioral impact environmental factor will influence how and why he/she chooses to consume greenhouse gases energy daily , e.g. impacts of a housing development, or a wind –farm that supplies greenhouse gases with power. So, the householder's greenhouse gases energy consumption behavior which will depend upon individual personal and subjective perspectives and value.

So, the householder's useful behavior or attitude of greenhouse gases energy product which will influence how he/she/ the family use or consume greenhouse gases energy, such as the householder individual environmental protection attitude which can impact how he/she/the family spends the quantity of greenhouse gases energy every day at home, if the householder does not expect our air or water or land is polluted , due to extraction of any natural gas resources to be manufactured any kinds of greenhouse gases products. Then, this environmental pollution issue will influence some householders choose to reduce to use more quantity of greenhouse gases products every day. Another environmental factors include the bio relates the (unsustainable) use of resources to avoid wasting much greenhouse gases energy to cause greenhouse gases energy supply shortage, avoiding the cause negative impacts of quality life , e.g. noise causing when the extraction of any natural resource from lands to the householder's house is near to the natural resource extraction land and health impacts, e.g. when the greenhouse gas householder user who often use the kind of greenhouse gas product when it is used to cook or heat any equipment to cause they to breathe dirty air at home often. These impacts can be measured in different ways include: monetary costs or loss, physical quantities of resources used or waste or pollution produced and the burden the greenhouse gases energy place on environmental resources. All of these external environment factors will impact the householder individual attitude or behavior how to use or consume greenhouse gases energy product at home.

All these environmental factors concern householder greenhouse gases energy consumer individual consumption attitude is influenced by environment pollution, greenhouse resource supply shortage challenge, greenhouse gases influence the householder's negative quality of life, negative health impacts, noise, waste money , raising economic cost to the householder which will impact whether how the householder choose to use the quantity of greenhouse gases product or the kinds of greenhouse gases products or other kinds of electricity energy products.

However, these are other external environmental factors which can impact how the householder decides to use greenhouse gas product at home. They include: the changes of energy regulation, e.g. the country government has quota number implementation to prohibit to import above the limited quantities of any kinds of greenhouse gas products to any countries. So, when the greenhouse gas energy supplying quantity is decreased, but if the country has may householders who need to buy different kinds of greenhouse gases products to be used at home. Then, the different kinds of import greenhouse gases energy products prices will be raised in possible, due to demand is more than supply in the country's greenhouse gas energy product market. Consequently, if the greenhouse gas energy price us risen above the general social acceptable level to the home greenhouse gas energy product householder consumers. Finally, it will influence them to choose to buy other kinds of gas energy products to replace the greenhouse gas energy product to use at home.

Another side, if the country's greenhouse gas energy

manufacturing supplier sudden changes its greenhouse gas energy production technologies to choose to concentrate on manufacturing other kinds of energy products. Then, the greenhouse gas energy supply quantities will be only decreased, even future one day , it will cause greenhouse gas supply shortage challenge to let the country's home greenhouse gas householder consumers who can not buy enough quantity of any kinds of greenhouse gas energy products to satisfy their electricity needs at home every day. Consequently, when future on day , the country greenhouse gas energy manufacturer has none any quantity of greenhouse energy products to supply to the country's greenhouse energy householders to use at home. The, they must only choose other kinds of new energy products to replace the traditional useful greenhouse gas energy products to be used at homes.

In conclusions, these non-controlled external environmental factors can impact and influence the country's every householder consumer individual attitude or consumption behavioral change to how any why the country's householders either choose to buy much or less quantity of greenhouse gas products to use at home.

The effect of house space occupancy and building characteristics on householder electricity energy use

In general, society believes large space size occupancy house building characteristics factor which will influence householder use more energy at home, e.g. in summer, when the householder is living at the large space size occupancy house, who ought turn on all air conditions or fans at sleeping rooms or eating room or studying room. So, if the householder's house has two to three or more sleeping rooms. Then, he / she needs to buy more air conditions or fans in order to let all rooms' temperature to be fallen down to let he /she feel more cool comfortable feeling when the temperature is above 30 degree or more extreme hot in summer weather. Otherwise, when the temperature is low, e.g. between 0 degree to 10 degree or below 0 degree in winter weather. When the householder is living in one large space size occupancy appartment, which has thee to five sleeping rooms , even more and two studying rooms and one eating room, even more as well as every room has one heater. Then, he / she must turn on all heaters to let who to feel warm feeling when he / she is staying in the house. It brings these interesting questions.

Will large or small size space occupancy housing characteristics influence any householder often turn on heater or air condition or fan in whole house space occupancy area in order to the householder feels warmer or cooler feeling when he /she is staying in the house?

Has any space occupancy housing characteristics relationship to influence any householder to turn on heater or air condition or fan in whole house space occupancy area in order to the householder feels warmer or cooler feeling when he /she is staying in the house? Does it bring positive relationship between turning on long time fan or air condition or heater and the house occupancy space characteristics is large or small size?

I shall attempt to give psychological evidences to explain the householder's house space occupancy area large or small size factor whether it can influence the householder choose to do long time or short time turning on heater or air condition or fan behavior in order to let he/she/the family to feel more cooler or warmer comfortable feeling when he/she/the family is staying in the house in summer or winter weather.

Does the house occupancy space size characteristics factor is the only one or important factor to influence the householder choose to turn on long or short time fan or air condition or heater in the house to let him/her/the family to feel more cooler or warmer comfortable feeling in summer or winter weather?

I feel that it is not exact right , due to the householder's house space occupancy size whether it is large or small characteristics to influence the householder choose to turn on long time or short time fan or air condition or heater time to let him /her/ the family to feel more cooler or warmer when he / she / the family is staying at home in summer or winter weather. The reason is because that the lifestyle of living quality need is different between developed countries and developing countries. The lifestyle of living quality factor will change the country's householder's expectation about the quality of living life. For example, for Africa, Korea, China , Japan, Hong Kong etc. developing countries. On the lifestyle of living quality need to these developing countries' householders aspect, that will cause a high environmental burden when they need to often turn on air conditions to satisfy more cooler feeling when they are staying at homes in summer or they need often to turn on heaters to satisfy more warmer feeling when they are staying at home in winter. Due to if their houses are large size space occupancy characteristics and they have more than at least two sleeping rooms and studying rooms and eating rooms and toilets number. Then, these householders who are developing countries' large space occupancy size characteristics houses, they won't like often turn on heaters long time to keep more warmer in their indoor whole space area in winter or they won't like often turn on air conditions or fans long time to keep more cooler in the their indoor whole space area house environment in summer .

The reason is possible because that the developing countries' householder chooses often to turn on their heaters or air conditions or fans long time in their houses when they are staying long time in their houses and their houses space occupancy sizes are very large, it will bring the electricity energy to be used more to these developing countries' householders' large space occupancy size characteristic houses. It means that the electricity fee will be also increased due to they often turn on heaters or air conditions or fans long time to keep their indoor temperature to be more cooler in summer or more warmer in winter. So, it seems that the developing countries' householders are living in the house whose space occupancy have very large size characteristics and more than two rooms house characteristics in the developing countries as above. Then, they won't often choose to turn on heaters or air conditions or fans long time to keep more cooler or warmer feeling in their house whole indoor space occupancy environment when they are often staying at home long time.

Their lifestyle of living comfortable feeling are lesser than the developed countries householders. Consequently, their lesser cooling or warming comfortable demand of living lifestyle factor will change their attitudes to use air conditions or fans or heaters turning on time in order to limit heaters or air conditions or fans turning on time to be shorter than the developed countries houeholders' heaters or air conditions or fans turning on time at homes. Due to the long time turnong on air conditions, fans , heaters at the developing countries' householders' homes, it will cause to spend much electricity energy to lead electricity fee charges to be raised to the developing countries' householders ' homes when they are often staying at homes in summer or winter weather. Hence, the house space occupancy large size characteristics ought not influence the developing countries householders choose to turn on air conditions , fans or heaters long time in order to let them to feel more cooler or warmer at homes in summer or winter weather.

So, the developing countries' house space occupancy large size characteristics householders won't be more acceptable to pay higher electricity energy fee when they are staying at homes at summer or winter weather. Due to they do not often choose to turn on heaters, air conditions or fans long time during they are staying at homes. Otherwise, the developed countries, e.g. UK, UK , France, Germany, Swiss, Singapore, Italy etc. countries. In general, these developed countries' householders' living lifestyle quality needs are higher than the developing countries. So, when the summer or winter weather is coming, if the temperature is extreme cold, e.g. below than 0 degree or it is extreme hot, e.g. higher than 30 degee.

Then these developed countries' householders will easy accept to turn on air conditions or fans or heaters long time at home in order to keep their appartment in door temperature to be more cooler in extreme hot in door environment or more warmer in extreme cold in door environment when these developed countries' householders are often staying at homes long time at night after their day time working time or schooling time. Because these developed counties' householders‘ quality of living lifestyle needs or demands are higher than the developing countries' householders. So, they won't consider that they will pay more electricity fee , due to they often turn on air conditions, fans or heaters long time to let them to feel more comfortable in cooler or warmer indoor large size space occupancy environment. So, it seems that the electricity energy efficiency will be raised to the developed countries‘ householders who are living in the house space occupancy large size characteristics and they will be possible to pay more electricity fees during they are often staying at home in extreme hot summer or extreme cold winter weather.

In conclusion, due to the living lifestyle quality need (demand) is different between the developed countries' householders and the developing countries‘ householders. It will influence the householders' long time or short time spending time on air conditions or fans or heaters indoor space occupancy size characteristics environment in order to achieve more cooler or more warmer feeling in their houses. Consequently, the long or short time of turning on air conditions, fans, heaters for the developed or developing countries householders‘ activities factor will be more influential to compare the house space occupancy large or small size characteristics factor to influence their cooler or warmer feeling in their houses. SO, the house indoor environment electricity energy consumption efficiency degree to the developing or developed countries' every householder house in summer or winter to the developing or developed householders in summer or winter weather , which is more influenced by the living lifestyle qualty factor to the either developed countries or developing countries householders. Hence, any developed or developing countries‘ electricity suppliers need to consider the building areas of property development market buyers their living style quality demands (needs) whether their living style quality demands are higher or lesser than the other building areas of property development market, they ought not consider whether the building locations of the houses' space occupation sizes whether they are large or small sizes in order to evaluate the householders will live at the building areas of property development locations ,whose electricty energy spending efficiency more accurate.

How to help low income houehold earners to reduce not essential electricity energy expenditure spending at homes

Has it relationship between the householder income and the electricity energy needs? How to evaluate the subsidies and social tariffs to assist lower income earners to analyze household energy consumption more accurate?

Electricity energy is essential needs for every householder at home, e.g. lighting, cooking power, healthcare, sanitation, cooler or warmer temperature indoor control at home. However, for lower income household earners, it its burden when they need often to use electricity energy to supply power to any home electricity tools to do any acticities at homes. If any these countries' lower income householder earner target can not get the reasonable subsidies to assist them to solve any electricity energy tools' electricity energy poer needs. Due to their lower income leve, it is possible that to knfluence them have enough electricity supply to help them to use to cook rice and food and vegatabe to eat, boil water to drink, turning on light tools to help them to read, watch TV, listen radio, music any entertainment or essential needs at homes at night or morning afternoon time. These lower income household earners will be easy to sick , due to they have no enough electricity supply to help them to use use electric bottles to boil water or cook food to eat. Then they only drink not boiled water or not cooked food to eat at homes in possible, due to they have no enough income to pay electricity fees every month.

Hence, how to evaluate the lower income household earners' electricity fee need (demand) level in order to provide the reasonable subsidies amount to assist every country's low income household earner to help them to pay the reasonable electricity fee which is one important issue to every country's government today. It brings this question: How to evaluate or analyze or predict every lower income household individual or family earner's every month electricity energy demand (need) more accurate?

It is one essential issue to be value to consider to every country's government. Moreover, to the estent that energy subsidies must be essential to be provided by public sources to all low income household earners or that a social tariff may be designed for improving access to energy for certain low income social earner groups. Hence, how to structure the energy subsidies between energy and income levels to be better target, such public mechanisms, and to avoid regressive subsidies unfairly. For example, India and China these both countries ' income poverty and energy poverty population are the large number. So , these both countries' governments need to focuse on more aggregated effects and analyze the effects of rural electrification at the local level on the decrease in energy poverty in rural low income poverty and energy poverty householders. Therefore, every country government needs to point regressivity of the subsidy for electricity. There is room to analyze to what extent low income household earners along the income distribution demand some forms of energy, and to suggest better and fair low income targeting household earners energy subsidies supply policies.

Each government does not only consider energy issues from a social point of view, it also needs have a manner to consider a possible link between energy, hunger reduction, and food security for each country's low income household earners group. So, every government has responsibility to calculate the determinants of different sources of energy consumption at the low income houehold earner level for urban and rural both populations in order to evaluate the electricity subsidies and to test whether every low income householder earner characteristics plays a role in determining energy consumption.

In general, in the use of energy measured as that for cooking, such as LPG reduces the exposure of households to hazardous, increases the consumption of different types of foods and medicines, improves the distribution of time between household memners, enables studys with more light, reduces the use of digital computer entertainment tools at home, and moderates the use of wood as fuel, preventing deforestation. These methods are the best suggestions to help low income householder earner groups to reduce time to use electricity at homes. When they spend less time to use electricity to do any not essential activities, e.g. watching television, playing electric games from home computers, listening music. They only use electricity to turn on light read, to turn on rice cooker to cook, when they feel hungey to eat. Then, I believe that these social low income household earner groups will reduce to pay much not essential electricity energy expenditure at homes. Hence, every country government ought need to persuade low income household earners to avoid to use electricity to do any not essential activities in order to raise electricity energy consumption in long term time.

It will bring less amount of energy subsidies expenditure benefits to every country's government. Hence, the success to persuade any countries' low income household earners to reduce to spend much time to do any electric entertainment activities of consumption behaviors at homes often. This is the most efficient and the most successful energy subsidiary method to help them to reduce electricity energy expenditure when they are staying at homes. Hence, if any country government expected the low income household earners can continue really reduce electricity energy expenditure, they need to learn to do the meaning essential activities which are needed to use electricity at home habitally. Then, they can change their electricity useful entertainment living habit, e.g. using computers to play games, listening music, watching television entertainment habits at homes to cause essential daily needs of electricity useful living habit, e.f. using cookers to cook rice or cook food to eat, turning on lights to read , turning on heaters to bath, turning on air conditions to keep cool temperature or turning on heaters to keep warm temperature at homes. Consequently, they won't need to pay much electricity expenditure at home, due to their waste useful electricity entetainment living habits have changed to do any essential useful electricity activities at homes.

Another kind of method to reduce the determinants of energy demand to the low income householder earners. The governments can persuade them to consider the variation factor can influence their electricity energy expenditure are increased or decreased at homes. It is not the electricity or gas price is increased from the electricity suppliers. It is that their bad living habits of waste electricity or gas to do any not essential activities at homes. e.g. the householder often turn on light tools to read or listen music or watch television in whole night, he/she ought need to sleep at night, but he/she does not go to bed to sleep in whole night. He/she chooses to turn on light to do these activities. Then, he/she will waste much electricity at whole night. Also, some householders like to bath more than half hour, even one hour, when it is winter, they need to turn on heaters to provide electricity to cause the bath room has warm water to provide to them to bath, Their long time bathing behaviors will be also waste electricity or gas energy from long time heating in bath rooms. So, they need to change their waste electricity consumption living behaviors at homes.

So, I suggest that some low income household earners will need to be taught to change their bad using electricity enery living habits from governments' public relation promotion in order to change the low income household earners' bad or incorrected useful electricity or gas living attitude to achieve and to avoid them often to do electricity or gas energy waste behaviors at homes. So, different countries' governments need to teach them how to do the correct or right electricty or gas useful activities (living habits) or let them know or feel how to use their electricity or gas which can help them to reduce to waste the not essential extra electricity or gas energy. Consequently, they must reduce electricity or gas expenditure as well as electricity or gas shortage challenge won't be caused by their

electricity or gas useful waste behaviors (activities) at homes.
In conclusion, energy subsidies method is not the best solution to help low income household earners to reduce to use electricity or gas energy. Because it is only short term benefit to reduce their electricity or gas expenditure at homes. The best solution is that to let them to know or feel why and how they have responsibilities to change their incorrent or wrong electricity or gas consumption bad habits in order to avoid global electricity or gas energy is waste to be used, even it is caused shortage from householders' energy waste behaviors.

Factors influence householder energy efficient consumption behaviors at homes

What factors can influence householders how to use energy in efficient way at homes. It depends on different countries householders' living habits to cause their choices to use energy efficiently at homes. In general, global householders energy every day consumption or use aims include cooking, heating, and cooling or warming rooms, lighting , water-boiled use and computer playing games entertainment etc. activities at homes every day. Some activities are often essential at homes, e.g. cooking, cooling or warming temperature in rooms, lighting , water-boiled use. So, their activities must not avoid to use energy at homes often. Otherwise, some activities are not essential at homes, e.g. playing entertainment games from computers, cooling rooms in summer, listening music, watching television etc. these activities. The householder can choose either to use energy to turn on these equipment tools or not to do these non essential activities at homes often. In general, householders rely on energy to make ourselves lives comfortable, productive and enjoyable. However, global householders need to learn how we can use energy resources wisely because global every householder has responsibility to manage resources includes: reducing total energy use and using energy more efficiently in order to avoid energy shortage crise occurrence. The choices are make about how we use energy, e.g. turning machines off when not in use of choosing to buy energy efficieny appliances will have increasing impacts on the quality of our environment and lives.

Energy conservation includes any behavior that results in the use of less energy. Energy efficiency involves the use of technology that requires less energy to perform the same function. For example, a compact fluorescent light buld that uses less energy to produce the same amount of light as an incandescent light buib is an example of energy efficiency. So, a householder's decision to place an incanadescent light bulb with compact fluorescent is an example of energy conservation. So, as individuals, every countries' householder choices and actions can result in a significant reduction in the amount of energy used in each sector of the economy.

So, I bring this interesting question: What factors can influence householder to choose to do any efficient energy consumption or useful behaviors at homes? I believe every countries' householders will have their different living attitudes and their living attitudes can influence their behaviors or activities to choose hoe to use energy at home. I shall indicate some countries' householders' living attitudes to explain the factors can influence them to use energy efficiency at homes as below:

Is the low income and rising price of modern fuels both factors best to influence Nigeria householders choose to use energy efficiently?

Firstly, for Nigeria householders energy consumption habit at homes example, it is richly with natural resources, modern energy resources which provide many householders with biomass (mostly firewood) and some other householders modern energy sources, such as kevosene, liquefied, petroleum, gas and electricity for their use. So, it is one country which can manufacture to provide energy for itself to use. It doesn't need to depend on other countries to import any kinds of energy to householders to buy to use at homes. But, it has social challenge, the poverty problem in Nigeria goes beyond low income, savings and growth rate, due to its low level of education, poor governamce, high level of unemployment factors influence.

It is important to know how Nigeria householders meet their basic energy needs between poverty and energy can bde described in terms of quality and quantity of energy used. Generally, most poor householders use biomass fuels because of affordability and they (householders) do not have energy equipment (such as, gas cookers, electric cookers etc.) . So, it seems Nigeria householders won't demand their living quality to be improved. It implies that they will use any kinds of energy efficiently at homes, e.g. gas, electricity, due to they find themselves in energy poverty. Although, this country has enough nature resources to manufacture energy to provide to householders to use, but due to many people are low income group, so they won't spend too much expenditure to buy much energy to use at homes. So, the rising prices of modern fuels, such as liquefied, petroleum , gas (LPG) and electricity and their erratic supply have made many householders revert to the use of traditional fuel, such as firewood and charcoal.

It brings this questions: Is the low income and rising price of modern fuels both factors best to influence Nigeria householders choose to use energy efficiently?

The hypothes is predicated on the economic theory of consumer behavior. However, when income increases, householders not only consume more of the same goods, they also need higher quality . So, it applies economic theory to householder's energy consumption behavior at home. It explains why low living standards induce greater dependence on firewood and other biomass fuels owing to a combination of income and substitution effects, such as Nigeria low income household energy home users case. it explains why Nigeria householders can accept to use firewood and charaval traditional energy to replace liquefied, petroleum , gas (LPG) and electricity modern energy . So, economic theory explains the Nigeria household energy users why they can accept to use traditional energy to replace modern energy and their energy useful or consumption behaviors are efficient at homes. Although, Nigeria has enough natural resource to manufacture modern energy to supply to householders to use at homes. But, due to these modern energy products prices are raised to the price level of householders who can not accept. it causes to Nigeria householders only choose to buy the cheap biomass, firewoods to replace high price of modern energy products to use at home often. So, they can accept their quality of living to be fallen down. So, expensive modern energy product price is one factor to influence some countries' householders to choose to buy cheap traditional poor quality of nature energy, e.g. firewood or biomass, to use at homes. Hence, they can raise energy efficiency to use when they choose to use traditional nature energy to replace modern nature energy at homes.

Does season factor influence New Zealand householders' energy consumption behaviors at homes

Secondly, for New Zealand householders energy consumption habits at homes , for example, their living quality needs are general comfortable need feeling. Their countries' houses of space heating was found to average 34% of total housholder energy use. The relation to space heating includes low indirect temperature are associated with persistent under-heating , whether some space heating sources tend to be higher or lower in winter indoor temperature than others and winter indoor temperatures are compared to international benchmarks and established healthy temperature ranges. So, New Zealand occupant's perceptions of winter indoor temperature conditions are presented and explored in relation to heating patterns and household energy consumption. So, it seems that NZ winter temperature is low. Moreover, it will influence householders need to turn on heaters to keep more warmer feeling indoor. Then, they will use more electricity energy. In special, if the householders' houses spaces are large sizes . Hence, their heaters need long time to keep whole houses' areas or spaces or rooms temperature to be rised up in order to let they do not feel very cold in winter. So, NZ's winter extreme cold weather will influence householders‘ energy use or consumption to be increased in winter.

The electricity efficiency to every NZ householder is very high in winter to compare spring, summer, autumn seasons. Hence, if NZ electricity suppliers expected to forecast electricity consumption more accurate in NZ. In order to ease the life for both electric net designers and electricity suppliers, it was decided to find out, how the NZ weather conditions and every householder's house space size factors to influence the power consumption to NZ householders. If there is a clear trend observed , then this relation can be used for power consumption forecasts to NZ householders.

Why does NZ weather condition factor and householder's house space size factor can predict householders' electricity consumption at homes. Due to geographic location on the global the lowest south sets specific conditions for weather, such as NZ's south island geographic location is near to south ocean in our earth. It is a country where average annual temperatures are well between 10 degree to below 10 degree at NZ south island special geographic location to near to the sourth ocean in our earth at the same time.

However, large part of mankind is living in the conditions where there are four different seasons in NZ geographic location, dark winter, which is cold and snowy, spring with rising temperature and high precipitation, sunny , dry and rather hot summer, and windy and wet autumn. These conditions lead to different patterns in electric appliances use in NZ householders, in special, in NZ south island householders. If trends in electric energy use have substantial correlation with weather conditions, this can help NZ electric energy suppliers and producers to forecast electricity consumption and thus organize and manage production of electric energy.

Consequently, it will lead to much more stability in energy supply to NZ every householder. For example, when the NZ energy supplier gathers data concerns every householder's house space size data, e.g. the house has how many sleeping rooms, toilets, bath rooms, eating rooms and reading rooms number, even the house has how many family members are living in every NZ geographical location. Then if it can follow different location of NZ houses spaces sizes whether they are large or small space size as well as whethe every house has how many family members are living to evaluate whether how much electricity efficiency can satisfy their comfortable living needs in winter. Then, it can evaluate whether they will use how much electricity efficiency for their needs in different seasons. If in winter, many householders are living in the large space size house in the geographic location. Then, it is possible that the geographic location is householders will use much electricity efficiency and where geographic location hosueholders who will be possible to pay the most highest electricity fee to compare the other geographic location of small space size of house householders. Hence, weather factor is the most influential to change NZ householders ' electricity energy consumption behaviors at homes.

Urbanization level and income per capita both tangible factors as well as temperature (weather variation factor) will have close relationship to influence China householder energy consumption or useful needs at home every day

For China householder energy consumption habit example, what factors can determine to impact this country's householders energy useful behavior at homes? Can the impacts of these factors be quntified? What are China householder energy consumption trends and characteristics? I shall explan as below:

I believe the influential factors include these three aspects to China householder energy users: Income per capita, urbanization level an annual average temperature (weather). These factors will influence any China householder energy useful or consumption behavior at homes.

Temperature (weather variation factor) is intangible from eastern region to western region of Chin, variances largely depend upon economic level and the provincial level. So, some regions were warmer and cooler temperature will influence the regional China householder how to use electricity. In addition, th influence of urbanization level varies according to income level as well as the urbanization level has more significant impact on the structure and efficiency of China householder energy consumption thatn on its quantity. So, the urbanization level and income per capita both tangible factors will have close relationship to influence China householder energy consumption or useful needs at home every day. Moreover, these two tangible factors (urbanization level and income per capita both factors) have the more influential to impact China any one of household family energy consumption or useful habit to compare temperature factor at home. Because temperature can only influence than to choose to turn on heaters to keep more cooler in summer or turn on air conditions (fans) to keep more warmer in winter.

The electricity energy needs for these equopment tools which will be influenced less. Otherwise, the urbanization level and income per family householder how to choose to spend more or less electricity or gas etc. energy at homes. Because in behavioral economy view point, when individual householder has more income and the urban in the China geographic location is lising many high income and high household families memebrs to every house. Then, the urbanization household energy household enery useful or consumption level will be raised. Such as China household electricity users case, e.g. large cities have many high income and many houses have more than four families members to live on one house together. Then, the electricity or gas energy efficiency will be influenced to rise. The city urbanization and per capita income level is high to these large cities have high to income population, who are living in these cities in China.

Moreover, the impact of lifestyle on energy use mainly reflects types and purposes of fuels are chosen by different China households factor which will influence the urbanization level of energy choice use. China is a country with typical binary economics and social diversity and these is significant difference in the consumption pattern between urban and rural regions. Urban residents consume high-quality energy, such as electricity, natural gas , heating power, solar energy and gasoline. For rural residents, usually use coal, and bismass energy because they are cheaper price energy products which requires much time and labor and are heavy indoor pollutants . The difference in energy consumption pattern between urban and rural China residents is closely related related to living of quality needs, building structure, e.g. steel or stone etc. different materials, manufacture, easily access clean and effective feels through the electric grid, natural gas network and district heating systems.

Therefore, it explains why urbanization level is as an integrated variable reflecting social progress situation to influence urban and rural regions, such as large cities , small cities and rural countryside regions' household energy consumption or useful behaviors which have differnet kinds of fuel useful demands and energy efficiencies qualify and quantity demand, or needs at homes. Consequently, it explains, urbanization level and income per captia level both factors are more influential to China household energy consumption at home to compare temperature (weather , seasonal) factor.

Employment rates or gross domestic product macro economic variation factor, residential space size factor, and the government's implementation of energy labeling schemes provide significant impacts on Taiwan residential electricity consumption .

For Taiwan householder electricity consumption characteristics in the residential sector, which has different factors and pattern to compare China householder electricity householder electricity consumption habit at home. Although, they are the same Asia country. I shall explain these reasons as below:

For Taiwan electricity householder factors influence their energy useful or consumption behaviors at homes. The main factors can influence their electricity energy useful patterns include: employment rates or gross domestic product macro economic variation factor, residential space size factor, and the government's implementation of energy labeling schemes provide significant impacts on Taiwan residential electricity consumption . However, the impacts of electricity raising price and the energy supply reducing shortage efficiency standards do not significant to influence the Taiwan residential electricity consumption behavior at sources.

It means that it won't influence Taiwan householders to use electricity or gas or any kinds of energy number to be reduced, even the Taiwan government energy suppliers sudden raise, any kinds of energy price and reduce to supply energy to satisfy Taiwan householders daily essential needs at homes.

In fact, Taiwan had improved gross domestic product (GDP) and it had raised employment rates recently. So, many Taiwanese has jobs to work, due to Taiwan economy had improved to be better. So, growth had also raised. The economy improvement causes many Taiwanese had enough jobs to work, due to new businesses are set up. Many consumers excit any kinds of businesses are invested to Taiwan from overseas or local investors. So, consumption is grown, the electricity consuming applicances are selected, as the household consumer focus grousp number if also influenced to be increased. So, Taiwan economy had improved to be better, it will encourage many electricity consuming applicances products are encouraged to excited to be selected to seel in Taiwan. Due to many different kinds of electricity consuming appliances are supplied to attract Taiwanese to choose to buy to bring to their homes for cooking, boiling water, or keeping rooms to be cooler or warmer temperature confortable feeling intention in winter or summer seasons. So, these electricity consuming appliances, e.g. rice cookers, heaters, air conditions, fans, bathing gas heaters etc. different home electricity consuming appliances will be increased to supply to satisfy Taiwan householders' needs. When they decide to buy any news electricity consuming applicances to bring to homes to use.

Environment scientists' education message how to influence Greece householders home energy consumption behaviors from primary energy to change secondary energy

Finally , I shall indicate Greece, this western which will influence this country's householders have desires to do household energy conservation patterns or conservation energy consumption behaviors or energy conservation activities at homes. I shall explain the social economic variable, such as consumers' income and family size variation factor which can influence the different Greece family household members differences towards energy conservation preferences. IN addition, the variable, such as environmental information feedback and consciousness of energy problems are characteristics of the energy saver consumer.

Why and how can environmental pollution , environmental protection, energy conservation information message can influence Greece householders to choose to do energy use consumption conservation or less energy useful behaviors at homes. It is one interesting energy efficient use behaviors , due to Greece householders are influenced by energy conservation or environmental protection message.

In fact, scientists agree overconsumption of natural resources is a major threat to oue lives in earth. Environmental problems like greenhouse effect, ozone layer depletion, and acid rain effect are not any more problems of a specific region or environmental problem. Also, economic theory is indicated that in order to gain comfort and time households are becoming excessive energy users, neglecting the environmental impact of their choices.

Environment scientists bring these environment pollution message to influence Greeks (Greece householders) to change their energy consumption behaviors at homes. The environment scientists' message indicate that we are facing global warmth and natural resource and energy shortage challenges. Due to our Earth have limited natural resource numbers to supply to us to manufacture energy, but global population has been increasing every year. Thus, it is possible that we have energy shortage crisis. Also, manufactures are spending too much energy to waste to manufacture any products, the energy will cause air or water pollution in manufacturing process or drivers are driving their vehicles to pollute air on the roads.

Hence, environment scientists‘ message influence Greece householders began to consider these questions concern to reduce fossil fuel energy. Why do we need to Safety in using fuel and handle gas leaks? Why do we feel town gas smell? How is electricity located at electric station far away from town area? How to solve problems caused by the use of fossil fuels? How to reduce the use of fossil fuels?

Greece householders consider to solve the problems, the best way is to reduce thir used of fossil fuel. This helps prevent fossil fuels form being used up too quickly. Also, it helps them to reduce environmental problems because fewer pollutants are given out when less fossil fuels are used. Can human help to reduce the use of fossil fuels? Fossil fuels are mainly in power station. Although they use some fossil fuels for our gas cooker and car, it won't make much difference if I use less. Fossil fuel is not used renew primary energy. Most of energy Greece householders use come from fossil fuels, for example, the electricity we use is generated in power stations by burning fossil fuels. The buses they ride use diesel oil. Therefore, they can help reduce the use of fossil fuels by saving energy in Greece daily lives.

The actions that Greece householders can take such as: setting the air-conditioner to a higher temperature, walking instead of using lift, taking a short shower instead of a bath. This reduces the use of the hot water and thus the energy needed to heat the water. Thus, many people can help a lot to reduce our use of fossil fuels to avoid fossil fuel shortage risk occurrence.

Greeks (Greece householders) had been beginning to conern that they will face energy shortage challenge if they can not adopt more energy conservation actions. Because the Greece government began to bring negative environmental pollution and energy shortage challenge message if they often waste to use any kinds of energy, e.g. electricity , gas excessive number efficiency at homes. Then, they will be possible to fac energy shortage and environmental pollution challenge to their country in future one day. So, this energy shortage and environment pollution message has bring predictive negative worries to influence many Greece householder energy home users choose to reduce to avoid the waste of any kinds of energy use at homes.

So, their reducing energy use actions that had encouraged them to cause habits to avoid to waste excess energy to do any non essential electric appliances useful or consumption activities at homes often. Moreover, the environment protection and energy conservation message has changed many Greece householder to make decision and activities to change their lifestyle to b low living quality from high living quality. So, the environment protection and energy conservation message factor has much influential to change Greece household energy users' daily energy conservation or less energy use consumption activities at homes.

Greeks feel greenhouse energy can be environmental protection enegy. A greenhouse can trap heat in the sunlight and keeps the air inside the greenhouse warm enough for plants to grow. The glass roof and walls of a greenhouse let in sunlight but prevent heat from escape, this makes the greenhouse warm inside. Similarly, some gases in the Earth's atmosphere can trap heat from the sun and keep the Earth warm. This is called the greenhouse effect. The gases energy that can trap heat from the sun are called greenhouse gases. It is future one kind of potential primary energy to reduce environmental pollution new energy products for human consuming. So, environmental protection message influence them to consume greenhouse enegy at homes.

So, environment scientists' environment pollution message had influence Greece householders concern to apply seconday energy (environment protection) to replace electricity energy to use at home. They will change energy to use at home. The scientists' messages have more influential Greece householders energy change consumption behaviors at homes. The messages are as below:

There are different forms of energy, e.g. light, heat, sound, wind, water, electrical kinetic, chemical and potential energy. Some form energy is primary energy and it can not renew to use, e.g. light, sound, wind, water, fossil fuel etc. Some form energy is secondary energy and it can renew to use in possible, e.g. nuclear, electric charge battery etc. Why does human need to concern how to manufacture secondary energy? Because it is possible that our natural resource will be consumed all, thus we will face primary energy shortage risk. If human can invent any new form of man-made secondary energy to renew to use in order to avoid primary energy shortage to supply to use to use, then human won't only depend on our Earth natural resource energy supply numbers. We can invent any new secondary energy to renew to use again either replaces primary energy or instead of primary energy limit number supply.

What is energy change? For television energy change power case. Firstly, electrical energy changes to television power to be used by television itself, then it changes to light power, next it changes to light power. How to choose fuel form to use? Due to energy can change to different form of powers to supply different form of power advantages to supply to human to use, so it is possible that we can also invent any secondary man made renew used energy to change different form powers to supply us to use, e.g. nuclear energy changes to light or sound or heat form of powers ; electrical charge batteries changes to light or sound or heat form powers to satisfy our daily life needs.

The environment scientists' energy consumption education influence Greece householders concern how to change to use secondary energy to replace primary energy at homes as below:

For primary natural resource fuel energy example, different fuel has different feature, e.g. easy to burn, safe to use, gives out a lot of energy, inexpensive, produces little air pollution, easy to transport and store. How can we use in different channels, such as heating food, hot pat, driving vehicles.

For example, although coal is not expensive to cause electricity energy for past transportation tool, e.g. traditional coal energy train or our daily home cooking, but it has negative influence to environment air pollution. Hence, we ought to follow the primary natural resource energy's feature to decide how to apply what aspects of our life needs.

For example, if the country's people hope to reduce pollution when who use any kind of energy, e.g. US , Europe energy markets. The energy entrepreneur ought concentrate on manufacturing the kind of energy which can reduce environment pollution to be the least level to supply the country people to use, e.g. electric charge battery supplies to these countries' drivers to drive their vehicles on the roads, wind energy or water energy to manufacture electricity power supply to reduce air or water pollution ; or if the country people hope to buy the inexpensive energy to use, even the energy's quality and performance is worse, e.g. China, India, Hong Kong markets. The energy entrepreneur ought concentrate on manufacturing the lowest cost and enough supply of natural resource to manufacture the kind of energy to sell cheap price to these countries to use, e.g. China, Africa can accept to use e.g. gas, coal, fuel energy to use to compare developed countries people, e.g. UK, US; or if the countries people who hope to use energy which can easy to transport and store, e.g. light coal. The energy entrepreneur can choose to concentrate on manufacturing much coal to supply to the countries people to use, e.g. China, Arica Thus, to choose to manufacture which kinds of energy supply to the countries market people to use, the energy entrepreneur how decides to manufacture which kind of energy, it depends on which kinds of fuel advantages of the countries people most concerning.

What is energy meaning? It is defined a dynamic quality, it is a fundamental entity of nature that is transferred between parts of a system in the production of physical change within the system, and it is usually regarded as the capacity for doing work, and it is usable power (such as heat or electricity) or the resources for producing such power.

Why does secondary energy own investment worth? Because the different forms of primary natural resource energy will have supply shortage crisis, such as natural resources coal, gas, solar, wind, water, geothermal, biomass(organic material) etc. However, human can attempt to explore any undiscovered Earth or Space resource to manufacture any kinds of secondary energies, e.g. nuclear energy, electric recharge battery energy to supply to electric vehicle or space robots transportation tools to use or satisfy our daily life needs in future one day. So any kind of undiscovered secondary man-made renewed used energy resources have potential commercial worth to any energy entrepreneurs, it is possible that they can replace traditional primary energy to supply to human to use for our different aspects of life needs. In the future, the secondary energy demand will increase, when primary energy supply number has decreased form natural exploration. So, it will cause the effect of any demand of secondary energy product to be raised and prices to be increased in possible. Due to global population has been growing up, considerably China and India both countries populations have been increasing rapidly. Scientists predict there are more than 1.2 billion people worldwide will lack access to electricity, and more than 2.5 billion still use wood, charcoal to cook and heat in the future when primary energy has no enough number to supply to us to use. Hence, the fact that demand is this much greater than supply to make energy a prime market for further growth.

Although, secondary energy will have much investment worth, but energy like all other investments will carry risks. The internal and external risk factors include such as: policy is always changing to prohibit which do energy trading more easily between the energy exporting and importing countries, the secondary energy manufacturer itself own abilities to invent and to manufacture any kinds of secondary energy, improved technology can quickly make an technology obsolete, geopolitical rifts can happen overnight, the country's energy consumer (user)'s preferable choice to use which either kinds of secondary energy or secondary energy. So, it seems that (man-made) renewed used secondary energy industry can provide above-average returns, but it can also bring high risk commercial investment.

Traditionally, energy supply companies will apply those methods to operate energy providing businesses. For Shell,. Exxon examples, which had own gas stations, explore and drill for gas on their own. Other companies specialize in a part of the energy market, e.g. leasing oil rigs for example, or operating a pipeline. Energy supplying companies can choose to manufacture any kinds of energy to supply, e.g. trade oil, gas, coal, uranium, electricity etc. Any energy price and supply is demanded on the countries energy users' which kinds of energy most choice need or certain energy commodities to be chose to use popularly. For example, if US most people prefer to use secondary man-made renew used energy more than primary energy. Then, US energy manufacturers ought concentrate on manufacturing much different kinds of secondary man-made renew used energy to prepare to supply to its domestic US market in order to raise secondary energy price to sell in its country. So, the energy manufacturer's energy manufacturing choice, it is depend on which the country's people prefer to use which kinds of energy for their daily life needs.

However, scientists predict secondary energy market will have large market share, due to primary energy will have shortage to explore to supply in our earth and future energy consumers(users) prefer to choose to use more efficiency, less energy consumption, none environment pollution cause, cost effectiveness, renew to use of any kinds of energy. For example, the electricity recharge battery secondary man-made renew used energy is one kind of reducing air pollution power to push any electric battery vehicles to be driven to compare gas energy during drivers are driving their cars on the roads. They can reduce noise and air pollution and drivers can drive safely, who only need to buy one electric recharge battery to recharge in any electric recharge battery stations on streets when the electric recharge battery has no enough power to push their cars and they need to recharge their electric recharge battery drive when they had driven between one to two days. Due to primary energy, e.g. fuel , gas, the kinds of primary energies will have shortage to supply to global drivers to drive their traditional cars.

Thus, the electric recharge battery or any undiscovered secondary energy will be future driving market needs. So, man-made renew used secondary energy, e.g. biofuel, hydro-electric, nuclear, will be one kind of efficient, clean, less pollution cause, cost-effective of energy to supply to our global vehicle market, even any other undiscovered new markets. Supposing they are popular to be used for electric vehicle market globally in future one day, then their prices will be decreased and constructed to average car requires up to 1,700 gallons of oil. Also supposing that making average computer requires more than ten times or weight to fossil fuels, every calories of food eaten in the US requires roughly then calories of fossil fuels. Hence, cheap energy will be one successful factor to influence future potential energy consumer (user) individual choice needs. Conversely, ion good economic times, people are more willing to travel, to buy products, and all of which success demand and low process for energy.

In the future, secondary energy will be the best choice to food production market. The modern food production system is essentially a success of changing fossil fuels into food. So, raising energy prices are almost higher food costs and even shortage for fossil fuels energy. If one day, one kind of discovered secondary man-made renew used energy can supply to any restaurants or homes to be used to cook at the cheap price, then the profit is very high for this kind of food production energy. Thus, future food production secondary energy consumption market is large and because the primary energy inputs for agriculture are higher than the energy outputs of the food. However, future secondary man-made renew used energy for food production system is only one part of whole energy consumer in food industry. The food production is related to whole food consumption market which includes: household cooking energy market, agriculture or vegetable, rice, fruit etc. foods farming machines energy market, food manufacturing factories market, food machine package market, transportation food delivery market, supermarket or fruit/ food sale stores market. They must need any energy inputs to achieve the food production or food transportation or warehouse / stores electricity supply or cooking energy needs. Hence, these food suppliers relate to any whole food factory manufacturers, food retailers, food wholesalers, farmers and home/restaurant cookers, all of them must need to use energy to carry on their food producing or food cooking or food transportation activities every day in overall food industry. Thus, it seems that undiscovered any second energy demand will be increased, when the primary energy supply number is decreasing. Also, when people can accept to use secondary energy to replace primary energy to be used for any cooking, transporting food, manufacturing food, food retail stores or warehouse food delivery energy need activities. Then, the secondary energy price will be fall down to attract many food energy consumers.

Nowadays, the food industry energy may includes primary nature resource gas energy or electricity energy for house house families or restaurants cooking needs, food delivering lorry drivers driving needs usually. If future second man made renew used energy is invented successful popular to be used, e.g. hydrogen, electric recharged battery energy for electric vehicles or restaurant/home families cooking needs or food factories machine maufacturing energy needs. Then, the seconday energy will have possible to replace primary energy to be food industry energy market.

Wiley, composition services graphics indicated that global primary energy consumption had been increasing 30 billion tons from 1830 year to 510 billion tons in 2010 year as well as global population size had been increasing from 70 billion 1830 yeat to 510 billion in 2010 year. Thus, it seems that global primary energy consumption will be needed largely after 2010 year. If future global nature resource primary energy is explored full number and it had not enough energy number to supply global human to use. Then, it will being many people feel uncomfortable and inconvenient,e.g. Some countries won't have enough energy to supply transportion tools to be driven, some homes and restaurants won't have enough energy to supply to cook to eat or to provide restaurant clients to eat etc. daily activies, due to human's much activities which are needs energy supply. Thus, it seems that global primary energy comsumption will be needed largely after 2010 year.

Wiley, composition services graphics also explianed that why the primary energy consumption demand can be needed to achieve the same level to the global population size increasing in 2010 year. The graph showed these reasons why cause the same level of global population size and global primary energy consumpion demand which may include: The graph showed that after a nation is developed, its per-person energy use hegins to level off. In North Ameruca and Europe, where energy demand has remained flat, or fallen dightly, in each of the past few years. But the 1.3 billion people on those two continents are far outweighted by the 5 billion people in Asia and Africa, e.g. Chinese and Indian. who currently have more energy need to comapre average per man to North America and Europe per man, ensuring that overall energy demand will rise for years to come.

Wiley, composition services graphics also predicted that the growth in primary energy demand. China will have 4,500 million tons in 2035 year. India will have 3,000 million tons in 2035 year. Other developing Asia will have 2,000 million tons in 2035 year. Russia will have 1,500 million tons in 2035, Middle East will have 1,300 million tons in 2035, other rest of world will have 1,000 million tons in 2035. Hence, it implied that China will be the largest primary energy need country in the future.

China will be future the primary potential energy consumer market. The primary energy includes water, coal, wind, fossil oil, gas ,solar, geothermal energy, biomass (organiz material) etc. different natural resource primary energy. Otherwise, US, UK, Europe will be secondary energy potential need market. For example, electrical recharge battery energy will be raised demand to supply to any future new design electrical charge battery vehicles in US, Europe, UK markets.

Due to US, Europe, UK people concern environment protection, so they will invent many electric charge battery vehicles to consume electrical charge battery to replace polluted gas energy to avoid air pollution when the drivers are driving cars on themselve countries' roads. For example, second man-made renew used nuclear energy can be applied to rockets to pusch them to leave our earth to fly to other space far away and consuming nuclear energy will be cost efficient, and nuclear energy saving will be more when nuclear to spend long time to be used in any long time space journey. Hence, nuclear energy and electric charge battery secondary energy will be popular to be applied to vehicles and rockets energy needs in US, Europe, potential marketss, even our daily energy needs in global second energy market.

Who are your energy business's competitors (peers)? How do they compare? How have your energy business company performed cyclically? How to choose to manufacture to sell which kinds of primary or secondary energy product(s), either manufactures only primary energy product(s) or manufactures only secondary energy products or both? Which countries do you plan to sell your energy product?

Illustration by Wilsey, composition services graphiss showed that these natural resources to energy product the world's electricity percentage, such as below:

41% of coal, 5% of oil, 21% of gas, 13% of nuclear, 16% of Hydro, 3% other renewable secondary man-made energy.

Hence, coal will be future the major natural resource to produce electricity. The energy entrepreneur ought attempt to explore any coal resources, when who choose to supply electricity power to consumers for future energy consumption country markets.

Wiley, composition services also predicted that the expectation is that North America coal will supply the expectation is that North America coal will supply Asian demand, Us export terminals have a total capacity of 173 million tommes output. China will drive 16% of the nations total output. China will drive the sea-born demand for coal over for the forcessable future. Chinese energy consumption will grow more than 12 % between 1980 and 2009 years. Though, China heads global demand, India is growing faster in terms of coal imports. Much of the global coal demand will be supplied by Indonesia and Australia. Colombia, Russia, South Africa and Mongolia are also players in global export coal energy resources.

Hence, environment scientists‘ education messages influence Greece householders believe that secondary energy will be one kind of new energy product to replace traditional primary energy product for human energy consumption market global needs. Hence, it is right time any energy entrepreneur needs to research how to explore any undiscovered man-made renew used secondary energy products to avoid primary energy shortage crisis occurrence. Greece householders will be the highest population number to choose secondary energy to replace primary energy to use at homes. it means that environment scientists had changed Greece householders' energy consumption behaviors at homes.

In conclusion, different countries will have different factors influence how the country's householders energy consumption behavioral changes. Hence, it seems that any country's householders‘ energy use of consumption behaviors will be possible influenced by extermal environment factors influence. Also, every country's energy providers can attempt to find whether the country has what kinds of unique factors to influence its householders' energy consumption efficiency to increase or decrease in order to find the methods to solve the energy efficiency demand reducing challenges successfully.

How artificial intelligence impacts energy consumers using behaviours

Nowadays, many countries began to educate citizens who have responsibilities to use energy at homes or offices or public places or any indoor environments in avoiding to do energy wastage behaviours or misuse energy wastge attitudes as well as teaching them have responsibilities to protect their earth's natural environment to reduce air, water pollution in order to void rising temperature to bring globl warm challenge to influence our quality of life to be poor, even facing death threat, due to our natural environment is damaged and polluted by our energy wastage behaviours.

In fact, I feel the energy wastage eduction is not one efficient or effective method to persuade every energy consumers, such as householders, office workers, factories workers, any entertainment places workers or enjoyers, such as cinema service staffs, shopping center staffs etc. entertainment places to reduce to use any electricity for light or any entertainment aims to consider themselves working environment or entertainment environment to satisfy, e.g. cinema movie to satisfy customers' needs. For example, private vehicle drivers, public transportation tool drivers, householder energy users, businessmen energy users who still only consider themselves passengers comfortable aims, e.g. spending much electricity often to turn on light in buses, taxi, cars, trams, trains, underground trains in morning or afternoon time. So, these public transportation tools are popular to waste electricity because they expect their passengers to feel comfortable in summer , so they will often turn on air conditioners to keep colder in summer or turn on warmers to keep warmer in winnter all the transportation working hours. So, these drivers are doing energy wastage behaviours. Moreover, these private car drivers only expect to feel comfortable , so they will open air conditioners to keep colder in summer when they are driving cars, even they are stopping cars on the road. So, they are also waste energy.

Hence, they will be negligent to consider how to use energy in efficient attitudes or energy saving behaviors in order to avoid energy shortage challenge occurrence. However, since (AI) technology began be popular to be accepted to use by human. (AI) scientists began to carry on researching how to apply (AI) technologies, e.g. big data gathering , robotics to assist human to adapt or learn to use any kinds of energy in efficient and no wastage attitudes or using behaviours habitually.

I shall explain how to apply (AI) technology to assist human to adapt to use energy in order to avoid to do energy wastage behaviours easily to every energy users as below:

In consumer psychological view point, the behaviours of individuals can have a standard rational choice model, in which people, such as energy users objectively weigh up the costs and benefits of investing time and money into " greening" their homes or offices or any working places or entertainment places or transportation tools being more energy efficiently. So, the social, cognitive and behavioural factors are important in explaining why many energy users, such as householders, vehicles owners or public transportation tool drivers, office workers, businessmen who are neglient to avoid to spend much excessive energy to drive their vehicles on the roads , to turn on lights in offices or any working environment or entertainment places or at homes all days. When they feel that they need more enjoyment, raising productivity, raising service performance to satisfy customers' needs. So, when they weigh economic benefits and cost. They will choose to use more energy to achieve their profit growth or customer number growth or improving quality of life intentions.

Hence, it also explain why education method is not effective to achieve energy saving aim for every energy users, e.g. it has no reward to compensate to their losses, when they choose to reduce energy consumption to cause that they have economic losses. So, it seems any country's government or schools energy saving education method which won't achieve the best energy saving consequency nowadays.

Why does (AI) influence energy users to reduce and use more energy in order to achieve their energy -saving habitual impact easily than education method? I shall explain as below:

(AI) technology can be one auto-manual tool to help householders to protect their homes to be more green environment and be more energy efficient. For example, householders can install (AI) auto-energy efficient measurement tool to record whether they will spend how much money for energy . e.g. electricity , gas consumption at home every day. So, they can know whether they will pay how much money for electricity or gas fee. (AI) auto-energy efficient measurement tool can also change householders' energy consumption behaviours to save more electricity or gas when they discover that the day' electricity or gas using number is excessive to cause they will be pay more extra electricity or gas expenditure on the day. Then, they will find whether why or how or what reasons cause them to spend excessive electricity or gas energy at homes, then they will change their energy wastage behaviours to save energy more easily. So, their energy -saving behaviours are influenced by the (AI) auto-energy efficient measurement tool's daily electricity or gas using record at homes.

So, (AI) auto energy efficient measurement tool can help householders to save energy and money when they need to use electricity or gas energy at homes. But making the kind of improvements that have these effects is not always simple, they usually require some planning, time to prepare to adapt how to do avoiding energy wastage behaviours at home habitually . So, (AI) auto-energy efficient measurement tools can focuse on what householders might be able to do and further encourage the uptake of energy efficiently measures as well as it might be able to motivates householders to act through restructuring existing incentives and using collective rewards.

When, they discover that the (AI) auto energy efficient measurement tool shows either electricity energy or gas energy or both using energy number is excessive too much to compare the normal energy using number on the day suddenly. Then , they will attempt to find what reasons influence their energy spending number is excessive on the day, in order to change their energy using behaviours or habits and they will be more acceptable to adapt to do energy saving behaviours because they can earn energy expenditure saving rewrd and money saving reward in order to avoid further the excessive energy using number to be increased to pay more electricity or gas energy expenditure , due to they often do unnecessary energy using habitual behaviours at homes.

Hence, (AI) auto-efficient energy measurement tool will have much effort to persuade householders to choose to do energy saving behaviours habitually at homes, due to it can provide the more acceptable number concerns their daily electricity and gas energy using record at homes to let them to know how and why their energy expenditure changes to spend more suddenly in order to let they can understand the reasons why and how cause their needs to pay extra excessive energy expenditure at homes.

The main important reward is that the householders can be encouraged to measure their energy using number and find the reasons why and how their energy using behaviours cause their extra excessive energy using number on the day. Then, they can find what the factors are to cause their electricity or gas energy using number to be increased suddenly on the day and change their energy using behviours to avoid the energy using number to be continus increased in order to avoid to pay extra excessive electricity or gas fees on the month immedicately.

6.1 How to apply (AI) technology to improve energy efficiency and better climate change and the security of energy supply as well a resource efficiency?

Increasing energy efficiency involves using a reduced quantity of energy to achieve the same or improved product, process or sevice. It is generally measured in a physical unit as the ratio between energy output and energy input. Similarly, resource efficiency refers to the ability to use a reduced quantity or volume of resources to produce the same or an improved service or product and it is measured as the ratio betweenn useful material output and material input, both measured in physical terms (Dahlstrom and Ekins, 2005).

Hence, if it was only (AI) technology can increase energy efficiency or reduce resource effifiency to improve service performance. Then, it will reduce energy wastage. So, it bring this question: How to apply (AI) tool to reduce resource consumptin indentified by analysis of historical resource efficiency?

It presents an historial analysis that seems have relationship between energy and resource efficiency improvements and resource consumption across a number of different sectors of activity, including iron, and steel production, electricity generation from coal, oil and natural gas and motor vehicle travel.

So, future(AI) technology needs to fight social and behavioural barriers to energy efficiency in the housing sector. If future (AI) technology can improve energy efficiency for home renovations and it can consider the social factors. It is a qualitative investigation technology of the decision making process guiding to teach householders hoe to use overall energy was reduced by the householders‘ house renovation. It will also bring another question: How can (AI) technology can help householders to do decision making to reduce overall energy consumption by householders' houses renovation, such as reducing energy using when the householder needs to renovate whose house's design, e.g. extensions and additional bedrooms or bathrooms . So, future (AI) technology can be needed to help low income householders to increae energy efficiency and reduce energy consumption when their homes need to renovate whose houses‘ design ,e.g. extensions and additinal bedrooms or bathrooms or bookrooms or children toy rooms at hoomes.

Due to low income householders were concerned about energy consumption for environment and economic reasons, upfront costs rather than life-cycle costs were considered more important when the low income householders need to renovate to extend extra bedrooms, bathrooms, studyrooms to buy extra electronic appliances to install them in these rooms to use. Then, they will be concerned energy awareness how will be more consume when the low income householders choose to renovate their homes design to extend more rooms to feel more comfortable, or large size, but they also need to consume or use more electrciity or gas energy for extra electronic appliances in these rooms possible as the same time.

Hence, future (AI) technology needs to assist these low income householders how to reduce or avoid to ue extra more energy, when they renovate their homes' designs to cause to need to buy extra more electric appliances to use more electricity or gas energy at homes. Moreover, future (AI) technology ought have effort to help any countries' buildings to be efficient energy saving buildings to be efficient energy saving buildings to help householders to use less energy to live in their builsing efficiently. When the country's overall buildings can use energy efficiently , it won't only bring energy saving benefits, even it can bring the country's economic cost to be reduced , due to any building' energy efficient using high technological method. So, future (AI) energy saving technology will concentrate on how to help any buildings to use energy efficiently , in order to achieve energy -saving efficient buildings to let the householders and office energy users to either live or work in energy -saving efficient buildings to avoid energy wastage aim.

Hence, future (AI) energy -saving technology needs to focus on how changing energy users' energy wastage behaviours to energy -saving behaviours. How to apply (AI) energy-saving technology to assist energy users change their behaviours to spend unnecessary excessive energy to use habitually daily.

I recommend that future (AI) robotic cans be such as energy-saving machines to help any factory workers to cooperate to work to achieve efficient energy -saving aim, but they can also raise productivities. So, factory robotic are as learning tools, allowing factory energy users (factory workers) to teach themselves how to use less energy to achieve the productivity won't be decreased intention. So, when the robotics and factory workers work in the factory environment together. The robotics can give feedback to let these factory workers how to cooperate to use lesser energy to work efficiently in factories.

Other information and advice achieving better understanding and control of energy use in factory. So, future factory robotic machine men are such as teachers teach students in classrooms or trainers provide training to train trainee in factories. It means that robotics and factory workers can learn how to understand to do every working steps to avoid to spend extra excessive energy , but they can also raise productivities as the same time in factories.

So , future (AI) robotics will be demanded to invent to be one energy-saving machines to assist factory workers to use lesser energy to manufacture any products in manufacturing process, but they can also have productivity and efficiencies won't be reduced in the efficient team work method. So, every factory robotic machine mman is needed to be designed to own the advanced manufacturing technological skills or manufacturing methods to assist the factory workers to manufacture the kind of products in team work together in order to shorten time and using the most efficient manufacturing methods to achieve and produce the best quality products and the highest productivity in energy-saving working environment in factories. For example, when every team watch factory's factory workers who need to operte with ten workers per team in the watch manufacturing factory. One robotic machine with ten workers per team will need to raise to manufacture at least fifty watchs number per hour to compare only ten workers per team can manufacture the maximum fifty watchs number per house, when the robotic machine participates to every team to work together.

The robotic machine must need to help them to use lesser time and electricity energy to manufacture more than fifty watches number pe hour in order to achieve long tem energy saving and time saving and efficient raising productive economic benefits to the watch manufacturing company. Hence, the watch factory's every watching manufacturing robotic machines can encourage the watch manufacturing firm to choose to use them to assist every team watch manufacturing workers to work in order to achieve high efficient productivities, high quality of watch manufacturing, reducing every watch manufacturing , reducing every watch manufacturing time and the important intention is energy -sving efficient benefit to reduce to spend more extra excessive electricity for long term expenditure.

So, in the future , every robotic machine will need have these benefits to satisfy manufacturers' every -saving needs in their participative manufacturing process in order to achieve energy expenditure to reduce for long term economic benefits to persuade them to use these energy-saving efficient robotics in factory attractively.

9 798886 678376

Printed by Libri Plureos GmbH in Hamburg,
Germany